Children's Ways
of Knowing

Nathan Isaacs

on

Education, Psychology, and Piaget

Edited, with an Introduction, by
Mildred Hardeman

Teachers College Press
New York and London

Library of Congress Cataloging in Publication Data

Isaacs, Nathan, 1895-1966.
    Children's ways of knowing: Nathan Isaacs on education, psychology,
and Piaget.

    CONTENTS: Hardeman, M.   Introduction.—Children's "why"
questions.—What is required of the nursery-infant teacher in this country
today?   [etc.]
    Includes bibliographical references.
    1.   Cognition (Child psychology)   2.   Educational psychology.
3.   Piaget, Jean, 1896-   I.   Hardeman, Mildred, 1921-   ed.   II.   Title.
BF723.C5I85   1974   370.15'2   74-3103

Acknowledgments

Mrs. Evelyn Isaacs is to be credited with the idea of making Nathan Isaacs' works available in America. Grateful acknowledgment is made both to her and to Frank Jennings for bringing these works to the attention of Teachers College Press.

A computer program specially written by William E. Blumberg, of Bell Telephone Laboratories, greatly facilitated the preparation of the index.

Grateful acknowledgment is also made to the organizations and individuals who kindly granted permission to reprint Isaacs' works. These are specified on the title page of each essay.

M. H.

Contents

Introduction

It is paradoxical that human beings are said to be distinguished from lower animals by their extraordinary capacity to learn, while many children seem unable to learn in the classroom. A collection of writings by Nathan Isaacs is of value both because of the clarity he brings to the issues underlying the paradox and because of the solutions he proposes.

Isaacs lived and worked at a time when broad dissatisfaction with the education of young children in England paved the way for the "activity" or "open" classroom in the British infant school. Isaacs' position concerning the psychology of cognition and the kinds of educational practice that are appropriate and productive provides—among other things—an unusually enlightening theoretical framework for study of that innovation.

For approximately forty years, Isaacs was concerned with issues involved in the psychology of young children and educational practice, beginning with his association with Susan Isaacs in the Malting House School. During all these years, his thinking was stimulated by the discoveries and theories of Piaget; and he became known for introducing and interpreting Piaget's concepts to teachers and students in England.

Isaacs was born in 1895 at Frankfurt-am-Main, of a Polish-Jewish family.[1] His childhood was spent in Switzerland; his family moved to England when he was twelve. He became a British citizen in 1917, and served in the British army in the First World War. Much of his life was spent in the merchandising of metals; and for special contributions in this area during the Second World War, he was decorated with the Order of the British Empire.

In 1922 he married Dr. Susan Brierley, who became an outstanding pioneer in child psychology in England. Together they worked out the theoretical basis and the policy of the experimental Malting House School in Cambridge, of which Susan Isaacs was director from 1924 to 1927. He was closely associated with the planning of Susan Isaacs' two classic works on the educational psychology of young children: *Intellectual Growth in Young Children*[2] and *Social Development in Young Children.*[3] The essay entitled

---

[1] The editor is indebted to Mrs. Evelyn Isaacs for providing biographical information.

[2] Susan Isaacs, *Intellectual Growth in Young Children, with an Appendix on Children's "Why" Questions by Nathan Isaacs* (London: Routledge and Kegan Paul, 1930).

[3] Susan Isaacs, *Social Development in Young Children* (London: Routledge and Kegan Paul, 1933).

"Children's 'Why' Questions" in the present collection was an appendix to *Intellectual Growth in Young Children.*

Throughout his life Isaacs was interested in the clarification and development of the theoretical issues underlying psychological and educational problems. As a member of the Aristotelian Society, he contributed papers on epistemology and language, approaching issues with a highly disciplined but fresh point of view. In 1949 he published *The Foundations of Common Sense,*[4] a work in which his own epistemological theory is developed.

After the death of Susan Isaacs, he married Evelyn Lawrence, Director of the National Froebel Foundation; and as a member of the Governing Body of this society, he devoted much of his time to writing on the education of young children and lecturing to teachers. He died in 1966.

The papers in this collection were selected to represent Isaacs' two-fold contribution to problems of child psychology and educational practice. The first contribution is the demonstration of the necessity for adapting educational practice to the nature of the child, as opposed to the more frequent custom of adapting the child's nature to educational practice. In itself, this is not a new doctrine; but it is reformulated by Isaacs with the intention of examining the issues in a more rigorous and comprehensive way than in the past. Specifically, he examines the ways that infants and very young children find out about the world, their own special ways of knowing their environment. He examines traditional classroom practices in England, shows how the rich cognitive abilities that young children bring to school are often by-passed and ignored, and demonstrates how the child's own ways of learning should instead be understood, encouraged, and strengthened.

His second major contribution is in the area of the psychology of cognition itself. According to Isaacs, the various schools of thought in the psychology of cognition have produced only fragmentary and peripheral accounts of cognition that are lacking in perspective and inadequate as a basis for educational theory or practice. He proposes a reconstruction of the psychology of cognition such that the entire cognitive life history of the individual may be examined. Such a genetic approach would have the advantage of providing perspective on other theories of cognition, and would offer the possibility of more fruitful implications for educational practice.

Examination of Isaacs' views on the cognitive equipment of the child reveals that he places great emphasis on two works by Piaget, *The Origins of Intelligence in Children,*[5] first published in 1936, and *The Construction of Reality in the Child,*[6] first published in 1937. In these works Piaget presented

[4] Nathan Isaacs, *The Foundations of Common Sense: A Psychological Preface to the Problems of Knowledge* (London: Routledge and Kegan Paul, 1949).

[5] Jean Piaget, *The Origins of Intelligence in Children,* trans. Margaret Cook (New York: International Universities Press, 1952).

[6] Jean Piaget, *The Construction of Reality in the Child,* trans. Margaret Cook (New York: Basic Books, 1954).

his detailed observations of his own children in their first 18 to 21 months of life, demonstrating that early infancy is the time when intellectual growth begins and that the basic way in which infants learn is through their own actions.

From the first weeks of life, by using his sensory and motor equipment, the infant creates experiences for himself. Piaget traced through six stages the kinds of activity the infant engages in from birth through the middle of the second year. Beginning with a predominance of reflex activity, the infant soon repeats his reactions, combines sensory responses, and discriminates in his perception of objects. New kinds of activity are stimulated that bring satisfaction, new interests, and new abilities. There is increasing capacity to act with purpose, to elaborate and to differentiate, to explore, to manipulate, investigate causes and effects, and distinguish between means and ends.

It is by means of such activity that the infant comes to know the world around him; and for Piaget, to "know" means, not to receive a photographic copy of the outside world into a blank mind, nor to be the passive recipient of stimuli, but to organize and integrate. Within the first 18 months of life, the infant has constructed for himself, through his own cumulative activity, a rough map of the world in which he has found himself. Gradually, for the infant, the world comes to be meaningful, intelligible, and predictable.

By the age of about 18 months, the infant has thoroughly mastered his lessons, acquiring an intimate, living knowledge of his world. He has found out that objects have a separate existence of their own, that they exist even when he does not see them, and that they exist in a spatial order so that one object is *here,* another *over there.* He has found out that events occur in a temporal order so that one event occurs *before,* another *after.* Further, he has discovered that some events in a temporal sequence are related in an especially interesting way, namely, they are causally connected.

These lessons are examples of what Isaacs terms "living learning." And so thoroughly does such learning enter into the total history of the individual that life is not imaginable without the integrative concepts of time, space, object constancy, and causation. Within these early months of life, the child has already acquired the most necessary and basic learning needed for the remainder of his life. The infant is not usually given credit for what actually is a momentous achievement, so momentous that Piaget termed it a "Copernican revolution." The remainder of the individual's cognitive life will be spent in filling in the gaps of the world picture he has already constructed in infancy, enlarging it, correcting it, elaborating its details, and further organizing and unifying it.

According to Isaacs, the way in which all of this highly important learning takes place in the infant is a prototype of the way that all meaningful learning takes place throughout life, namely through the active engagement of the learner. No meaningful learning can take place unless the learner is active, for it is he who has to do the integrating of new material into his own world picture. No one else can do the integrating for him.

In the present collection, in the article entitled "Piaget: Some Answers to Teachers' Questions," Isaacs gives a brief summary of Piaget's work, the implications he finds for education, and his own criticisms. He views Piaget's account of cognitive development in the first 18 to 21 months as constituting a full story of the single, cumulative process of intellectual development. However, it is Isaacs' further view that Piaget did not continue to account for the total process after the time of infancy. Instead Piaget concentrated on only one aspect of cognitive growth, namely the development of formal logic. Isaacs, however, points out that the processes stemming from the child's own activity, begun in infancy, continue to develop, enriching and expanding his world map.

Soon, in the life of the very young child, language comes to be a potent instrument that can open up vast new areas for exploring, organizing, and integrating. Isaacs points out that if language is closely connected with the concrete living realities of the child's experience, it can make an abundant contribution to his learning. However, there is a danger; the language used by adults in giving information and explanations, if not actually assimilated into the child's own "living learning," may help to create a world of "verbal twilight learning." To the extent that the child's language stays in intimate contact with his own living reality, we see the manifestations of logical thought expressed verbally in questions, logically valid comments and objections, and other connected ideas. The child verbally points to similarities and differences, he distinguishes, orders, organizes, makes judgments, criticizes, and argues.

It is in the child's question-asking ability that Isaacs' main interest lies, and he sees language in its most constructive and productive use when children spontaneously ask questions. He was concerned with the way such questions function in the lives of children, and reported the results of his study in "Children's 'Why' Questions," which is included in the present collection. Analyzing the spontaneous "why" questions asked by children at the Malting House School as well as others reported in current psychological literature, Isaacs formulated four categories of such questions. He was primarily interested in the open-ended "epistemic" questions.

Epistemic questions have their origin very early in life, when the infant develops expectations of what will happen next in his life. All goes well when such expectations are fulfilled. But his behavior shows marked responses to conditions that do not conform to his expectations. Such expectations may be regarded as a very early aspect of the child's cognitive history, for they are his assumptions or incipient beliefs about the nature of things. They are an essential part of the child's cognitive map, and provide him with a readiness to respond in certain ways to various objects and events.

By the age of three or four, the child has constructed a fairly elaborate scheme of knowledge, a complex organization of assumptions and beliefs. His cognitive map, or picture of the world, has become larger and more coherent. He is aware of some of the constancies of his environment. He has acquired a more extensive set of expectations and beliefs about his world. His world model, his scheme of knowledge, on the whole, functions as a guide. And the small child, like the adult, is functioning each moment according to what he assumes will happen next. Much of the time situations do in fact turn out in accordance with his expectations. However, his world model is still very incomplete, and in many ways not tested; and often his expectations lead him to stumble in an area where they are not justified, or circumstances somehow turn out to be different from what he expected.

According to Isaacs, when the child's expectations are not fulfilled, a "cognitive jar" or "cognitive shock" results. This experience may range in intensity from mild surprise to confusion, fear, pain, or a sense of danger and a feeling of helplessness. And the child's verbal response to such unpleasant occurrences is an open-ended "Why?"

Isaacs termed such questions "epistemic" because actually the child is concerned about the state of his *knowledge.* He is aware that something is not right about his knowledge. It needs to be corrected in some way, but he does not know in what way. Such questions may be interpreted to mean: "What I thought was the case is not correct. What's wrong with my knowledge?" Such situations occur frequently in the life of a child, and he develops a fear of betrayal by his own knowledge. The credibility of his whole world picture seems to be in jeopardy.

Thus the child is pushed by his own painful experiences into an *interest* in *knowledge.* He wants his knowledge to be correct, clear, and sufficient so that he is not again betrayed. He needs knowledge of what to expect, so he can be confident.

When a child asks an epistemic "why" question, he is asking for help, for an explanation which he cannot supply for himself. If an adult is genuinely helpful, with an explanation of where the child went wrong in his expectations, he is once again confident in his world picture, which is now amended and more stable. At the ages of four and five, the epistemic question is a very frequent expression of cognitive shock. Afterwards, the number of purely epistemic "why's" decreases, partly because the child learns to ask for the help he needs in a more discriminating way, partly because he has gained more knowledge and is not betrayed so often, and partly because adults are not always helpful. Adults do not always answer children's questions intelligently, nor do they often give much encouragement to children's questions.

By the time the child enters school, about the age of five, if his environment has been reasonably favorable, he possesses a rich assortment of cognitive abilities. These include what Isaacs terms proto-logical and proto-mathe-matical abilities: comparing, contrasting, sorting, arranging, counting, measuring, generalizing, thinking up explanations, challenging explanations. The child also possesses proto-scientific abilities, namely curiosity about the world and concern about the clarity, correctness, and sufficiency of his knowledge. He also has a very powerful urge to understand causes. In addition, the child has constructed for himself a cognitive map of the world, an extensive network of beliefs, assumptions, and expectations. This map has resulted from the child's own cumulative interaction with his environment. He has therefore had several years of rich experience in learning meaningful material in his own warm-blooded experiential way.

In addition, the child has very strong motivation to learn. His motivation to learn stems from three sources: pleasure, power, and security. Sheer delight results from exploring, experimenting, finding out, observing, understanding, constructing. The child's urge to gain increased power in his daily practical world also pushes him toward greater understanding and competence. Finally, the child needs knowledge of what to expect next, in order to feel secure.

What happens when the child enters school? In England, says Isaacs, if the child is fortunate he may have one or two more years in which he can continue the living, integrative learning in which he has been so fruitfully engaged. However, by the age of seven, most children enter a classroom of an entirely different kind. In the usual classroom, children are required to renounce their own living interests. This means that they must leave their own cognitive equipment outside the classroom, forgetting the objects of their genuine curiosity and their eagerness to explore and construct. They must become passive, receptive, take in what the teacher offers, follow his directions, live their lives under his constant guidance, allow the teacher to fill their minds. Above all, they will need to listen to the spoken word, for it is through words that the teacher issues directions, explains, and drills them in reading, writing, and arithmetic.

Under such circumstances, according to Isaacs, very little takes place that has any educational value. Many children reach some level of proficiency in verbal and mathematical skills and turn away from them as rapidly as possible. Some children become interested in a "subject," but this remains a "school" interest and does not pass into the stream of living learning. Many children "learn" the things they are required to "learn" and forget them immediately. In Isaacs' view, the active cognitive drives of most children either stay alive only outside the school, or wither away completely.

In this kind of classroom, the kind of learning that is likely to take place is "verbal twilight learning." Children are given information, explanations, directions, are "taught" concepts that they cannot find a way to integrate into their own experience. Such verbal material is not meaningful to children. Around the central integrative learning which children have been actively engaged in building up, there develops a large world of vague, shadowy quasi-meanings. Much of the vocabulary that they have now been "taught" is part of this verbal twilight world.

According to Isaacs, when "knowledge" is presented to children in verbal form, they may hear sound-patterns that are divorced from their own living experience. These sound-patterns are meaningless. In trying to be cooperative, children try to attribute meanings to the sound-patterns that they hear. But the meanings the children provide are not at all the same as those the teacher intends. Such activity, then, is a waste of time for both teachers and children.

Such waste is a result, not of refractory human nature, nor of the stupidity of children, but of a fragmentary and ill-conceived educational psychology. A psychological view of children's ways of learning that issues in such classroom activities would have as its basic assumption that children are passive, their minds essentially a blank tablet, and that learning takes place best when the teacher is active and the children passive.

In opposition to such an educational psychology, and in opposition to the usual classroom in which the child's own astonishingly rich learning capacity is by-passed and ignored, Isaacs proposes an entirely different program of education. His program is based upon the implications of the Piagetian model of building up intelligence and upon the children's own cognitive equipment. It is, he says, the only kind of educational program that makes good psychological sense.

Such a program would require that educators find out how to use the child's native equipment in every respect. The teacher needs to find out what the child's living interests are, encouraging, strengthening, supporting such interests, so that they are either reinforced or lead to new interests. The teacher would stimulate the child to ask questions and to look for his own answers. The teacher would need to make comments, ask questions, make suggestions for new directions, always pointing to the need for additional knowledge in order to answer the child's questions.

Such activity also requires the genuine understanding by the teacher of her own active role, for a laissez-faire attitude on her part would result in frustration for the children, a dying out of their interests, and general chaos. Little learning would occur, and probably no meaningful education. When children have been discouraged in their active pursuit of knowledge by home conditions, educators need to find ways to revive the urge to grow mentally.

In his "Memorandum for the Plowden Committee," included in the present collection, Isaacs outlined a program for education for each of five stages in the lives of children, ranging from the age of three to twelve or thirteen. The emphasis is on strengthening children's yearning for knowledge by capitalizing on their cognitive assets, postponing systematic "chalk and talk" teaching until the children are eager to know "all about" some area of knowledge. Always, the test of whether they are actually ready for such systematic teaching is their ability to translate the newly acquired knowledge back into their living learning. Isaacs recommended to the Plowden Committee a twenty-year pilot study in order to test his proposed educational program.

The question of whether and how science should be brought into the elementary classroom is considered in "Early Scientific Trends in Children" and "The Case for Bringing Science into the Primary School," both of which are included in the present collection. Isaacs takes the position that we must broaden considerably our view of what science is, and humanize it by viewing it in its historical context.

Science should be regarded as one of the humanities; like literature and art, science is a human achievement. About four centuries ago, a new emphasis developed in human culture, an emphasis on learning about the world by observing it and thinking about it, and then checking one's observations or beliefs by consideration of data from the context of relevant facts. Isaacs points out that human beings did not at that time suddenly acquire a new set of cognitive abilities. Rather, people simply began to use in a different way the cognitive equipment they already possessed.

Now children, before arriving at school age, have already developed the equipment needed for these two aspects of inquiry that constitute scientific method. They have a natural interest in the world, and they are alert to the need for clarity, correctness, and adequacy in their knowledge. Again he stresses the crucial role of the teacher, who must find ways to encourage and strengthen such cognitive drives. In his view, the teaching of science as a "subject" in the primary school results in fragmented knowledge. Further, most children are not capable of the sustained logical discipline that is necessary for mastery of any one of the sciences.

Instead, the teacher who has a wide understanding of what is involved in scientific method, and in the proto-scientific drives of young children, will encourage the development of these drives by helping children again and again to ask the kinds of questions about their beliefs in all areas of life that would assist the children in testing them. Isaacs points out that in our daily lives our standards of evidence for our beliefs, like our standards of explanation, are extremely low.

According to Isaacs, it is necessary that these methods of scientific inquiry be experienced by the child in his very bones, that he experience the "inwardness" of scientific inquiry. This kind of experience can develop only through the child's integrative learning, through help toward belief-testing in the areas of his life that are of vital concern to him. Only in this way can the scientific heritage that rightfully belongs to human beings become integrated into the main stream of children's lives.

Isaacs' second major contribution to the psychology of children and educational practice is his proposal for a total reconstruction of the psychology of cognition. In his view, such a reconstruction is needed because the theories of cognition already formulated by psychologists, in terms of which their empirical studies are carried out, do not do justice to the cognitive life of human beings. With the exception of Piaget, psychologists concerned with cognition have mainly studied only certain very limited kinds of learning that can easily be examined in the laboratory, or those that can be observed in animals, or they have been preoccupied with attempting to find a physiological basis for learning. Such attempts to understand cognition have not only resulted in focusing attention on fragments, but have also resulted in the consideration of cognition as a faculty entirely apart from the on-going stream of life. Isaacs' proposals for a psychology that would avoid these limitations—and also those in the Piagetian framework—are presented in the paper entitled "On a Gap in the Structure of Our General Psychology."

What would be the subject matter of such a reconstructed psychology, and what would be the tasks of the psychologist of cognition? The subject matter would be the cognitive map, or world model, or "complex cognitive organization" that each of us has constructed gradually since birth, and the role of this cognitive map in our life history.

According to Isaacs, the key to understanding human cognitive life is the truth-falsity distinction. Psychologists have overlooked this distinction because of a fear of being caught in a web of philosophical problems. But the decisions that we make as to what is true and what is false are crucial determinants of our behavior. And to ignore this distinction is to by-pass the central part that our expectations play in our total life history. Attention to what is involved in making truth-falsity distinctions is needed.

Freud demonstrated that our affective life is largely unknown to us. Isaacs points out that our cognitive life too is largely unconscious. We are simply not aware of the complicated network of beliefs or assumptions in terms of which we go about our daily life. At each moment of waking life, our behavior is at least partially determined by what we unconsciously assume will happen in the next moment or at a later time.

Now if our expectations were always fulfilled, it seems likely that we would remain completely unaware of our cognitive framework. But there are failures, the situations in which our expectations are not justified by actual events. Our assumptions or beliefs are wrong. And it is when a customary expectation is *not* fulfilled that we become *aware* of the belief in terms of which we acted.

"But I thought . . . !" we are likely to say. And in this statement we render explicit the heretofore implicit belief in terms of which we acted. One of the tasks of the psychologist interested in cognition would be to find additional ways to render explicit the cognitive organization of individuals.

Another task of the psychologist would be to explore the cumulative impact of the truth-falsity distinction on our total life history. Isaacs states that the role of knowing (and not knowing) in our lives is as dramatic and powerful as the role of affect. The history of an individual could be understood in terms of the rhythm of things happening according to expectation and things happening otherwise. Such a rhythm, he points out, is a powerful one in the area of cognition, as also in the area of affect. The psychologist would also need to be concerned with the relation between cognition and affect in the individual's life history. Attention is needed for both, for human behavior cannot be explained in terms of either of these alone.

What Isaacs is proposing is that the psychologist of cognition should make a behavioral study of the total inner cognitive history of individuals, comparable to Freud's study of the history of affect in individual life. He points out that Piaget has elicited behavioral responses from children that reveal the presence or absence of logical structures. It would be possible to elicit and study overt evidence for other aspects of the implicit world model.

What are the implications of such a reconstruction in the psychology of cognition for educational practice? One implication is explored by Isaacs in an article included in the present collection: "What is Required of the Nursery-Infant Teacher in This Country Today?" Above all, the teacher of young children needs a broad, integrated, and meaningful psychology of cognition, in terms of which various kinds of growth, such as intellectual, moral, emotional, and aesthetic, may be understood as aspects of one integrated on-going mental life. Usually, Isaacs thinks, the teaching of psychology is not very effective because the subject matter consists of fragments that do not add up to an integrated view of human life. He believes that the psychology he is proposing could be illuminating to the teacher, giving her more enlightenment about herself, about children, and about all human beings than she had ever thought was possible.

Such a psychology is also suggestive of important activities in the classroom. If truth-falsity distinctions are so critical in our lives, the child could be helped to examine his criteria and to develop more adequate criteria for distinguishing between truth and falsity. He could also be helped to become more aware of his cognitive network and to explore the vague, shadowy, untested aspects of it.

Much-needed perspective may be gained by examining the education of children in the light of Isaacs' proposed reconstruction. Questions may be raised as to how classroom learning contributes—if indeed it does contribute—to the world map or scheme of beliefs in children. Does it make substantial contributions? Does it strengthen and encourage belief-testing? What *is* the impact of classroom experience on the total life history of the individual?

We may conclude that in Isaacs' view human beings, from a very early age, have an extraordinary capacity to learn. Yet many children are unable to learn what they are supposed to learn in the classroom. The fault lies primarily in an inadequate educational psychology that misconceives the nature of the young child's cognitive abilities, ignores the nature of cumulative living learning, and disregards the total role of cognition in human life.

Although his criticisms of traditional classroom learning were directed specifically to schools in England, his concerns with the nature of the child and how the child should be educated are universal problems. The precept that educational practice should be based on the nature of the child, advocated earlier by such thinkers as Rousseau, Froebel, and Dewey, is now given a new empirical basis by the work of Piaget.

And Isaacs develops the implications of this work. He has presented a difficult program of work to be accomplished: ". . . starting everywhere from the native educable forces and drives in the child and learning how to use them to carry him forward in all the chief directions of human growth." Such a program requires work by psychologists, teachers of children, and educators of teachers.

Isaacs' total philosophy, a deeply humanistic outlook, is an antidote for views that tend to regard the child as a passive object to be manipulated, that consider intellectual growth in terms of too narrowly conceived behavioral objectives, standardized tests, and grade point averages.

It is a correction for views of education that promote miniaturization of knowledge and dehumanization of the learner.

It is a correction, too, for the romantic view that if we leave the child to his own devices he will learn all that he needs to know. It demonstrates that children are far more eager for knowledge, and even knowledge for its own sake, than we usually give them credit for.

An integration of Isaacs' broad perspective could have an enlarging and exciting effect. It might also have a sobering effect on the lively faith in magic that creates expectations of a new technological device or other sudden innovation that will quickly and easily solve educational problems. It might correct the tendency to ask inappropriate questions: How can we speed up children's cognitive processes? How early can verbal and mathematical skills be taught, and how can they be taught most quickly? Learning from Isaacs, we might ask instead: Considering the ways that children have at their disposal for learning, what are the *optimal* conditions that might be provided for their education?

Nathan Isaacs was endowed with a mind both gracious and painstaking. Lillian Weber, leader in informal education in America, wrote that when she first heard him lecture, she suddenly became aware that "this was a rare *mind* at work, examining very deeply questions vital to education. He spoke slowly, sharing every step of his reasoning, sharing the evidence, not trying to overbear or persuade in any other way."[7]

---

[7]Lillian Weber, "Nathan Isaacs: An American Appreciation," *The New Era,* 49 (March 1968): 73.

Isaacs' writing is accordingly careful, precise, generous in explanation if not always in example. The articles in the present collection (arranged chronologically) are reproduced just as they were printed by their various publishers in England: often with multiple subheads or in outline form; with British usages, spellings, punctuations; with a few stylistic inconsistencies from paper to paper. The marvel is how little "editing" has been needed.

The style is not always conducive to rapid reading. But the work is so alive, so carefully thought through, so full of implications for the education of children, that the interested reader is richly rewarded.

Children's "Why" Questions*

Isaacs' interest in children's questions stemmed from his association from 1924 to ᾽1927 with the Malting House School in Cambridge and from his study of Piaget's work.

The Malting House School was an experimental school, designed to encourage active inquiry in young children and to provide them with direct experiences in all areas of interest. The children, ranging in age from two to ten, were from professional families and were above average in mental ability. Detailed records of the children's classroom behavior were kept by members of the staff. The purpose of such records was to present, with as much objectivity as possible, the cognitive behavior of children in situations where their free inquiry was encouraged.

Piaget had made a study of the spontaneous questions of a six-year-old boy, analyzing them according to the kinds of answers the child presumably expected. (*The Language and Thought of the Child*, 1926, London.) Isaacs believed that "why" questions could be examined more constructively by inquiring into their various *functions* in the lives of children. Analyzing many children's spontaneous "why" questions, he demonstrates the existence of "epistemic" questions indicating that young children are interested in the sufficiency and clarity of knowledge as such.

In carrying out his theme, Isaacs differs from Piaget on several major issues: whether egocentrism is an innate characteristic of the child's mind; whether a clash of views between a child and his peers promotes cognitive growth or simply helps the child to develop interpersonal defenses; whether differences between children's and adults' logic are best explained by the presence or absence of certain "structures" or by more or less experience of the world.

*First published in Susan Isaacs, *Intellectual Growth in Young Children, with an Appendix on Children's "Why" Questions by Nathan Isaacs* (1930) by Routledge and Kegan Paul Ltd., London. Reprinted with the permission of Mrs. Evelyn Isaacs and the publishers.

CONTENT OUTLINE

Section I: Theoretical Analysis

1. A Thesis.
2. The Problem.
3. A Suggested Answer.
4. A Closer Survey:
     A: The Reality of the Stimulus.
     (a) The groundwork of the reaction.
     (b) Functional reinforcement.
     (c) Reinforcement by consequences.
     (d) Frequency of occasions.
     (e) General functional significance.
     B: The Character of the Effect.
     (a) The epistemic question.
     (b) The openness of the answer.
     C: The Key-function of "Why".
     D: The Multiple Meanings of "Why".
     E: Children and the *Word* "Why".

Section II: Some Evidential Facts.

1. Prefatory Note on the Most Distinctive "Why".
2. The Data Drawn On.
3. Some Specimen Clear Questions.
4. Some Rejections of Faulty Adult Answers.
5. A Doubtful Case.
6. Testimony from the Adverse Evidence.
7. A Batch of Typical Evidence in Support.

Section III: Theoretical Problems and Issues.

1. A Case for Adequate Inquiry—and Its Conditions.
2. The Outcome so far.
3. The Conflict with Piaget's Views.
     A: An alternative to Piaget's interpretation of the differences between the child's and the adult's "why's".
     B: Attempt at re-interpretation of Piaget's findings.
     C: Epitome of result of this re-interpretation.

Section IV: Conclusions and Applications.

1. Children's "Why" Interest in the Concrete.
2. The History of the "Why" Interest.
3. "Why" and the Development of Causal Interest.
4. Explanation and Education: A Possible Moral.

SECTION I: THEORETICAL ANALYSIS

1. A THESIS

The topic of children's "why" questions is, I believe, worth special attention in connection with the general issue of the relation of child thought to adult thought. Contrary to such views as Piaget's, these questions seem to me to bear witness to the essential identity of structure and function of thought throughout our life history. And their evidence at the same time throws a great deal of light upon the fundamental dynamics of cognitive development whenever and wherever it occurs, in the adult as in the child.

The child's "whys"—or rather, one important and common class of them—appear to me to show him actively interested in his knowledge as such and directly concerned with the question whether it is (*a*) correct, (*b*) sufficient, and (*c*) clear and unambiguous.

I am naturally not suggesting that any child would or could *formulate* any concern of such a kind, but only that children do in fact *act it out,* and that their "why" questions can be shown to represent this acting out. Even so, it may well seem a wildly improbable concern to impute to the child. It may be thought quite out of harmony, not only with Piaget's findings, but with the whole trend of present day psychology, with its stress on the primacy of the instinctual life, and the *late* development, at the best, of any "disinterested" concern with knowledge as such.

There are, however, powerful reasons, good instinctual reasons, for such a concern from the beginnings of the child's life, and I hope to give evidence that the capacity for it is not lacking. And as will be seen, it has to be a "disinterested" concern, i.e., a concern only with knowledge as such, otherwise it will not serve. The instincts and needs it is called upon to help will not be helped by it. But it is there all the same to serve them, and it is sustained by them.

I believe that the foregoing view seems improbable only because we are still too liable, under the influence of our philosophic tradition, to take a *faculty* view of cognition, even if we avoid it everywhere else. We treat it in separation from the active current of our lives, and in the very problem of its relation to the rest of our life, we try to relate it as if from outside. It is the relation to life of the *faculty* of knowledge—a thing distinct and apart, whether superordinate, co-ordinate, subordinate or even illusory—that we consider.

2. THE PROBLEM

Now if I am right, "why" questions are capable of yielding just that evidence and insight which might most readily assist us to break down this false division. They can help us to integrate knowledge into that *cumulative history of interaction* between the human organism and its environment which provides the main substance of our human psychology. But under the influence of the self-same philosophic tradition, we approach "why" questions in a way which is bound to miss this most important aspect of them. We examine them only in relation to our theoretical ideals of knowledge (causal or logical explanation, etc.). We treat them as logical entities, corresponding to those other logical entities, explanations. We note the child's "why's" as evidence of his attitude towards causal explanation; we find him capable or incapable of appreciating physical or mechanical causality, interested or uninterested in it; we observe his proneness to anthropomorphic assumptions and draw conclusions from this as to the structure of his thought. But all the time we remain within an abstracted *world of knowledge,* of pure theoretical interests and beliefs. It is a world of contents, not of events. It is the world of the *faculty* of knowledge.

But for the psychologist, "why" questions should before everything else be psychic *events.* They are definite acts of behaviour, and his problem should be: what are their causes and functions? In what situations do they arise? What is their relation to these situations?

We know of course that they are demands or appeals for explanation. But what is it that causes these demands? We need the answer to this question in order to determine the psychological function of explanation itself. It is a question of fact, not of logic, and we must start, not from types of explanation, but from "why" questions as the prior psychological fact.

What kind of situation is it then that happens to or in the child and produces the need or demand expressed as a "why" question?

3. A SUGGESTED ANSWER

Now we naturally have to take care not to assume that all "why" questions express the same kinds of needs and arise out of the same sort of situation. There are, in fact, several different types which need to be carefully distinguished. The customary treatment of children's "whys" covers some of them (though not, I think, very satisfactorily, because always from the point of view of types of explanation). I wish, however, to focus attention here upon one particular type of question which this traditional static approach has tended to disregard. It is based upon a situation that seems to me to be peculiarly important and to throw an essential light not only on the meaning of children's "why's", but also on the relation of our knowledge to our total life-history.

This situation is that of a sudden clash, gap or disparity between our past experience and any present event.

Some fact is met which is contrary to expectation, or unexpected, or creates confusion or difficulty as to what to expect next. Something has gone wrong with our habitual knowledge or assumptions. We need to find out what it is and to put it right. We are pulled up, thrown out of our course, caught unprepared, or left without any clear guidance, and we have to deal with the obstruction.

This kind of state is, I think, the key to the most distinctive meaning of the "why" question—and a meaning as real for children as for adults. The question serves as expression or formulation of this state, and, when addressed to others, as an appeal to them for help in remedying it. Explanation, in its corresponding sense, is the provision of the right remedy.

That it is the surprising or anomalous that starts off thought is of course a commonplace of genetic psychology. But as a consequence of our faculty philosophy of knowledge, this has tended to be conceived as a mere stimulus action which sets the machinery of thought in motion, the nature of its motion being then a function of the nature of the machinery; e.g., for Stern, the innate category of causality, for Piaget, the ego-centric structure of the child's mind, etc. But the point about the type of experience to which I am referring is that it is not merely a stimulus or release; it presents a specific problem. It demands specific thought directed to the problem. There is a contradiction to be resolved, an obstruction to be overcome. Some x has to be found which will actually achieve this.

The effect, in the case of the young child, can only be a state of puzzlement, and a process of fumbling and groping and random activity until in the easiest cases some sort of solution or at least get-away is chanced upon. But that will not carry the child very far; in general, this type of difficulty is almost insuperable unhelped, because its very cause is the breakdown of the machinery for self-help. The latter is based upon successful and satisfactory knowledge; but the state with which we are concerned is one in which our knowledge suddenly fails us, or some fact actually contradicts or subverts it.

The significant fact, however, is that there is one discovery which it is fairly easy for the child to make. He discovers that there is a definite way in which he can secure adult help in his difficulty. He finds out that the word "why" will carry the meaning of a wish for help in this situation: he learns to use it in order to ask for an explanation.

With the help of the explanations thus received, he comes gradually to be able to do more for himself in similar situations. He learns to distinguish different kinds, to recognise them rapidly, and to tell in what directions to look for a solution. In a large number of cases, he becomes able to ask at once for the *right kind* of explanation, and this permits him further to answer an increasing proportion of his questions himself. But he also remains liable still to the original experience: a sudden sharp breakdown, at some point, of his cognitive organisation up to date, with at least temporary at-a-lossness and helplessness. In such cases he can still only resort to the original open "why", and appeal for an explanation at large, whatever it may prove to be.

We thus get "why" questions as general responses to cognitive challenge, but also as specific responses to certain recognised types of challenge—as demands for explanation as such, but also as demands for certain recognised types of explanation.

This applies alike to children from about four years onwards and to the most mature adults. Both types of question are represented in both, and the only difference is that the second type, which grows by experience of explanations actually secured, is much more highly differentiated and systematised in the adult. But it is the first type which is the primary one. It is and remains the one directly concerned with the correctness, sufficiency and clarity of our knowledge as such. And it is clearly and definitely represented in children from about four years onwards. I hope that the evidence to follow will sufficiently establish this.

4. A CLOSER SURVEY

The foregoing gives the broad plan of the argument. Let us consider it somewhat more closely before going on to the evidence.

A: The Reality of the Stimulus

The first essential point is that the jars and jolts, breakdowns and confusions which arise from disparity between past experience and present fact are as *real* and as *important* for the child as for us.

(a) The Groundwork of the Reaction.—As is well known, vigorous reactions to the unexpected or anti-expected occur as early as the first year. By the third year there are, moreover, striking negative responses to *mixtures* of the familiar and unfamiliar (Stern and Groos).[1]

(b) Functional Reinforcement.—It is easy to see how much these immediate reactions must be strengthened by the very nature of the child's development. From his first recognitions and pre-adjustments onwards, he goes on piecing together, from the repetitions and recurrences in his experience, an organisation of beliefs and expectations which covers more and more of the field of his experience, and more and more determines his course in advance of actual perception. He comes to approach most of his situations with a definite, even if unformulated, expectation set, a certain momentum or pressure towards some assumed development of the situation. If it then all at once breaks away from this development, the prepared expectation set collapses, and a sharp jar and confusion or a sudden drop into helplessness are bound to occur.

---

[1] See W. Stern: *Psychology of Early Childhood*, p. 495; a penetrating analysis, but Stern fails to follow up the clue, because he identifies "why" questions with the child's innate causal interest, and treats causality as a fixed category. [William Stern, *Psychology of Early Childhood up to the Sixth Year of Age: Supplemented by Extracts from the Unpublished Diaries of Clara Stern*, trans. Anna Barwell (London: George Allen and Unwin, 1924).]

(c) Reinforcement by Consequences.—But there is more to this experience than the mere immediate experience. It can hardly fail to carry some degree or shade of *ominous* significance for the child. It will inevitably link up in some degree with the character of the practical consequences which are *liable* to go with unpreparedness or wrong preparedness. The child, like ourselves, is continually committing himself on his expectations; he is behaving *now* according to what he believes the situation *will be.* At the best, error may mean failure or disappointment. But the anti-expected or unexpected encounter may also mean danger and fear, shock and practical helplessness, or actual hurt, of every kind and degree. Such consequences are very well fitted to leave their mark on anything associated with them. The child has good reason to pay *voluntary* attention to situations of failure or breakdown of expectation, over and above their direct power of forcing attention to themselves. Even if beyond the momentary jar of surprise, there is nothing in particular in them, they may well carry some reminder of past occasions when there was, and some warning of future occasions when there may be.

(d) Frequency of Occasions.—Again, these failures or breakdowns of expectations are unluckily no rare accidental affair, but a regular periodic consequence of the mode of functioning of our knowledge. Error is indeed the price we pay for our successful truths. It is unfortunate for us that it happens to be liable to prove some time a ruinous price, destroying at one stroke more than we may have gained by a lifetime of accumulated truth—in fact destroying us. But it is a price we can only try to bate down, not one we can avoid paying. This bating down is a matter for slow and painful *learning,* and we—i.e., the child—thus start from a maximum liability to be carried into error by our successful truths. We are simply led on by their efficacy into carrying them too far. We go on automatically with our successes until they lead us into failure, and this is our only way at first of learning their limits. Later on, we learn ways of allowing in advance for the limits of some of them, and of positively looking for these and testing them. But always from time to time we come upon cases where this has never occurred to us; where we have just automatically assumed the indefinite application of our successful habitual beliefs; where their limits have once again to be first brought home to us by their sudden actual failure. The difference between child and adult consists primarily in (*a*) the number of limits which the adult has learnt from failure, and (*b*) what he has learnt about the *risk* of failure from its occurrence.

But this learning is just what the child is engaged in; that is the general burden of my argument. My present point is merely insistence upon the *frequency* of his learning occasions, to complete the case previously based on their *efficacy.*

(e) General Functional Significance.—That frequency, however, must in its turn be understood only as a relative fact. What it is relative to is the overwhelmingly greater frequency of our successes. In the vast majority of cases, what happens, or what we perceive next, is congruous with what we expect. The further course of experience fits into the expectations which some given beginning has released. They run ahead from this or that datum, but the further data follow their course. This applies not only to specific inferences, beliefs or judgments, linked to particular data, but also and most of all to our general familiar picture of the world. The latter is in fact not so much a picture as an immensely complicated pattern of *unformulated assumptions,* representing all the tenor of what has been constant in our experience and of what makes it experience *within a constant, familiar world.* This pattern supplies what we *take for granted* in each situation or setting in which we move and act. We have at any moment only such and such data; the rest is assumption, based on past familiarity; and it is always assumption, among other things, as to what data we are going to get next. It functions wholly implicitly so long as it functions successfully, though disturbance or failure at once makes its presence and anticipative character plain. But the whole time when there is no disturbance, it is in full functioning. It is being successful in a hundred thousand ways; the next data as we move, turn, or act are what we assumed them to be, and the next again, and so on in a continuous process. We are paying no attention to this, we are intent only upon some end-objective and what is specially involved in our way to it, whilst our just assumptions as to its familiar containing setting, which the latter is continually verifying, never become conscious at all.

Now this automatically functioning knowledge, I have suggested, sooner or later leads us into local error. But it is because it is so much greater than any local errors, that local errors can be profited by and corrected. In what can still be safely taken for granted we find the firm ground and the leverage with the help of which we raise our knowledge up again at the point at which it has collapsed.

However, because our knowledge is thus a continuously functioning organisation of expectations and assumptions, *unexpected* collapses anywhere involve some sense of strain, some shaking of security, as regards the whole. This is a part of the repercussion of our key situation of sudden jar or disparity. We are led into this present mal-functioning or failure to function through past successful functioning. The question then is not only: what was all unsuspectedly wrong with the latter—but also: how are we to know when anything is wrong? How are we to get rid of this perturbing *liability* to be let down at any time?

From this seed no doubt the philosophical problem of knowledge develops—in suitable soils. But the seed is present everywhere. Even young children can be assumed to be liable to some such sense of insecurity and perturbation. They do not have to be supposed to reflect about it. They need only be thought capable, after a number of experienced jars, of developing a certain general fear of them. This fear will then be stirred up again, even if only incipiently, by each one of them, and will form a part of the total reaction to it. And it will then be not merely a matter of specific feared consequences, but of the general liability to be all at once left helpless, of finding oneself betrayed by what one was depending on.

For as the very outcome of his successful knowledge, the child is all the time becoming more and more dependent on it. Upon this successful knowledge and its immense preponderance rests the whole growth of his adaptive intelligent behaviour. Upon the correctness of his earliest anticipations, his earliest pre-adjustments are built. And stage by stage, further and further anticipations, and further pre-adjustments, adaptations, purposes and plans are piled upon these foundations, because they hold, and upon each stage in turn because it holds. The local collapses that occur can disturb our confidence, but they cannot really disturb the general structure. On this completely depends our every power of doing or avoiding, all our ability to plan, the whole of the safety we actually possess; and so long as we are alive at all, that structure must be holding good in a myriad ways.

However, once we have such a structure of successful knowledge (and even the child of three must already have built up a very extensive and complicated one), we are not concerned with its myriad successes, upon which we are reckoning; but with its occasional failures, which let us down. These then are more than a mere matter of local patching-up. When such sudden and unforeseeable breakdowns occur, the credit and dependability of the general structure is involved, and we can hardly help being in some degree concerned about it *as such*. And though this formulation is worlds away from the child—as from the ordinary unsophisticated adult—the attitude and feeling and direction of behaviour corresponding to it are just as much forced upon him as upon us. What happens to him, what he has to fear, and what he needs are the same, and he has to feel his way to the same only remedy. He needs to be able to depend freely and securely on his knowledge, and there is sustained pressure upon him to learn to pay attention to its dependability as such, to be alert to any challenge to it, and if and where necessary to set it right.

B: The Character of the Effect

The second essential point of the total argument is accordingly that the cumulative effect of the situations in question, of clash, jar or disparity, is to stimulate the child to a genuine interest in the revision, extension and re-organisation of his knowledge.

In other words, the immediate involuntary experience leads to a voluntary directed activity aiming at the prevention of future similar experiences; at first on particular similar occasions and eventually in general.

(a) The Epistemic Question.–The immediate experience turns into a sense of *something wrong with knowledge,* some unsuspected error, insufficiency, or confusion–or else of something wrong with the perception of the supposed fact.

There is accordingly generated a striving or endeavour to locate what is wrong and to put it right. Is there a definite error, or something missing, or something ambiguous or unclear? If any of these, it must according to the case be corrected, supplied or cleared up. If none of these, then what has happened?

Let us separate the tangle of competing possibilities which are more or less confusedly and vaguely envisaged. Has some previous expectation or belief to be henceforth limited, and if so, to what kind of cases? And by what signs are we to know when to apply it and when to inhibit it? What new and different expectation has to be formed for such different kinds of cases as this one, where what we thought the right expectation has broken down, or where we were taken entirely unprepared? Or were we just hasty or premature, is there nothing to "explain" except the presence of some circumstance for which we might have looked out, and is there nothing to alter except our own degree of attention or vigilance? Or is there still less to "explain" because the apparently recalcitrant fact is a mere misperception and closer inspection dissolves the whole seeming problem?

(b) The Openness of the Answer.–All these are possible alternatives, and the need of the situation is to find out which or what is the right one. And also, what the readjustment is to be if readjustment *is* needed. The possibilities, once again, are not set out side by side as such. But there is what as behaviour corresponds to them: there is a fumbling and groping and turning all round for something that will satisfy the need of the situation, whatever that thing may be. The obstruction or difficulty must be resolved: something must be found that will establish such a relation between fact and knowledge that the latter will once again be a true, clear and sufficient guide. How it is to be done–whether by altering the "knowledge", interposing new, or re-attending to the fact–is just what one does not know. That is what has to be found out. The situation is an open one; its need is not this, that or the other way out, but a way out. It has happened in the past that ways out were found or offered; when they were offered, they proved real ways out. What is wanted is something which when found or offered will in the same fashion *prove* a way out.

C: The Key-function of "Why"

We are thus brought to the third essential point of the argument, which is that "why", in one of its senses, is the appointed symbol for the conveyance of the above situation and need, and is so taken up by the child. In this sense "why" means therefore open-minded puzzlement, a demand for any sort of help which will actually help to put one right.

D: The Multiple Meanings of "Why"

Here, however, we come upon the question of the confusing multitude of meanings of "why", which cannot be too carefully dealt with. An adequate analysis of all these meanings is not possible here, but I hope that the following will sufficiently clear the ground for my present purpose.

Over and above the meaning considered here, there are a considerable number of others which may in the first place be roughly divided into two groups; one notably different, the other, distinct but still closely connected.

These meanings seem to me to be all originally related in some way to situations of anti-expectedness, unexpectedness or confusion of expectation, but the first group have become specialised in a way that has almost severed the connection.

(i) In this group we have the familiar meanings of "why" which express inquiry about motives, intentions, purposes, uses, functions, or the specific causes of human or animal behaviour or states. These are typically mere demands for special familiar classes of information, not for explanation. They are more nearly allied to categorical question forms such as "where", "when", "what", "who"—questions, that is, of simple ignorance—than to "why" as the question of puzzlement. The distinction is of course functionally a most important one. Questions of ignorance and information arise out of the *successful* functioning of our cognitive organisation, and remain part and parcel of it; they provide a scheme which fully predefines the character of the answer, and leave only a specified *blank* to be filled in. They *continue* our previous course. Questions of epistemic puzzlement and explanation, on the contrary, start typically from an intrusive, obstructive *presence,* which falsifies or challenges our course, and forces upon us the search for some way of *reorientation* or *readjustment* (unless, as we say, the hampering fact can be "explained away"!).

Nevertheless, the above distinction is not an absolute one. An intermediate link is provided by the different types of information which are found or offered as explanation in *particular kinds of situations of puzzlement.* These then come to be asked for more and more directly as the kind of information appropriate to the given kind of situation. Questions of motive, etc., are merely very early and extreme cases of this type, which have been developed into practically pure informational categories. They represent the first and most marked divergence from the epistemic root-meaning of "why".

(ii) The second group of distinct but connected "why's", on the other hand, represents later derivatives from this root-meaning and remains dominated by it. This group comprises questions of causal intervention, causal control, causal deduction, and causal selection or analysis. Here the real interest remains explanation. It is true that a special kind of explanation is presupposed in the question, so that it is informational in a secondary sense, but in the first place this kind of information is peculiarly related to the main function of explanation as such, and in the second place there is usually some puzzlement or sense of difficulty or hitch latent in the question, and the information will only be accepted if it *explains*—otherwise we readily get an open "why" again.

Questions of this type by young children will be given. Their causal implications will be returned to later, but in this connection it may be worth pointing out at once that where causal interest is really quite free from any element of epistemic puzzlement, it is not usually or naturally expressed in the "why" form. In other words, it is then a simple informational question, and has its own form as part of our ordinary smooth cognitive functioning. We ask: what makes, what causes, what is the cause of; and in straightforward cases where we use these forms, we should not say "why".

(iii) A quite different third type of "why", neither explanatory nor informational, is that of demand for what Piaget calls "logical justification". This class, no doubt, as he points out, links up with "why's" concerning behaviour via the intermediate class of "why's" for rules, commands, prohibitions, etc. But it also bears an instructive relation to the original why-reaction to clash or unexpectedness. Just as "why" begins by being addressed to actions, behaviour or states which are strange or anomalous or take us by surprise, so we address it to beliefs or statements which strike us in the same way. However, our *attitude* is very far indeed from being the same as in the case of physical jars or surprises. The real situation, superficially so similar, happens to be very different. The anti-expectedness or unexpected-ness of other people's beliefs or statements is not as a rule a matter of fear or danger to us. There is no active functional disturbance about it, no association of disappointment, danger, helplessness or hurt. We pay a handsome tribute to the practical sanctions behind our why-interest in physical facts by our altered attitude where we find ourselves—at least for the moment—freed from those sanctions. We tend to deal with this form of clash in a way which is the very opposite to that forced upon us by the critical practical significance of clashes with hard facts. We assert ourselves against the clashing views, refute them, rebut them, spurn them or disregard them. We have indeed provided ourselves with a logic which never leaves us without approved methods of maintaining rebuttal or producing self-justification—even if those methods cut both ways and the net effect is mere deadlock. Thus the "why" of dialectical challenge is very different in nature and trend from that of genuine demand for explanation. It may of course be—and very often is—open to reason and evidence, and in so far as this happens, it does represent a valuable development from the original sensibility to risk of error, and readiness to attend to any possible indication of this. But that is a matter of individual disposition and training, a voluntary addition, as it were, and not inherent in the dialectical "why" demand.[2] The latter must be distinguished as a quite separate usage of "why", like that of inquiry as to

[2]See Note 1 [p. 55].

motive or purpose. (As such, however, it becomes generalised in its turn as a recognised form of elicitation of the grounds or basis of any proposition, irrespective of its relation to the beliefs of a particular person. In this form it makes a different sub-type again.)

(iv) In addition to the above collection of types of "why", there are others which are not questions at all but exclamations, but which yet should not be omitted altogether, because they very clearly bring the affective or dramatic features of the primary situation out: they signify protest, anger, helplessness, surprise, surprised recognition and other variations on the same theme.

E: Children and the Word "Why"

The foregoing rough survey of the main kinds of meaning of the "why" question is intended in the first place to make clear by contradistinction the special type, and as I think the original and most significant one, with which I am concerned here. I have given at the end a table of "why"-meanings and modes of explanation which may assist a general survey of the field. [See page 53.]

There is, however, a second reason why the complexity and confusion of the meanings of "why" needs to be underlined for the purposes of the present argument. The main import of the latter is that children from four to five years onward clearly and freely show "why's" of the epistemic type and derivative types, and through them display the identity of the dynamic of their thought with that of ours. If this can be established as a fact, it is all the more impressive because (*a*) the earliest usages of "why" to the child can only bring a motivational or other psychological meaning home to him—when "why" is addressed to him, *he* is not in a state of puzzlement or surprise; (*b*) the later usages indicated above, as the child comes across them, must make up the most bewildering shifting medley of meanings, and the child must have a very powerful intrinsic drive of attention and interest in the right direction if he is to pick out the distinctive epistemic meaning of "why" from the tangle. He does so, if I am right, because the experiences and needs which this meaning meets were waiting in him for a means of expression from his very first years, so that he is ready to grasp at anything that looks like such a means even from afar. On the other hand, if we take a random collection of children's "why's", we have to remember, firstly, the bias we give to the meaning of this *sound* by its first introduction, in favour of motives, purposes, etc.; secondly, the multiplicity and confusion of our own usages of the sound to or round the child, from which he has to collect its meaning as best he can. We may therefore have a great deal of work to do upon the interpretation of the verbal material, before we begin to draw any conclusions as to the beliefs of the child, true or mistaken—let alone then the peculiar "structure" of his mind. Where, however, *in spite of these obstacles and difficulties,* the child plainly testifies to the identity of his cognitive attitude and relation to the world with ours, it is evident that we need not ask anything better.

SECTION II: SOME EVIDENTIAL FACTS

1. PREFATORY NOTE ON THE MOST DISTINCTIVE "WHY"

Coming now to the consideration of actual questions, it may be worth while to distinguish a little more clearly what I have so far lumped together as concern with the correctness, sufficiency and unambiguity of knowledge.

The occasions for the first two concerns are plain enough. We may, on the one hand, have the most dramatic clash, where a definite belief or expectation is or seems suddenly falsified by some facts. Or on the other hand, we may get dramatic failures of knowledge, where we come up against some fact that is totally unexpected and unprepared for, a fact that reveals a quite unsuspected gap in the knowledge or expectations which we had been acting on as sufficient in some given situation. In both these kinds of case, attention to our knowledge is immediately made important. In suitable circumstances it occurs and leads to a search for readjustment. But the actual dramatic experience and its consequences may distract or distort or overwhelm the mere epistemic interest. There may be no opportunity or no appetite for any question, and the demonstrated reality of error or insufficiency may leave no room for anything but hasty abandonment or correction, without as much as any question how we came to fall into it.

For the *ideal* conditions for epistemic interest we must rather turn to kinds of occasions which are never anything more than mere *risk* of error, viz., occasions of ambiguity or confusion of expectation. There is no happening in them, only observation. Of course their ultimate practical significance is that of *future risks* of disastrous clashes or gaps; these are to be forestalled by getting the ambiguous rule or control of the situation quite clear here and now. That, however, is a pure epistemic issue. The question is: why does this, so far similar to that, suddenly begin to diverge? Why do these similar things behave differently? In general: "Why . . . whereas . . . ". The apparent similarity which one might have adopted as one's guide is evidently not satisfactory, reliable or sufficient: what is the right controlling rule? These "why's" of difference, divergence, or contrast, between otherwise similar things or situations to which one might have applied the same rule, are perhaps the most characteristic class of "why's", the most open-minded and the most attentively explored. They obviously lead by insensible gradations to definite anomalies or anti-expectednesses in one direction, to sharp unexpectednesses in another. But in them we can most clearly see the epistemic interest, not only the rectifying, but the pre-rectifying and forestalling function, of "why". Merely possible rules or natural or plausible expectations ("one would think", "one might expect", etc.) are envisaged side by side with their difficulties and apparent flaws. What is sought for is differentiating, delimiting or controlling knowledge. These "why's" of difference, divergence and contrast are in continual use among adults, and one need, I think, only invite attention to them to make their epistemic character plain. I hope to show that they are as easily illustrated from the questions of young children. They appear to me to constitute the *clearest* evidence of the reality and the meaning of the child's concern with his knowledge.

2. THE DATA DRAWN ON

In going on now to the factual data, I do not propose to confine myself to the "why" questions collected from the Malting House records, which in any case happen to be very few. I do not quite know why this should be so; one may suppose that far more must have been asked, but that as this matter had not been singled out for any special attention, they did not get recorded. When one child stood out by the copiousness and persistency of his "why's", they became a focus of attention and were put down. But ordinary occasional and scattered "why's" were not specially heeded. If my view is right, this is much to be regretted. A complete record of the "why's" of children under conditions such as those of the School would have been very illuminating. I rather imagine that those conditions would have been reflected in a different distribution of "why's", some kinds tending to be more infrequent, whilst others would be increased. However, this is idle speculation, and in fact the School records are particularly meagre, especially when the performance of the one child Phineas is subtracted. I have therefore drawn on the general literature, as far as I have been able to find any relevant data in it, and all the more so, in view of the generality of my thesis; but I will say at once that the *quantity* of material I have found available is not impressive. However, I believe that it will readily be recognised as qualitatively representative. So much so that there is no point in using even all such data as I have collected, and a few typical instances are as good as a long, merely repetitive series. If I am not much mistaken, most people will have no difficulty in matching the *kind* of questions I shall use from their own experience of young children, and it will be obvious that these questions do not, as a whole, represent rare exceptions, but the sort of thing that is common and ordinary with intelligent children.[3]

[3]For this reason also it seems hardly necessary to give a special reference for each question. I will merely mention here that apart from the School records, and those given as appendices to this volume [Susan Isaacs, *Intellectual Growth in Young Children*], I have mainly drawn upon that notable paper "The Scientific Interests of a Boy in Pre-School Years" [see footnote 4 below], Sully's *Studies of Childhood,* and a few scattered sources. [James Sully, *Studies of Childhood* (London: Longmans, 1903).]

In connection with Sully, let me add that his account of children's "why's" still seems to me to hold the field as the best all round one available — at any rate of those known to me. He intellectualises his "why's" too much, and rather turns the child into a little philosopher; but apart from divergences on these points, the present analysis may be looked upon as a completion of Sully's account, and vindication of it against more one-sided views.

3. SOME SPECIMEN CLEAR QUESTIONS

I will begin by offering three examples from children under five years of age, examples which seem to me worth particular attention in the light of my general argument.

> (4;1) Why doesn't the ink run out when you hold up a fountain pen?[4]
> (4;1) Why does it get lighter outside when you put the light out?
> (3;9) Why don't we see two things with our two eyes?

I think it is reasonably apparent (*a*) that there is no question of motive or purpose in these enquiries; and (*b*) what their real occasion and meaning is. The first one especially is crystal-clear: the child is struck by the *anomaly* of this liquid *not* tipping out as liquids always do when treated like that. He is stopped and puzzled. He wants the difficulty smoothed out, the puzzlement removed. In other words, he wants an explanation.

This example is one of a definite clash between a familiar rule and a contrary present fact. The second provides a similar but less sharply defined anomaly. When the light is put out, it becomes dark, and yet you notice sometimes that outside, where it was dark before, it is now lighter. It seems queer. You would think it would get still darker. And you can't understand how something which makes it dark should actually be able to make anything lighter. Hence again perplexity, a sense of something wrong or lacking somewhere; and a demand for the removal of the anomaly, i.e., an explanation.

The third example is still of the same type, but not so closely tethered to a specific experience. There is no intrusive external fact of challenge. But there is an anomaly as soon as you come to think of it. At some moment the two separate facts of (*a*) two eyes, and (*b*) one thing seen, come together in the mind of an intelligent child and he sees the strangeness and surprisingness of their conjunction. Usually, when he attends to eyes, he attends to them as things seen, like any others; and when he attends to other things seen, he is not thinking of his *two* eyes. But if the two kinds of fact come together in his mind, how queer it suddenly seems that you don't see one thing each for each eye (which of course can see by itself) and so two of each thing because you have two eyes. Why, so unnaturally, does one see only one thing? Why doesn't one, as one would expect, see two? The child again feels that there is something wrong somewhere. Puzzled, he turns to the understanding adult for help—that is, for an explanation.

It so happens that a great many adults would no doubt give a teleological reply to this last question. E.g., they might very plausibly say: because there is only one thing there, and if we saw two, we should get completely muddled

---

[4] "The Scientific Interests of a Boy in Pre-School Years, By Two Parents." *Forum of Education* 6 (February, 1928): 22.

and lost. I do not question that such a reply would usually satisfy the child; whether it should quite satisfy the adult to give it is another matter. One might indeed have to agree that a more appropriate reply would be more difficult to make intelligible to the child; but it might be better to try and find some way of overcoming the difficulty than to give an irrelevant and misleading explanation—even though this might be much worse. The child cannot know any better, and in any case turns to the adult trustfully, ready as a rule to accept whatever he gets as the right help, since offered. Moreover he must in large measure form his standard of what constitutes right help, i.e., satisfactory explanation, from what he gets from the adult. The responsibility rests with the latter. But the important point, for the present argument, is not what the adult in his wisdom or unwisdom considers the right answer to give, but what is the state of the child when he asks the question. In that state, I suggest, there is nothing whatever teleological; the child merely notices a physical, almost an arithmetical, anomaly: two seeing eyes and only one seen thing. His interest is purely epistemic; he is held up by a contradiction and wants it cleared up. He does *not* know how to deal with it, and makes no assumption as to how it is to be dealt with; and it is just this state of being held up that he expresses by the question "why", and through it refers to the adult for his help or explanation.

4. SOME REJECTIONS OF FAULTY ADULT ANSWERS

However, it is not an absolute rule that the child will accept the adult's explanation, even when it is a teleological one. He is quite capable of applying a functional standard of his own—that of the functional need which generates his question.

Carrying the case a stage further, we may observe how even in cases where "why" specifically refers to human behaviour, it need not be motive or purpose as such, but their anomalousness or contrariness to the accustomed order which is in question.[5] The situation is in fact exactly on a par with physical anomalies; and in one important sense, the child might at least as truly be described as a universal mechanist, assimilating human behaviour to the physical world, as set down as a universal voluntarist, assimilating the physical world to human behaviour. He may assume similar causes in the former as in the latter; but he certainly also assumes a similar uniformity in the latter as in the former, and applies the same criteria. He is puzzled and put out by human behaviour that does not fit into what he has come to look upon as its law or invariable rule in a given set of circumstances, just as he is puzzled or put out by physical anomalies, the inverted liquid that does not

---

[5] A particularly clear example is the *first "Why"* of Scupin's boy, quoted by Piaget as follows: "The child's mother was lying on the ground. The boy wants to get her up: 'Du bis ya nicht tot warum stehste nicht immersu auf?' ['You are not dead — why don't you stand up?']" (*The Language and Thought of the Child* [trans. Marjorie Warden (London: Kegan Paul, Trench, Trubner, 1926)], p. 233.)

spill, the light put out which yet makes the dark lighter, the two seeing eyes that only see one thing.

Moreover, the child can make quite plain the epistemic character of his interest and question, by at once picking out the flaw in any explanation which fails to deal with the anomaly. This is exhibited clearly in the following two examples. The first in particular is a striking demonstration of the capabilities of child logic. What seems astonishing about it is that a boy of under four and a half years should be able so to *sustain* his criticism and to drive it home at last to such deadly effect.

I refer to the discussion quoted from Sully[6] on pp. 162-3. The terms are terms of human actions and ordinances. But the "why" question arises from a sense of anomaly, and presses for an explanation of the troubling anomalous fact. The child is pre-occupied with the killing of animals. He asks what seems to be an ordinary question of motive or purpose, not even in the "why" form, about the killing of seals. He is provided with a purpose. But that is not really what he wants: he quickly raises the same question about the killing of another animal where that purpose does not apply. "Why do they kill the stags? *They don't want their skins, do they?*" This time the issue is clear. The adult can only reply: because people want to chase and kill them. But that now only enhances and intensifies the anomaly. People do sometimes want to do horrible things, but in that case they are stopped, there are special people to stop them. What has gone wrong in this instance? "*Why* don't policemen stop them?" The adult is forced further; he has to define the situation still more plainly and sharply. People are not stopped, because killing animals for pleasure ("because they like to chase them") is allowed. "Allowed, allowed? People are not allowed to take other people and kill them." The adult's explanation of the killing is monstrous. In the process of looking for an explanation, the anomaly has simply become worse and worse. There is less than ever one, and yet there must be one. "You don't understand me." The adult can't be seeing that there is something here so horrible and contradictory to all acknowledged reason and order that there *must* be some explanation, something that somehow makes a difference. One can't have made him understand one. Killing is acknowledged as an abhorrent thing, yet animals are killed. Special motives may be offered in some cases, but they won't do, they clearly do not apply to others, one is only pulled up all the more by a case where they are not the explanation. But there must be an explanation—there must be something which if only one knew it, would somehow alter the situation, would make the killing of animals like stags in some quite unthought of way different, would sharply separate or free it from the horror of killing. For without some such explanation, there is the contradiction, there is the fact that animals are killed, though killing is something which everybody knows to be revolting. And then the adult makes

[6] [Sully, *Studies of Childhood*.]

the contradiction a hundred times worse: animals are killed for pleasure, and *allowed* to be taken and killed. That cannot be. Think of it with people, is it not monstrous and quite unthinkable? The boy could not feel anything else but that they did not understand him.

The above pedantic dotting of every *i* of the child's thought and expression is not of course offered to increase the force of his case (which speaks far more powerfully for itself), but rather as a study in the anatomy of the demand for explanation. Cases which make the articulation of this demand so clear and permit such a sustained and cumulative analysis are rare.

My second example is in fact of a much simpler order, with only one stage of criticism, and that immediately let go, together with the original question, in favour of a different direction of interest. However, the principle is the same. On p. 358[7] will be found Rose's question, at 3;8: "Why don't we milk pigs?" This of course is a clear epistemic question of difference or deviation, not of motive or purpose. The adult deals with it as such, but unfortunately gives an explanation which is thoroughly bad logically. "Because they (pigs) have little ones of their own to feed." This is presumably suggested by the particular circumstances of the actual case, but of course it cannot explain the difference in treatment of cow and pig; it does not constitute a standing difference between them. The child instantly seizes upon and answers the bad logic. "So do cows have calves!" Try again, mummy! Only, she now suddenly sights a better game, a real first-rate leg-pulling game, and amusingly twists her first theoretical interest into that, and drops her merely logical quarry.

With the above two cases, it seems natural to associate a third, where "why" is used in one of its more divergent and less epistemic senses, but where the same criteria of control of the answer can again be seen applied. In the episode on p. 145,[8] "why" is employed in connection with a rule, as children easily and quickly learn to do. This use of "why" can in some respects be classified with "why's" of purpose or motive, and is no doubt also related to the later "why's" of logical justification, but in much of its import, it approaches close to the primary functional import of "why". A rule is like an unrelated kind of fact, often an unexpected fact and one that interferes with one's course and may easily stop it. One needs to be able to foresee the rule, to adapt oneself to it in advance, or at the very least, when one comes up against it, to learn to link it up in some way with things one already accepts, understands, and has in some sense mastered. The "why" question

---

[7] [Susan Isaacs, *Intellectual Growth in Young Children*.]

[8] "12.11.24. While Mrs. I was sitting near Benjie (4:1), helping him to put on his shoes, he said reflectively, 'Why do we have to pick up things that we put on the floor?' Mrs. I replied, 'Well, if we left them on the floor, and were running and trod on them, we might break them, mightn't we?' He said, 'We shouldn't break those big bricks, should we?' Mrs. I: 'No, but perhaps we should hurt our feet on them.' This seemed to content him."

thus comes to aim not merely at any sort of familiar motive or purpose for
the rule, but at a ground or justification which will make it clear what there is
to make this rule necessary or desirable. If the child can get it translated into
terms of actual things and their behaviour and effects, he can feel that he is
on known firm ground. He can foresee what rules will be called for by those
things from occasion to occasion, instead of being taken by surprise by them.
And in the converse way, he will not run the same amount of risk of suddenly
finding that some rule of which he does not understand the ground or basis
lets him down—does not apply in this or that case. Therefore he asks for the
means to his own understanding, which signifies foresight, control and
security.

But therefore also what is proffered in reply must *serve.* An alert and
intelligent child may accordingly at once weigh up what is offered to him,
and reject it if not up to standard. The logic of the situation is the same as
that of the previous examples. The ground supplied must cover all cases of
the rule, else it is not the right ground for that rule. If it is merely based upon
some special feature of some cases of the rule, it is fallacious and useless for
its function. You cannot understand the rule through it, nor use it as a key or
control as to where the rule will and where it will not apply.

But adequate objective grounds for rules are not easy to produce
point-blank on demand. At the best they may happen to be very complicated
and at many removes from straight-forward external facts; but it may also
happen that no sufficient grounds exist!

The latter type of rule the Malting House School tried hard to avoid, and
even the former was minimised as much as possible, though of course it could
not be avoided. And simple and easily intelligible objective grounds, which
would in fact give the child the utmost possible power of understanding the
rules and foreseeing them, were always valiantly tried for.

Thus the child's challenge was met at once; in fact a little too quickly. The
objective basis or firm ground offered for the rule about picking up things
was the risk of breaking them. But if you start giving reasons to an intelligent
child, the child may reward you by applying reason to them, and in that case
it is as well to make sure in advance that one can afford to risk that reward.
The child instantly perceived that the ground offered did not match the rule.
It might have been a ground for a rule of picking up breakable things, it was
not a ground for picking up things at large. He lodges his perfectly valid
objection: "we shouldn't [i.e., wouldn't, couldn't] break those big bricks!" A
better reason is needed; the firm ground he wants is not there yet; try again,
"Mrs. I.".

Well, "Mrs. I." tries again, but alas, only tries a further special reason for a
further special case. One hopes that the child quoted by Sully would not have
let himself be put off like that. He would have found a case where no hurt
would happen either to what was left about or to those who were using the

room, and he would have gone on insisting for a valid reason (or a sufficient collection of reasons) for the rule. But it needs no doubt a strong motive, as well as unusual powers of resistance to casuistry, to go on resisting a *succession* of *plausible* reasons which merely happen not to be sufficient. There would not be many adults who would not have let themselves be persuaded that "Mrs. I.'s" second ground, added to her first, cleared things up. One is certainly continually accepting this mixture of reason and suggestion in everyday life. It is not surprising, and not discreditable to him, that Benjie seemed content; he had not got a sufficient reason for his rule, but he had a pair of quite good reasons. And of course he also had the prestige of the adult to back them, and his inevitable great plasticity to this prestige. Moreover, as has already been remarked, whatever the child's original functional standard may be, through turning to the adult for guidance he offers his very standard, at least in some degree, to the adult's moulding. One can even say that, up to a point, the more helpful guidance he gets on the whole, the more he may lay himself open to take over any unhelpful leads as well—as if they were one of the forms or degrees of helpfulness, drawn from the superior wisdom of the adult. The responsibility for the right or the wrong help rests with the latter.

5. A DOUBTFUL CASE

I have dealt in some detail with these striking cases, because they belong to ground where, if anywhere, the child's mere concern with purposes or motives might be expected to exert the fullest sway, whilst yet a sharply critical epistemic logic has in fact been found present. It may now be worth glancing at a special case provided by the School records, where "why" has certainly degenerated in some measure into mere automatism and it might seem that there is nothing to be expected from it. Yet closer inspection once more shows clearly that underneath the automatic degeneration of the function, its genuine characters still remain present and operative.

Phineas' "why's"[9] are probably in part a function of his temperament, and express a certain vehement impatience with anything of any kind that offers opposition to his knowledge, understanding or purposes. Accordingly he is often mainly concerned to discharge this feeling, and just passes on from one such discharge to another without settling down to any attempt to clear up the obstacle. Explosive protest takes the place of the prolonged and held state of puzzlement. Hence he is in fact much of the time relatively uninterested in explanation; when he has made his protest and so relieved his feelings, he can go on to the next thing.

But one reason why he goes on so often is no doubt just that he is not really left at a loss. Since he overflows into "why" at the least touch of

[9] See, e.g., pp. 148-149. [*Ibid.*]

anything like obstruction, he does so frequently when the obstruction is one which he need only bother with to overcome. He needs no help, or only the barest touch of it; he can supply his own explanation.

Thus, note 24 and 25.2.27 (p. 149). As soon as his "why" is retorted on him, he gives his own perfectly just *physical* explanation. No doubt in some cases—though hardly in 24.2.27—the retort of his question helps to turn his attention to the explanatory fact; but even so, it presents no difficulty to him, he has only to read it off. Of course, the "why's" in question are not "why's" of pure open puzzlement, "why's" of breakdown of knowledge or sharp clash between knowledge and event. They belong to the class of causal derivatives. They represent indeed unexpected and uncustomary events; but of a kind which plainly suggests the interposition of a special cause. So that "why" here means merely: what special *disturbing* or *interfering* cause or fact produces this disturbance of the usual or expected course of events. We get this clearly in "Why won't it burn?" (25.2.27), as in all the large class of *negative questions* of this type. They are definitely questions for preventive or interfering causes. They represent one of the most important lines along which causal interest branches off from epistemic. Incidentally, they are sufficient of themselves to vindicate the causal interest and capacity of young children, since their causal meaning is as a rule quite unmistakable, and leaves no room for any anthropomorphic or purposive interpretation.

Even in Phineas, however, we get "why's" of very genuine puzzlement, based upon sheer disappointment of expectation. E.g., when on 27.1.27 (p. 148) his starch did not turn blue, as Miss C.'s had done, and on 2.2.27 (p. 149) he applied a match to every hole of an old gas-fire, and asked, "Why won't it burn?" this time really at a loss. The spate of "why's" on 21.1.27, when he was only 3;11, connected with the picture of the station has been dealt with in the main text (pp. 85-86). It would certainly seem here that whilst some of the "why's" taken separately are mere pointers and exclamation marks, and others simple demands for motives or purposes, the meaning of his whole behaviour is a reaction to the unfamiliar and unrelated construction of the picture, as against his experience of actual stations. He notices and challenges where the picture fails to meet the obvious demands of real trains, the stoppage of the railway lines at the margin, the fact that you could not see the railway go on, etc. If this was a picture of the station, why wasn't it like the station?

6. TESTIMONY FROM THE ADVERSE EVIDENCE

By way of clinching the case so far, we may now glance at some of Piaget's own records of questions.[10] These emanate from a child of 6-7, i.e., a rather later age than my argument calls for, but on the other hand this is a child whom Piaget definitely finds to be in the precausal stage. Let us consider the following:

Why haven't little goats any milk ?

Why are there waves only at the edge of the lake ?

Why can you see lightning better at night ?

Why do ladies not have beards ?

Why are the funnels (on a boat) slanting ?

Why do wood and iron rub out pencil marks ?

Why do animals not mind drinking dirty water ?

Why have you got little ears and I have big ones although I am small ?

Why is my dadder bigger than you although he is young ?

Why has it (a dead caterpillar) grown quite small ?

I suggest that all these are definitely epistemic "why's". Their subject matter—i.e., whether human, animal or physical—is immaterial to their meaning. An element of vague supposition of possible motive or intention may be admixed in *some* of them, but it is at the most only an element; there is no evidence whatever of it in other instances, and it does not affect the common character of all these questions, which has nothing to do with motive. They are all cases of anomaly, deviation, contrast or difference; and the "why" question is a demand for help in dealing with them, since past experience leaves the child at a loss about them. Why should the little goats not have milk, while the big have? What is there about little goats that makes the difference?—Since there are waves at the edge (i.e., in one part) of the lake, how is it that there are none elsewhere, what is there that makes the difference between the edge and the rest?—At night most things can't be seen or only very poorly; why should lightning actually be seen better then?—What is it that prevents ladies from having beards like men, what underlies this difference between them and men?—Chimneys always go up straight; that is part of the picture of a chimney. Now all of a sudden, on the boat here, they are bent. What a queer thing, a bent chimney. What makes them be different like that?—You often write with a pencil, and that is what a pencil does, it makes marks. You presently try writing on a table or a stove, and the pencil marks either do not come out at all, or seem to go off at once, as if the wood or iron rubbed them out as they were made. Of course you notice that that happens when you are writing on wood or iron instead of, as usual, on paper. (Perhaps even, when you find that the table or stove rub out the marks, you now specially try other things, and you find that it is always wood and iron that rub out in this way.) And so you ask: what is there about wood and iron (as against paper, or different from paper) which prevents a pencil from leaving the proper pencil marks?—Dirty water is something that seems disgusting to you and to everybody else to drink; yet animals do not mind it. How extraordinary! Why is it not disgusting to them? What makes them not mind it? What is it that makes the animals feel or act so differently from us, so contrary to everything one would have imagined?—You expect little ears in anybody small, big ears in anybody big. How does it come about that it is the other way round here?—In the same way, as people grow older,

[10] [Piaget, *The Language and Thought of the Child.*]

they grow bigger. Yet my daddy who is young is bigger than you (evidently taken for older). How is that?—How strange, a thing like a caterpillar grown much smaller than it was. You might expect it to *grow* bigger, and anyhow, not smaller. This dead caterpillar: what has happened to make it go small? And is there perhaps a connection between death and growing small? "When I die, shall I also grow quite small?"

Piaget takes a different view of these questions, (which are scattered among his various categories), and finds that they either demand, or at least fit into, his general scheme of the intentionalising attitude and assumptions of the child. In the presence of the impressive body of evidence he has brought together, which seems plausibly to demand conclusions such as his, some attempt to meet the force of his data and intrepretations is clearly called for. My general case will, I hope, seem reasonably established as far as it goes, independently of this attempt, but the questions are: what relation does it bear to those other data? How are the two sets, pointing such different ways, to be harmonised? Do Piaget's data limit or qualify the interpretations offered here? Or if my view is just, what re-interpretation in its light do his data permit?

But these questions will come better after a further and larger body of supporting instances, to which therefore I now proceed.

7. A BATCH OF TYPICAL EVIDENCE IN SUPPORT:

3;6 It (exit of a tunnel at a distance) looks very weeny. Why does it?

3;7 Why can I put my hand through water and not through soap?

3;7 Why do ponies not grow big like other horses?

3;7 What's there? (Of houses behind a fence at night.) *Houses.* Why can't we see them?

3;9 Why are the snails in the water?

3;10 (About a spinning-wheel when the strap had slipped off the wheel.) Why won't it work?

3;11 Why won't it (wet raffia held in fire) burn?

3;11 Why didn't it (starch paste) turn blue?

3;11 Why won't it (old gas fire) burn?

3;11 Why does it (Bunsen burner choked with matches) burn?

3;11 Why did it (burner held in water) go out?

4;0 (Seeing word PULL on lavatory Pull), Why are there two l's? We don't need two, do we? One would do, wouldn't it? Why has it got PULL? We know what to do, don't we? We don't need that, do we?

4;1 Why does the soap look smaller in the water?

4;0 Why don't they (shadows) go before us?

4;1 Why is there no shadow when there is no light?

4;3 Why can't we see the stars in the day-time?

4;4 Why doesn't the butter stay on top (of hot toast)?

4;5 Why does the water spread out flat (in the bath)? Why won't it keep up in the middle?

4;5 Why do you see the lightning before you hear the thunder?

4;5 Why am I not in two all the way up?

4;5 Why does the glass look different in the water, but it doesn't if you just put water in the glass? The water can't really bend the glass, can it?

4;11 Why can't we sharpen them (pencils) like they were when we first got them, all round and smooth? (*And note the boy's own answer:* I know, it's because they're not done with a knife; they're done with those things that you turn round.)

5;0 Why does water go out of the way when anything goes in?

5;0 Why don't trains stop and start off suddenly express?

A few examples from older children may be noted also:

6;0 Why does the beam of sunlight stay so narrow? Why is it on this side of the room in the morning and the other at night?

6;6 Why do the angels never fall down to earth when there is no floor to heaven?

7;0 Why can't you see the messages on the telegraph wires? How do they go?

7;0 Why does a square piece of wood look round when the lathe is working?

7;4 Hasn't it (a sparrow) any teeth? Why hasn't it?

In the above examples there is always, either directly presented or close to the surface, some habitual experience, some natural expectation from habitual experience, which appears falsified, or challenged, or at least confused, by present fact. The snail in the water, when snails are always found on land; the sparrow which so surprisingly is found not to have any teeth like the animals familiarly known to the child; the water that, unlike other heaped up things, won't make a heap; and also unlike other things, goes out of the way when anything goes in; the express trains that are supposed to go as fast as possible, but are so slow in starting and stopping; the pencils that can't be sharpened now as they certainly were sharpened at the start; the tunnel exit that looks so small, quite unlike any tunnel exit one has ever gone through; and so on, and so forth; all these are matters that need *explaining*. In other words, they need so dealing with that you will know when to expect the one kind of fact, and when the other, how the queer fact is brought about and the usual one prevented, or whether, by any chance, the queer fact is not so at all (one "thought it was funny"): whatever, in brief, you need in order to make this fact like other facts, and to get over the hitch or difficulty.

SECTION III:
THEORETICAL PROBLEMS AND ISSUES

1. A CASE FOR ADEQUATE INQUIRY—AND ITS CONDITIONS

I imagine that instances to swell the foregoing list could be collected from almost any child left free to interest himself in the world about him. Those given are mainly intended as illustrations.[11] For the chief purpose of my argument, for establishing the reality and the character of what I have called the *epistemic* why question in young children, the instances given seem to me sufficient. They range over a number of different children of five years of age and under, well scattered in time and place, and there appears to me to be good reason for thinking them representative. But, of course, a really wide and systematic collection of the "why's" of children under, say, six is needed to provide full scientific data as to the *extent,* and variations in extent, of children's epistemic interest. This interest might well be found to vary with individual temperament, with native trend of interest, with intelligence, with general social setting, and with educational influences in the widest sense. It would be important to discover how much in it was innate and uncontrollable, how much open to instructed and thought-out environmental control. Moreover, given a large body of systematic data, the detailed study of all the varieties of experience and response distinguishable within children's epistemic interests would also, I believe, add a great deal to our insight into the general functional development of thought.

Possibly the present argument may help to make the necessary record seem worth while to some among those who have the opportunity for it; and it may also suggest some very essential precautions which are liable to be overlooked. I have already stressed the importance of distinguishing between the thought of the child, and the sound "why" and its history. Observers of children have been liable to hail some child's first "why's" as if these defined his attitude to the universe instead of merely his reaction to a repeated parental sound. In any study of the first development of the use of "why", the parent's primary part, the history of his introduction of the sound, cannot in effect be omitted. It comes first, and must be taken first, and is the right and only possible key to what the *sound* "why" should or can mean to the child.

Furthermore: how children come to make the junction between their epistemic concerns and the sound "why" (with its first different meaning), would make a very interesting study. But if comparable data were to be obtained from different children, the parents' or adults' part in that junction would have to be much more consistent and uniform than it can usually be

---

[11] Quite by chance, a friend has just mentioned the following question of her boy of 3;8: "When a building has a corrugated iron roof, why is the corrugated iron always crinkly, and not flat like the other sorts?" This might have been expressly composed for my argument.

assumed to be. We fail to allow for the extent to which this highly variable extraneous factor enters into data which we treat as if they offered direct access to the thought of the child. What is needed, in fact, from the point of view of adequate scientific method, is a collection of studies of the development of the epistemic interests of different children, with a reasonable *shared* minimum standard of attention to the way in which they are provided with the instrument for expressing these interests.

This very exacting ideal is no doubt a long way off and will have to be made to seem much less pedantic and more practically useful before it will be seriously thought worth while. But so long as its conditions remain so very unfulfilled, I very much doubt whether the bravest show of statistical methods, percentage measurements, and even experimental results helps us any further. It may only succeed in seeming much more conclusive than it really is. So long as the data are not homogeneous or even clear, formal scientific treatment of them in the mass is liable to be a positive pitfall and a snare, and what may be needed in its stead is intensive qualitative analysis to establish the meaning of the data. But of course if abundant controlled comparative data are not available, the results of such an analysis can only be very preliminary. This limitation has to be fully recognised in the present case.

2. THE OUTCOME SO FAR

If we grant then that a great deal of essential *amplifying* information is lacking, I think that it is still reasonable to claim that the foregoing analysis establishes at any rate the widespread presence of a particular significant factor in the thought of children of from four to five years onwards. The data do not permit any scientific measure of its force or extent on the average, or in any large class of cases, but there are good theoretical reasons for supposing that it has a part of some consequence to play in the development of any child, at any rate in our civilisation.

This factor of epistemic interest and inquiry, as far as it goes, is in every respect the same in the child as in the adult.

To the four and five year examples, I have added a few more from children over six, in order to bring out the perfect continuity of type of these epistemic questions, but I might just as easily have illustrated this by instances taken from adults. The situation is the same and is reacted to in the same way. Intelligent inquiring grown-ups ask the same type of question every day. Some of the most important and fruitful scientific inquiries set out from just such starting-points. They are the typical beginnings of new and better *integrative* knowledge. They initiate revision, reorganisation, and new, previously unthought of lines of extension of knowledge. Why is, or isn't . . . ? Why should, or shouldn't . . . ? Why does, or doesn't . . . ? Why does this . . . whereas that . . . ? These are the ways by which isolated, anomalous or discrepant facts, unexpectedly or confusingly divergent facts, lead us, just as they do the child, to the most important corrections and fruitful expansions of our thought. By such questions, the child shows himself already capable of subjecting his beliefs to revision; by such questions we show our beliefs to be still liable to or in need of revision. They are the outstanding manifestations of the identity in function and mode of growth of the child's mind and ours.

3. THE CONFLICT WITH PIAGET'S VIEWS

A: An alternative to Piaget's interpretation of the differences between children's and adults' "why's"

There are, of course, notable differences—though also a large region of overlap—in the content of children's and adults' questions. Different expectations are challenged, different supposed knowledge is found wanting. But these differences, if I am right, are a function of experience, and of its cumulative effect. In the simplest case, we do not ask some of the child's questions, because through having asked them, or else by the right kind of offered instruction or experience, we have learnt the answer. Other cases are more complicated, but I believe that the character, range and limits of previous experience are in general a sufficient key. These factors determine the child's expectations; and the mere fact that he accepts factual challenges to them, and appeals or looks for a way of meeting these, seems to me to be evidence of this origin of his expectations or assumptions, and to give strong support to the view that they do not issue from a fixed internal assimilative structure of the child's mind.

They represent, rather, an accumulated psychic content, which may be more or less strongly established, but is still liable to be disestablished by the same kind of force and the same kind of process by which it was established. In responding to those challenges, the child demonstrates his ability to receive new and discrepant experience. He thus at least answers the possible argument that, whilst his experience may suffice to account for his beliefs, yet the structure of his mind limits his reception of experience, so that those beliefs still reflect what alone he can take in.

The full answer to this argument is, however, that there may well be respects in which the beliefs of children (and of adults) are structurally incapable of modification—respects in which we simply do not or cannot receive what would be needed to change us; but that the field of "why" questions is the last field in which to look for such fixed innate beliefs. It is mainly organised about experiences, situations and stimuli which *demand* and *initiate* modification. Loosely affiliated with it, there are, indeed, important fields which are dominated by specific modes of organisation of experience ("why's" of motive, purpose, etc.), but just through this affiliation, even these become open at suitable points, and through suitable stimuli, to cumulative reorganisation.

The general position is that we carry about with us beliefs or assumptions of all degrees of fixity, and that our "why" questions testify with varying degrees of force, both to their strength of lodgment (at the time), and to their liability to a greater or less measure of dislodgment. Epistemic "why's" testify mainly to the latter, informational "why's" mainly to the former; but the second may easily pass into the first. Our absolutely fixed and innate assumptions probably do not come into the open. When any do so, they have presumably begun to get unmoored (as Piaget himself illuminatingly points out). Those that do come into the open, however, as definite established assumptions, may offer greater or less resistance to change, in the child as in the adult. It is right and necessary in most cases that they should offer a certain amount of resistance, just on the basis of all that past successful functioning by which they have become established. The problem is, in fact, precisely to arrive at some sort of division or apportionment between past belief and present kind of fact, so that the former can be preserved where it *is* valuable and successful, whilst the latter can be done justice to wherever its occasion arises. Sometimes very little may thus be left of the original assumption; or it may break up altogether as pure stupidity, blindness or prejudice. Sometimes it may be only very slightly modified or simplified; or it may even emerge quite intact, the challenging occasion being resolved into mere misperception. But of course stupidity, blindness or prejudice, or *possibly* some absolute innate factor may prolong, fortify or cause resistance beyond any power of change. That, however, applies to adults as much as to children, and is to such a large extent explicable by the history, the acquired functional value, and often the social enforcement or reinforcement of particular beliefs, that the evidence for absolute innate factors must at the best be dubious in the extreme. Resort to them, foreclosing on the examinable causes, is therefore thoroughly liable to be premature and gratuitous.[12]

B: Attempt at re-interpretation of Piaget's findings

The foregoing seems to me to provide the main basis for the right understanding, both of the familiar anthropomorphism and intentionalism of the child, and of Piaget's further demonstration of this.

In detail:

(a) We must, of course, in the first place eliminate the regular and correct use of "why" for inquiries as to motives or purposes, where we should ourselves use it in exactly the same way as the child.

(b) We must not assume that the child is using "why" in this sense wherever he uses it—merely because he is an anthropomorphising child! Nor must we infer that because he is not using it causally (and in a particular causal sense), therefore he must mean it motivationally. The existence and

[12]See Note 2 [p. 59].

importance of the epistemic sense of "why", and of its various derivatives, makes this plain. There is also a certain amount of linguistic confusion and overlap, which makes it very uncertain whether some usages of "why" which we are in the habit of taking as purposive are meant as such or not. Often, no doubt, the child's own state is unclear (which, however, need not mean that it is "pre-causal"—causality being here frequently irrelevant). Stock examples such as "Why does kitty have fur?" "Why do cows have horns?" illustrate this. The former seems to me likely to be meant epistemically, the latter may just possibly be. We have, I think, to learn to consider each case on its merits, and to be prepared to find alike clear and straightforward ones, and all kinds of unclear and mixed ones.

Thus, the teleological meaning—or any other—may be absent, present but subordinate, present but fused with other elements in a vague, unanalysable whole, present and dominant, or solely present. Where there is any doubt, we have to try to decide which it is as best we can. "Can't she (a baby) talk? Why can't she talk?" or "Why can't the cat talk?" seem almost or quite pure epistemic-causal questions. The first case is one of clear exception to rule, with a corresponding demand for the cause or factor that prevents "her" from talking. The second case is more a matter of general analogy or rule. Cats are alive like us, they are persons, "Kitty", "Pussy", "Tom", "Peter", etc. They see and hear and eat and drink, they have a hundred shared and intelligible ways. And yet they cannot talk as we do: how does this discrepant fact come about? The question, "Why does kitty have fur?" may well be homologous with this, a question of puzzling difference or divergence, perplexity as to where one is to expect similarity, where difference—a demand for some delimiting rule. On the other hand, the child may be expecting a purposive reply, partly just because he so often gets it, partly because on so many occasions it is a helpful, an intelligible and satisfactory reply. Or the child's state may be vaguely and fluctuatingly intermediate between the two meanings. On the other hand, in "Why do cows have horns?" there is a suggestion of some active use or function about this additional equipment of the cow's, and the child seems likely enough to mean something like: what do cows *do* with horns? But here, too, there might be an epistemic factor present, a sense of the queerness of having horns, and puzzlement why they have them and we do not—on the same basis of confusing divergence from similarity. Very often in such cases, the behaviour, attitude and tone of the child may show whether he is under a sense of anomaly, or merely asking for a familiar type of information. And certainly the teleological meaning of "why" must not simply be taken for granted.

(c) When all subtractions are made, however, there is no doubt that the child will often use "why" in the sense implying motive or purpose, where this is pure anthropomorphism. Even here, however, we must distinguish between cases of simple, straightforward assumption that a motive or purpose will be forthcoming, and cases where, on the contrary, this very assumption is being shaken—there is behaviour so unlike that of known purposive entities that "why" is asked in discomfiture, and there is, consequently, some preparation for the possible reply, that it is not a case of purposive or rational action at all. In effect, any state of surprise or sense of anomaly opens the way to correction or revision.

However, even the case of assured assumption of intention or purpose seems to me no different from any ordinary plausible error—exactly such as we adults are prone to. They are the most familiar causes or key facts in the experience of the child, and the explanation he most often meets, where he is taken by surprise or left at a loss. He goes on looking for this cause or expecting this explanation until sufficient failure disabuses him. And he is more easily disabused than we are in many of our beliefs! He does not by any means try the category of psychological causes, either as information or as explanation, anywhere near universally; he asks straightforward causal questions outside the "why" form, (*what* makes, not merely *who* makes), epistemic-causal questions in the "why" form, and pure epistemic "why" questions which have nothing to do with purposes or intentions. He tries psychological causes, or looks to psychological explanations, only where something, some analogy, however remote or slight, prompts him to do so. And he learns gradually to demand closer and closer analogies, as the remoter ones fail him. He is capable of discovering or learning his mistakes as we do; and we are capable of continuing to make a given mistake as he is. We retain all the errors which we have not had an opportunity of discovering, all those assumptions which do not happen yet to have come to grief. From time to time, in fact, another one collapses, in order to prove that this is not idle philosophic scepticism. And there is very little more reason for inferring a compelling structure of mind to account for the first anthropomorphism of the child, than for inferring such a structure to account for our Newtonian assumptions prior to Einstein.

(d) A point on which Piaget insists as part of the universal intentionalism of the child is his lack of any notion of chance—his assumption that there are explanations for everything. Here again, we must first of all eliminate the linguistic factor. The universal application of the question form "why" may at least in part be put down to its becoming a more or less automatic verbal habit. In part, again, it is a natural error largely fostered by those round the child, whose answers to his questions offer little guidance as to any intelligible limits, or for that matter any limits, to the application of the why-demand. (So often "anything will do" as a reply to a child's "why's".) However, even after the linguistic factor is ruled out, we get, no doubt, some tendency in children to try for explanations where *we* should say, "chance"—or not ask any question at all. But this is still merely the same general law, just as applicable to us, by which any successful procedure gets extended and extended, and only failure or breakdown uncovers its limits for us. That is just the way in which we have gradually come to find that, in these or those cases, there is either no answer but "chance", or else no significant answer at all—so that such questions cease to be significant ones. It is experience alone which has shown us where we are dealing with unresolvable differences, the actual irreducible variety of the world; where with "chance", i.e., conjunctions or intersections of more or less unrelated courses of events, determined, but without any *single or constant* determining cause; and where with one sort or another of discoverable explanations—causes, controls, constitutive differences, differential circumstances, possible correction of rule, etc., etc. And over wide areas, we cannot be sure in advance even now what we are dealing with, and have developed a whole elaborate science of statistical analysis in order to try to sort out one kind of case from another. Furthermore, apart from chance, the facts for which we expect no explanation are often merely cases of *resigned* puzzlement: our attitude remains identical with that of the intelligent child. We crave an explanation, we cannot help feeling, at least at times, that there must be one, but through long trial and failure, we have come to accept a great many facts as being beyond our powers of integration. And as the child has to discover, for himself and his individual knowledge, where he can get further, where he cannot, so the scientist is still doing at the boundaries of our racial knowledge. The scientist's way of discovering this is, moreover, just like the child's, to note anomalies, unexpectednesses, unrelatednesses, every "why should" or "why doesn't", and to try these questions.

(e) There remains to be considered Piaget's direct probing of the *background* of children's "why's" and other questions (in La Causalité Physique chez l'Enfant), by systematic questioning of them. I cannot go into his material here in detail, although a close examination of it has convinced me that it contains many challengeable elements. I have, of course, in any case not questioned the fact that children do bring "pre-causal", psychological, intentional and mixed and confused expectations or beliefs to a large range of situations which to us are matters of obvious physical causality. But I have endeavoured to show, firstly, that they also bring very different states and attitudes (including very often straightforward causal ones); and secondly, that where they do assume psychological explanations, this is a natural product of previous experience, very frequently a readily modifiable one, and often enough in process of being opened up to modification by the very occasion and formation of the question.

The results, however, of Piaget's method of asking children for their own explanations, by putting their own kind of questions to them, might appear to show a much more systematic, consolidated and firmly entrenched philosophy of intentionalism than would be expected on my view. This, I think, calls for some consideration. If I am right, however, the apparent difficulty arises only because it is a complete error to equate the situation in which we ask children "why" questions, with that in which they ask us. The seeming precaution of putting to them their own kind of question is irrelevant, and only serves to hide from us the total difference of the two situations *functionally*. It allows only for the subject-matter, and hides the controlling features of attitude and function. The word "why" actually changes its meaning in the change-over of situation. It passes from its epistemic sense (where that had been operative) to the informational one—and naturally the most familiar informational one, viz., in the earlier years, that of motive or purpose. The epistemic sense belongs, of course, peculiarly to the situations in which the question comes to be *asked*. If my view is correct, it then marks points of possible new departure in growth of knowledge, points, often, of marked stimulus and activation, points of focal attention, needs and tensions for re-adjustment or extension of knowledge. But when such questions are put to the child, he is not involved, often not interested. He has experienced no shock or stimulus or puzzlement. In the case of many such questions, the particular child asked may, indeed, never yet have thought about their subject-matter. And now, they are sprung at him in the mere form of words, when he is worlds away from the state which creates such questions in him. But an answer is expected of him, questions from adults have to be answered, and he has to try to produce something. Sometimes, of course, no effort is needed; some children are ready verbalisers, and delighted by anything that gives them an opening for this accomplishment. Sometimes an effort has to be made, and the questioner may even have to register "no reply". Either way, however, the reaction is strictly relative to the very special situation prepared for the child. It must be interpreted in the light of this, and must certainly not be treated as transferable to other quite different situations.

We may distinguish two main types of reaction, according to the character of the child and the degree of intelligibility of the question to him. And here, as always, the linguistic factor has to be carefully separated and allowed for, before conclusions are drawn as to the intrinsic tendencies of the child. We are not dealing directly with the child's reaction to the problem *contained for us* in the question put to him. We are dealing, in the first place, with his reaction to certain sounds, and to the meaning which these sounds have acquired for him. This may throw light on his psychology, but it *may* only throw light on our verbal habits and our tendency to the psychologist's fallacy, or on our own "childish egocentrism"—the assumption that our words mean for others what they mean for us. How the child really reacts to the problem we *mean to put* to him may need a great deal of critical analysis, better attempts to present the problem, etc., etc. If we just take it for granted that the child has "got" our problem, we cannot avoid mistakes.

The two main types of reaction do in effect correspond to whether the problem does or does not reach the child. If not, we get this fact shown in a reply which is mere verbal association. The child picks upon this or that familiar word or group of words in the question, and replies with any sort of thing this happens to evoke in his mind. That is, no doubt, an instance of Piaget's concepts of "syncretism" and "juxtaposition"; but in the instances here in question, it is induced by the artificial situation. If the child replies to "Why does the sun not fall down?" by "Because it is hot". "How?" "Because it is yellow",[13] the answer is obviously not a belief, but an association. The question is anything but intelligible. In this and many other cases, Piaget's use of "why" seems to me definitely confusing, and hardly capable of conveying anything to the child—or, I should say, to many and perhaps not the least clear-thinking adults. If children ask such questions, either they mean something definite which they cannot *express* clearly, or they may be in a state of mere puzzled questioning without themselves knowing what they want, or else they may be carrying through an intentionalistic assumption. Which this is, has to be determined. But at any rate there is something present in the question which gives a meaning, at the least a symptomatic one, to the "why". But when such a "why" is put to children, it is likely enough just to mean nothing; the child simply ignores it, fastens upon any word in the question that does mean something to him, assumes he is asked to say something about that, and says something about it. The type of question and answer concerned represents an induced regression to the earliest associative levels. There is no control and no eductive effort, not only because there is no experienced interest or stimulus or context to provoke effort, but because even if it were to be volunteered, there is nothing for it to lay hold on.

The second type of reaction is far more significant, though still not comparable with situations of real eductive effort. Some effort may be made, but it is likely to be of a limited and low order. The higher orders are typically produced where a live concrete problem, epistemic or other, thrusts up in the child's path, and all that he is engaged in doing and wants to do rallies him into trying to counter-thrust through it. Accordingly, eductive efforts occur more often outside traditional pedagogic situations than within them, and formal questioning is in the main dependent for its stimulative value upon the *trained* habit and *prepared* resources of *formal answering*. The child, confronted with unconsidered "why's", either naturally assumes them to be meant in the most familiar sense of inquiry as to motive or purpose (wherever the content of the question will lend itself to this sense at all), or naturally falls back upon his most familiar system of explanations, whatever this may be. He then looks for the answer in his readiest knowledge of answers to "why" questions. And at the beginning, the staple of experienced explanations consists undoubtedly of motives and purposes. The fact that the

[13] *Judgment and Reasoning in the Child* [trans. Marjorie Warden (London: Kegan Paul, Trench, Trubner, 1928)], p. 229.

child is asked the question suggests that he is expected to know the answer, and so, that it has the sort of answer that he knows and has only to remember or identify. He responds to this prompting of the question by looking, as it were, into his stock of answers; and he tries to find some sort of intention, motive or purpose which, on this or that analogy, would fill the bill. Perhaps it will be right . . . or, yes, that must be right . . . but if not, then . . . . In any case, trying answers for the adult to say "right" or "wrong" to, and very often "wrong", is a familiar enough situation for a child.

This type of reaction may, however, be expected to be progressive. The stock of explanations develops with experience, and that of verbal explanations advances rapidly with schooling. They become differently adapted to different kinds of situation, and when "why" questions are asked, their content now refers the child to this or that part of his store of stock types of explanation. He has causal ones available for some kinds of situation, whilst purposive ones are restricted to other kinds. He is still liable to respond to the assumption latent in the question, viz., that he has only to try to think of an answer, and that it is there in him, and he still gives the nearest kind of answer by analogy available in his mind.

But the progression of answers of this kind with the years is undoubtedly extremely interesting and revealing, and its analysis seems to me an exceptionally valuable contribution to genetic psychology. Only, if I am right it is an analysis of the readiest *habitual* thought of the child at any period, and not in the least of his structural capabilities. The situation in which the answers in question are obtained is a situation producing regression to the next level below that of actual growth. The child falls back on the level of reaction that at this time carries him through ordinary situations of no particular difficulty or consequence, the sort of average organisation of knowledge that represents the effect of his learning of *last year* on his crystallised experience up to *then*. This average naturally rises with each new accumulation of learning, but it is well below the level reached in and through each new piece of learning itself. And of course it throws no light on learning situations as such—and takes no cognisance of their existence.

"Why", in questions addressed *to* the child, interpreted informationally and without any special significance for him, taps those earlier levels of merely applied organisation, without any learning stimulus or effort. The child's own epistemic "why's", on the other hand, represent some of his most significant learning situations, forced or voluntary, with genuine interest and effort.

C: Epitome of results of re-interpretation of Piaget's findings

It seems to me, in sum, that Piaget's data and conclusions merely offer a natural counterpart to the facts and interpretations presented here. They give the other side of the picture, the habitual level of functioning of the child's mind at any time, based upon a given degree of interaction of old and newer experiences; in contrast to the side here stressed, the challenging impact of new and different experience upon this functioning, and the consequent stimulus or pressure to work out a new and better adjustment—a mode of functioning which shall in future deal successfully with the new kind of experience as much as with the old. This complementary relation between the two sets of data is just what one would expect from the difference in the situations from which they are drawn; the spontaneous "why" questions which his own actual experience strikes out of the child, as against external ones merely verbally imposed upon him. The difficulty and source of confusion arises only from the fact that the sound "why" combines the epistemic sense here stressed, with a merely informational one which represents the child's automatic habitual functioning—and, to make confusion worse confounded, carries several intermediate semi-epistemic, semi-informational senses as well. This confusion I have tried to clear up to some extent, mainly by endeavouring to isolate and set in sharp relief the crucial epistemic sense and function of "why".

SECTION IV: CONCLUSIONS AND APPLICATIONS

1. CHILDREN'S "WHY" INTEREST IN THE CONCRETE

In conclusion, now, it seems as well to safeguard the case against the risk of over-emphasis which naturally goes with an attempt to make very sure of securing sharp relief. Such an attempt seemed to me to be rendered necessary in the present instance by the extreme complexity and confusion of the field in question. However, it need not imply any exaggeration of the frequency, efficacy or value of epistemic "why's" in the development of the average child. It is admittedly difficult to say what these "why's" amount to, and for how much they count, because the necessary comparative data are lacking. I have merely suggested that children do tend, at a quite early age—often between four and five, sometimes earlier—to develop some degree of concern about the truth, sufficiency or clearness of their knowledge, because they frequently stumble into situations which force just this concern upon them. They do not of course feel it as such; it merely acts upon them, and a number of their "why" questions—those I have called epistemic—show this, and at the same time show how they act this concern out. They are readily stopped by facts that do not harmonise with their habitual expectations, are not provided for by these, or confuse them; and "why" questions are a response to the challenge of such facts. They are discovered as a first and easy means of meeting these challenges, or, rather, getting them met, and they are taken up and exploited accordingly. This certainly affects the further development in knowledge of the child, but how much is so far only a matter for plausible theoretical appraisal.

One typical fact to take into account is that just as far as they are exploited, "why" questions may come to act as an easier and easier substitute for concern. They may become a more and more ready and even automatic response to jars or surprises, so quick a way of dealing with them that they hardly have time to develop. "Why" may then readily degenerate into a purely verbal habit, presently left behind in the process of growth.

What in fact happens to this basic epistemic concern is an open question, depending upon a great variety of factors. No doubt individual predisposition goes a long way in shaping its history, but a thousand outside circumstances also play upon it, help or hinder it, reinforce or dissipate it, organise or vitiate it. In the long run, indeed, what happens to it is governed for individuals by the type of civilisation into which they grow up, but, taken in the mass, it governs in turn the type of this civilisation itself.

2. THE HISTORY OF THE "WHY" INTEREST

In our civilisation a fairly regular kind of development of the "why" interest may be noted, at any rate in its early stages—much as is to be expected if the present analysis is just. In typical cases, when the child first begins to see the powers and possibilities of the "why" question, he rapidly extends his use of it until, in the familiar "stage of why questions", he is working it for all it is worth. But this as usual carries its own nemesis. "Why", as we have seen, may partly lose its function by becoming a mere automatism—the child just discharges it but is not interested in the answer. But in part, also, it proves more and more of a disappointment. The question may be rebuffed or derided, there may be no answer, or there may be a quite unsatisfying one. It may be ununderstanding and useless, ununderstood and useless, or wrong and misleading. Even if helpful for the moment, it may somehow get into a confusing jumble with other answers, also helpful at their moment, but quite different. The child thus gets ample reason for losing much of his enthusiasm for "why" questions; they are by no means the master key which at first they seemed to be, for unlocking every difficulty about the world.

On the other hand, at the same time as this is going on, there are also more fruitful processes making for a slackening in the "why" impulse. How far they will carry the child, however, depends largely upon his good or bad fortune as regards his environment, and most of all his human environment. As far as the impulse fulfils its function, and leads to his being supplied with more satisfactory and adequate knowledge in relation to most of the more obvious sources of puzzlement or epistemic challenge around him, it is no longer so often and readily needed. What is more important still, an intelligent child in the right kind of setting (including the right grownups) will be finding his way all the time to new active ways of exploring the world about him, and building up cumulative true knowledge of it. These ways will then express themselves in their own appropriate questions, and as new successful modes of knowledge to which progress is freely open. And they will take the place of a good deal of "why" questioning which was needed only where the way was barred.[14]

3. "WHY" AND THE DEVELOPMENT OF CAUSAL INTEREST

A very positive part in this latter development, perhaps the most important, falls, however, upon "why" questions themselves, and depends in turn upon the way in which they are dealt with by the grown-ups about the child. Adequately dealt with, these questions should lead the child from his first crude modes of associative belief to the increasing discovery of a specially valuable type of controlling knowledge, which offers the most direct and assured access to security and to practical ability of every kind. This knowledge is, of course, causal knowledge, in the full sense not only of mechanical causation, but of every form of dependence and inter-dependence of things.

Behind most of the checks which the child's expectations or assumptions receive from the world, there are unknown or insufficiently known or misconstrued *causal* facts; the right kind of explanation will disclose these to him. Endless unexpected happenings, failures of expected happenings, deviations or differences from the customary, will turn out to be explained by unsuspected causes, by intervening or preventing causes, unknown determining or conditioning causes. Thus, causes and causal relations should come to be looked for as the important controls of what does or does not happen; and new or better causal knowledge, as the most potent means to true and successful expectation, and the key to secure and controlling knowledge of the course of things. Thus followed up, "causes" branch out into activating events on the one hand, controlling structures, compositions, natures, relations, etc., on the other hand. They become extended to include every kind of relevant or possibly relevant circumstances or conditions or facts of immediate or wider setting; everything which, if it were different, would make any given thing different. Carried right through, causal inquiry becomes, of course, eventually the basis for our most systematic and comprehensive investigation into the constitution and controls, the general structure, of our world; in other words, the warp and woof of science.

How far any child will travel along this road must naturally depend on his own trend of interests as well as on the favouring or unfavouring character of his environment. Some minimum distance of causal appreciation and interest has, however, to be covered by every human being who is to be reasonably capable of assuring his own security, or of purposing, planning and effectively acting. This causal interest has other roots besides those of the jar or failure of expectation, e.g., in countless instrumental experiences and efforts; but for its fullest deployment, the epistemic root is the most significant. This comes out in the way in which the word "why" develops, out of its epistemic sense,

[14]See Note 3 [p. 62].

a series of derivative senses embodying definite inquiry for different kinds of causal information. (We thus actually come to treat "why" as if it meant causal interest, though we rarely appreciate the variety and complexity of the interests covered by the word "cause", or their relation to the much wider and often quite different interests covered by "explanation".)

In any case, the original epistemic "why", as far as it is reasonably and helpfully dealt with, brings causal knowledge and its crucial value into greater and greater prominence. The child learns through it, in his greater or lesser measure, to look for causal and controlling facts and factors, and to take a more and more voluntary interest in them, without waiting for breakdowns and obtrusive failures of knowledge. It thus points the way to new *causal* question modes, which then become a part of our regular equipment for knowledge, and the most powerful and important part. In this way, the *fruitful* use of the original "why" form leads to some extent to its own supersession or obviation. (In its secondary senses, the "why" form continues, of course, to be used to define problems for these new activities, but to a large extent, it can be dispensed with; and in fact, on account of its supposed commitment to purposes and ends, it is commonly, though mistakenly, looked at askance in connection with deliberate causal inquiry.)

Thus, for good and for bad reasons, the *epistemic* "why" form suffers a decline after the first spurt. Much of the part which it played at the beginning is divided up among its derivative senses; some is superseded by direct informational questions, some simply lapses—according to person and circumstance. But of course the epistemic "why" must retain its function as an occasional immediate reaction to surprise or discomfiture, unexpectedness, strangeness, etc. It remains indispensable where nothing but obstruction and confusion exists for the moment; where we are suddenly pulled up, where at the moment we do not know what is wrong, where our problem is—always for the moment—simply: just what is wrong? To such situations we continue to be liable; and they continue to be valuable and from time to time revolutionary opportunities for discovering unsuspected falsities or short-comings of our knowledge, and so, at times, for starting it on revisions or new extensions which may prove of vital significance.

4. EXPLANATION AND EDUCATION: A POSSIBLE MORAL

Finally, we may come back for a moment to the environmental factor in what happens to our epistemic concern. This concern, we have seen, can develop continuously from the stage of occasional spurts of extension or correction of knowledge under the sporadic stimulus of jars or breakdowns, into the most systematic investigation of the causal structure of the world. It has taken the race hundreds of thousands of years to discover the possibilities of such investigation; but yet it involves no new element in human nature and no new stage of internal growth. The powers, interests and activities demanded are rudimentarily present in the earliest human learning from experience. Their most highly elaborated form is merely the outcome of a cumulative multiplication of this process by itself. The child's "why's" are sporadic, casual, usually only mildly and passingly concerned. But they have the full germ of the matter in them, and the rest is mainly a question of where the seed has happened to fall. It took an immense time before a sufficient number of seeds happened to fall on favourable enough ground to get a good start in growth. In point of fact, most human societies have managed to develop express arrangements for choking their growth—often under guise of bringing it to its rightful fruition, as in set types of universal false explanation. But it so happens that a favourable juncture arose, the roots were allowed to grow, and we now know what the grown, or at least the vigorously growing plant, can be. We also know, or can know if we so desire, how its seeds germinate, where they are to be found, and what helps and what hinders their growth. Once the process of right growth has been racially accomplished, it has naturally become immensely simpler and easier to foster it in the individual. Nothing need be further from this fostering process than any design to *specialise* children in scientific interest or enquiry; that might in a majority of cases prove as impossible as it is undesirable. But some degree of growth in the ability to understand and determine the dependences of things, and to fulfil the conditions of true, clear and sufficient knowledge, has become an essential of membership of a civilised self-governing society; and here I believe that a just comprehension of the meaning and various kinds of explanation has a far more important part to play than has generally been appreciated. The adults round a child determine progressively his *standard* of explanation (i.e., of what is attainable or considered valid and satisfactory as explanation); and this standard will more and more determine when he will be puzzled, how he will then try to readjust or extend his assumptions or beliefs or knowledge, what knowledge or insight he will think possible or desirable, and when and how he will be satisfied.

But these are the factors that will beyond anything else decide the general character and level of his intellectual life. They will determine the degree of control which actuality is allowed to exercise over his notions and beliefs. Nothing can be more fatal to growth in adequate knowledge, or in the capacity for objective judgment, than the vitiation of that actuality-control by a low social standard of explanation. If it sanctions explanation by pretentious tautologies, by arbitrary selections of partial causes, by imaginary and mythological causes; if it seems to authorise endless irrelevance, the divorce of explanation from its occasions and function, its confusion with verbal and formal self-justification (and the substitution of the latter for enquiries into evidence). and if, moreover, it does this all together in one anarchic medley—the result will be self-evident. Such a social standard must continually tend to blunt alertness; to confuse the functioning of such native functional standards as we may possess; to discourage an interest which it hinders or leads astray from achievement; and in general, to make us drift towards a state of chaotic muddle-mindedness which then in turn can only, in a vicious circle, reproduce itself. By continuous efforts to counteract its consequences, impelled and sustained from the one direction in which we have achieved successful integrative growth, i.e., science, and the scientific attitude and method, we may indeed keep them under control and even very slowly and laboriously gain a little upon them. But at the very best, the most part of the work of our special socially delegated organ of cognitive growth must thus be wasted, so long as we are content with a general social and educational standard of explanation which lags so far behind that which science itself has reached, and which is the basis for all its achievement.

The alternative is to equip and guide the natural epistemic concern of children from the start, so as to turn it to its most fruitful and valuable use. It depends for a long time upon adults for its satisfaction, and they can either give every help possible to turn it into an active, enjoyed and freely advancing interest for the child, or they can rebuff, confuse, mislead and stifle it in endless ways. They can encourage or discourage the child's exploring activities, his causal interests and enquiries, his alertness to challenges to his knowledge, or to gaps in it. And it depends upon them whether they will strengthen or vitiate, develop or debase, the child's standard of control of beliefs by facts. He has a native standard which is active whenever he is arrested by a clash, disparity or unclearness between expectation and perceived fact. His "why" questions in these situations are governed by it. But by these questions the development of this standard is to a considerable extent placed in the adult's keeping. And if he thinks it worth promoting, he must go beyond merely answering "why" questions, even in the best possible way. He must aim at forestalling them by providing the child from the start with the amplest opportunities for active experience of every significant kind, together with well-planned stimuli and guidance for its most fertile use for growth. The child's knowledge will then develop all the time in the light of fact, and will to the greatest attainable extent be freely controlled by it, without having first to be falsified by it.

APPENDIX

By way of a schematic index to the foregoing analysis, I append the following summary of the main meanings of "why", and the principal modes and kinds of explanation.

"WHY"

(1) Affective and expressional:
    Protest, vexation, helplessness, surprise, recognition, etc.

(2) Epistemic:
  A. Primary:
    (a) Given contradiction or anomaly: Demand for its resolution, for reconciliation or mediation.
    (b) Given unexpected, unrelated, strange or odd fact: Demand for subsumption under familiar, or linkage with it; for missing general rules, determinants, controls or connections; for missing circumstances or conditions.
    (c) Given differences or contrasts, upon a basis of similarity: Demand for a differentiating or delimiting rule, cause, control, circumstance, etc.
  B. Derivative (causal and quasi-informational):
    (d) Given deviations from use and wont, or failures, absences,etc.: Demand for intervening, preventive or deflecting cause, circumstances or factor.
    (e) Given *general* relation or connection: Demand for *specification* of determining or controlling factor.
    (f) Given any so-ness: Demand for determining or controlling conditions, structure, basis, laws, etc.
    (g) Given any happening or event: Demand for determining history or events, for controlling basis, etc.
    (h) Given causal relation: Demand for subsumption under higher or wider or more familiar and accepted relation.
(3) Informational:
  A. Teleological:
    (a) Demand for purposes or objects.
    (b) Demand for uses.
    (c) Demand for functions.
  B. Motivational: Demands for motives, intentions, etc.
(4) Justifactory:
  A. Demand for *grounds* for rules, commands, prohibitions (i.e., not merely causes or motives, but principles or reasons, presupposing some standard by which what is given as ground will be judged— moral, social, conventional, practical, etc.).
  B. Demand for grounds for statements or beliefs:
    (a) Purely formal and deductive—major premise.
    (b) Material—evidence or minor premise.

EXPLANATION: MAIN FUNCTIONAL MODES
(1) Correction of perception (malperception or confusion).
(2) Correction of assumption or belief, with or without account of origin of error.

(3) Explanatory new knowledge:
    A. For specific facts or features of facts:
        (a) Intervening cause.
        (b) Unknown circumstance.
        (c) Unknown class membership.
        (d) Determining structure or factor.
        (e) Unknown rule.
        (f) Subsumption under known rule.
    B. For differences between similar facts: Constitutive grounds or causes of delimiting features.
(4) No explanation (usually given as if an explanation):
        (a) Irreducible differences.
        (b) Chance.
(5) Modes of pseudo-explanation:
        (a) Spurious: by "ideas," abstractions, verbal paraphrases, faculties, properties, imaginary entities, etc.
        (b) Misleading: by "the cause", as if this were a single thing, some arbitrary partial cause being thus suggested into the status of "the explanation".

NOTES

Note 1 (to page 24)

My reference to "why's" of logical justification is of course only a side-glance. To deal with them adequately would need a treatise to itself on the "Psychology of Formal Logic"—a theme, incidentally, which has already been trenchantly dealt with by Professor F. C. S. Schiller, throughout his writings, but which still permits of some extensions . . . and perhaps one or two minor modifications.

All that is essential to the present essay is to distinguish the "why" of logical justification together with other different types, from the epistemic "why", with which I am mainly concerned. In reinforcement of the distinction, however, I try to bring out the instructive *contrast* between "why's" about facts and "why's" about statements, even where they seem to overlap; in relation, that is, to situations of contradiction, clash or divergence.

But having gone so far, I should be courting misunderstanding and rebuttal if I did not go a little further. To be quite exact, I must note that where the attitude to a divergent view is completely undisturbed and self-assured, one does not bother even to ask for its "why", or reasons; one just rejects or refutes it at sight. If one asks "why", there is at least a formal tribute to the possible existence of a reason that one ought to know—a reason that might conceivably make a difference. But that tribute need not be more than formal; it may only be politeness or habit. And in fact it may even be merely intended as a preliminary to pounding all the more forcefully on the reason then exposed; which of course one knows in advance must be worthless and false. One's attitude may thus be completely "ego-centric" in an important and fatal sense, even though "why's" of logical justification are 95 percent of one's "why" score. And in fact all the more so. The innocent, trusting ego-centrism of the child, which offers itself up to every kind of shock, duly receives it and painfully learns from it (and so ought not to be called ego-centrism at all in any fixed structural sense), becomes most genuinely a structural affair in the entrenched and armed, impregnable and unanswerable logic of the adult. The adult, that is, who has fully discovered the possibilities of a formal enough logic.

However, it is also true that "why" does more usually mark a transition to some degree of pregnability. The reason to which it opens one up may in fact turn out to be unknown and impressive. Most people who ask "why" about divergent beliefs want at least to make sure that this is not so. And if they did get something which they had not discounted in advance, something sufficiently new and impressive, some of them at any rate might find themselves impressed by it (more or less, for a longer or shorter time, according to their degree). Moreover, passing by the intermediate stages, when we come to cases of merely new and unexpected statements or beliefs, where no factor of definitely contrary pre-judgment is involved, we no longer have any opposition to the functioning of "why" as the specially open-minded question which it should be. It then tends, however, towards another special *informational* sense—it is more concerned with material than with formal justification, with evidential new information rather than with logical deduction. The formal element must of course be potentially satisfactory, but it is only attended to as a rule if there is any ground for being doubtful or suspicious about it. But again there is continuous transition from cases where the key is actual unknown information to these other situations, where the question is not what the evidence is, but whether it is *conclusive* or not. And so we are brought at the end to logical justification proper, as an abstract impersonal demand, applicable to every proposition, for grounds which, in addition to being materially true, shall comply with a minimum formal standard of relation to the proposition.

So far, in accordance with my general scheme, I have only taken into account "why's" of logical justification from the questioner's point of view, not from the questionee's. The distinction is an important one for my argument all the way through. But whilst the questions asked by the child, not those addressed to him, are crucial in the case of epistemic "why's", the relation is rather the reverse in the case of "why's" of justification. Such "why's", specifically initiated by the child with a logical purpose, are a highly differentiated end-product of cognitive development, and not a factor in it. They are of course a social product, which can only arise out of a long differentiation of social verbal relations. But "why's" of the same type addressed to the child are a special form of active impact on him, operating from an early age, and gradually producing their own distinctive consequences in him.

Among those consequences one is of course that he finally gets the special sense of that impact and uses it in the same way on others. A more important consequence, however, is a cumulative impulsion towards retroflexive, self-searching, logical thought—the effect which Piaget stresses. The child is in fact stimulated to an activity similar in many ways to that produced by factual challenges, an activity which is turned back from the transitive continuance of its course to retracement of the way by which it arrived at the point of retroflexion. But once again, there is a crucial difference. The challenge is not to alteration of the course, but in some sense to its repetition; not to withdrawal or revision, but only to defence. Hardly, to begin with, even that; in effect, merely repetition and amplification. If this will not do, something else is groped for, and under pressure the situation becomes more and more one of sustained attempt at justification or defence. The challenge is itself after all nothing sharp or fixed, there is no question of any definite blocking of the course, one only discovers the fact of resistance by having to go on pressing against it, and it always only seems a question of pressing a little differently or a little harder. And so one is easily led on almost unawares into deeper and deeper commitment to defence, more and more express justification and maintenance of one's course, resistance or no resistance.

Thus we get again the same play of personal, non-cognitive forces, which makes "why's" of logical challenge, and discussion of conflicting views, so equivocal a factor in cognitive development. Under suitable conditions and with the right personal relations, it may be turned into an invaluable stimulus and guide to true cognitive development, closely integrated with direct experience and its progressive organisation. But left to itself it leads as easily in the wrong direction as in the right one.

Summing up, therefore, I am quite unable to agree with Piaget's view—although I acknowledge the powerful case he has made out for it—that it is discussion arising from the clash of views which (from certain stage of maturation onward) breaks up ego-centric assumptions and stimulates and guides the child to the development of self-critical and logical thought. Such discussion certainly leads to the development of formal logic and its processes and affiliated behaviour-modes. But that is another matter. The facts seem to me to be rather as follows: (a) The breaking up of assumptions, which is most fruitful for cognitive development and for the formation of an effective, objective logic, is accomplished by the direct impact of external facts on beliefs, and by the consequences of this impact; (b) the early assumptions in question do not imply nor need any innate ego-centric source or structure, but are themselves formed from anterior experience of facts (by revival and habit); (c) the impact of facts on these assumptions operates from the beginning, so that we get no chance of forming anything like a closed ("ego-centric") system of fixed assumptions, to wait until the time comes when the right social impacts can gain access to it; in the place of this we have learning of knowledge, logic and method going on all the time, under the exacting, ungainsayable pedagogy of experience. And (d), the social impacts can indeed be a very valuable reinforcement of the latter process, if it has already been well begun, and if at the time the impacts themselves, or at any rate a dominant group of them, are carefully guided; but if both or either of these conditions are not adequately fulfilled, the social impacts in question may bring about a definite aberration or arrest of cognitive development, a fixation in henceforth inaccessible assumptions or beliefs. They may lead to this because (i) there is *absent* from verbal social clashes or challenges of beliefs the most powerful element in the objective teaching process, viz. the compelling controls and sanctions, the hard, sharp facts which create and back the challenge; (ii) there are *present,* on the contrary, all kinds of extraneous factors tending directly to disturb or even counteract any cognitive effect; factors of *personal* challenge and defence, all sorts of affective personal elements and stakes; in fact an obscuration of the cognitive situation and *substitution for it* of a dramatic social and inter-personal one; (iii) we are still dominated by a logic, or set of standards and methods, which has arisen out of just this substituted inter-personal situation, is shaped primarily to its exigencies, and *sanctions* them; a logic focussed on the forms of inter-personal defence and attack, instead of on learning situations. (A logic of learning has of course been developed during the last eighty years or so, but it is itself still being fought over and judged—and meanwhile naturally kept stunted—by the standards of the logic of formal defence and attack. The interesting fact is that the difficulties and deadlocks discovered by the latter are usually set down to its superior, over-exacting and absolute standards, when in fact they arise because those standards are inferior, not exacting enough and full of gaps and flaws. Encouraged by the impregnability they produce in social situations, we apply them to factual clashes and challenges as well, in a small way, and secure a similar appearance of impregnability there, but have to be very careful either to limit this to matters of no consequence, or to keep it merely verbal and strictly divorced from action.)

Thus the upshot is that instead of a logic which counteracts the special limitations and aberrant temptations of social clashes of beliefs we have one which insidiously and powerfully reinforces them. And discussion arising from such clashes is so far from being the main agency of logical and cognitive development that it is in fact at present a major agency of mal-development, itself fortunately counteracted to a large extent (though not enough) by the more and more powerful cumulative prestige of that quintessence of successful objective learning: scientific knowledge and method.

It remains to add, since a case against Piaget's views has been stated, that I am only referring to those presented in the volumes referred to in the present work. I am aware that he has modified his standpoint in some respects, but am not sure to what extent this affects the views controverted above. I imagine, however, that his valuation of the social factor probably stands, and in any case I cannot of course simply assume conveniently that he has changed a view on which in fact he may still fully insist and which he may claim that his evidence entirely vindicates. At any rate, I am merely concerned with the view itself, which is certainly held in some quarters and has enough in its favour to merit the closest consideration. I will only take the opportunity here of expressing my immense debt of illumination and stimulation to Piaget's work, a debt which it would be a pity to allow the dominant controversial tone of the present essay to obscure.

On the actual objective question: what is the part of clashes of opinion in cognitive development? I have offered an answer which seems to me amply borne out by individual and social history. But I should add that I have only tried to deal with the *direct* effect of this factor on cognitive processes, under our conditions, and have neither denied or decried all its indirect stimulation value. As a mode of arousal of attention and interest, as an incentive to new enterprises of investigation, as a source of quickening of energy and effort, etc., etc. it may well have played a decisive part throughout our intellectual history, and may still do so in the lives of most of those who carry this history further. But for the purposes of the present essay, I have not tried to evaluate the *historical* part played by conflicts of opinion as a whole. And I have not in the least wished to suggest a case for *their* educational avoidance, but merely for that of certain avoidable features in our handling of them; together with a case against an interpretation which carries an implied sanction for just those features, at the expense of what seems to me to be needed to take their place.

It may be worth mentioning finally that one invalid reason which seems to influence some of those who tend to make the most of social, and the least of external objective factors in development is a reluctance due to thorough philosophic training, to lean on that doubtful or discredited hypothesis, the external world. Well, as far as it is a hypothesis, we need not lean on it, and my case, such as it is, certainly does not do so. Wherever I speak of "fact", "external fact", etc. this can be replaced, without making the slightest difference to the argument, by "the experience which we call the experience of external fact", etc. All the distinctions, contrasts, clashes, controls, and so on, which I invoke, are experiences within experience, and are invoked as such. What clashes with a particular state of belief or expectation (hence called erroneous) is itself an experience, and the clash is another. And so right through. My objective view, my suggested objective logic, and all the rest, are thus based just as much on experiences, and experiences of the same kind, as any social theory; and not on a metaphysical hypothesis, doubtful or otherwise. But I think that when we get our empirical psychology a little less selective and conventional, and a little more realistic and *complete,* there will be nothing metaphysical or doubtful left about the belief we call belief in the external world. Meanwhile, however, the question between the view here presented and the social view is a purely experiential one, viz., whether or not the experiences which I invoke occur as experiences at the time and in the order and relations which I have suggested.

Note 2 (to page 41)

My argument is that differences in experience suffice to explain even the most marked differences between the "why" questions of children and of adults, so that there is no reason for inferring any difference of structure between them. To guard the argument against misunderstanding, however, it seems as well to make its acknowledged limitations as well as its exact claims quite clear.

(1) Whilst I hold that cognitive development takes place throughout by the same sort of learning from the same sort of experience, unchanged in essence

from the first steps forward of the child to the last, up-to-date, of the scientist, I fully acknowledge the existence of an internal limiting factor which governs the *rate* of this learning. There is the fact of the protracted passage from the outlook of the child of say three to that of the adult, and no argument would be worth bothering with, which suggested that this passage could be abolished or merely seriously abridged.

But the *limiting factor left over* on my view is a totally different matter from any suggested process of *internal qualitative development,* fully determining and manifested in a succession of *qualitatively different* stages of cognitive behaviour and belief. On my view, the process of overt cognitive development presents rather the aspect of a constant force acting in a constant way, but limited in the *rate of production* of its cumulative effect by a kind of inertia or friction which is itself a constant character (variable only in degree) of its material.

The case for this view is of course represented by the analysis in my text, which endeavours to show that the hypothesis of sameness of experience and sameness of learning can, if rightly applied, account for all the facts alleged to demonstrate the contrary; and is indeed demanded by them when they are considered closely and concretely enough. The slowness of the learning process introduces a genuine limiting factor, but only as a rate factor and not as one of qualitative control. (Our concept of intelligence rather fits in with this view, since it puts differences in the comparative rate of cognitive development down to differences in respect of a *constant factor* of ability or capacity, characteristically problem-solving, and characteristically advancing to problems of *increasing complexity and difficulty.* We may conceive intelligence as the constant force operating on the successive matter of experience in a constant, adaptively organising way; with the resistance or opposition or mere novelty of new matter in relation to existing adaptations corresponding to the action of inertia or friction. The characteristic difference between the child and the adult may then be related to the simple fact that our world happens to be such that the amount of *new* matter, in proportion to repetition of what is familiar, diminishes progressively, and with it the broad proportion of resistance and opposition. The great bulk of our learning can be done and has to be done at the start.)

(2) In any assessment of the part played by experience, it is essential that it should not be thought of as a mere matter of information collected and extended, but as a succession of *actions* on the organism, with powerful and important consequences. If we take the former view, it at once becomes plausible to reason that if the difference between child and adult were merely one of experience, it ought to be possible to turn the child into an adult mentally by giving him the right kind of information and instruction; and if that is not possible then the difference must go beyond experience. The deplorable experiment in question has of course been tried by people who have taken this kind of view of experience, usually under the influence of the philosophic tradition of sensations or sense-impressions and the "laws of association". But what is wrong here is the concept of experience.

As against this tradition, we may emphasise the much more pregnant common usage which makes experience mean a more or less dramatic piece of undergoing or a biographic episode. We may also note the very penetrating meaning of the common phrase "learning from experience", and again the substantial ordinary sense in which it means the matter or span of some accumulated, direct, familiar knowledge.

The full sense of experience has in fact to take in everything that comes or happens to us throughout our history, or makes any part of the quality of what comes or happens to us; including our arena as the progress of experience makes us familiar with it, together with all the course of more or less dramatic "experiences" which happen to us "in" it.

(3) If we see the experience from which we have to learn in this comprehensive and at the same time dramatic way, we can, I think, find some reasons in the learning process itself (before we fall back on our unknown limiting x), which make it inevitably a slow one.

We have only to be careful to take our experience both widely and connectedly enough. We experience on a very wide front; in many different modes, directions, and relations in turn. Each experience has a series of effects spreading eventually over our whole front; some very markedly, some only negligibly beyond their immediate area. Our cognitive behaviour, or learning, is, like every other, the resultant of a large constellation of proximate and remote influences (even if we disregard the relatively inoperative remotest ones). Our learning or advance at any point depends on the remote as well as the proximate influences, and we cannot therefore get very far at one point until we have advanced concurrently at others, so that a larger and larger part of the total operative constellation becomes favourable. We cannot in fact often get the proper sense of some local experience-lesson until we can approach it in the light of some much wider one, but we cannot reach the light of the wider one except through a succession of local ones. We stumble out of this vicious circle at some easy place after a greater or less interval of failure and helplessness. But when we have done so once, we have made the next time easier, and the next time again, shaping the constellation more favourable to advance at each next point. And when this has gone on for a time, we may suddenly get a sharp acceleration of advance. The piecemeal movements consolidate into a wide reorientation, and we may have a more or less rapid and complete change-over to a whole new type of belief and behaviour, now readily and habitually applied all round.

This sort of thing may occur on all levels of generality, but naturally, the wider the reorientation, the greater and more difficult must be the necessary prior piecemeal advance. The widest kind of learning movements will be separated by long intervals, in the growth of knowledge of the individual as in that of the race. And when we examine the previous state in the light of each such movement one after another we get that appearance of a succession of stages, with a common set of characters running through each and a marked contrast between them, which so readily suggests a process of internal qualitative transformation.

But the transformation is of the same type and produced in the same way as any piece of local learning. It merely needs the concurrence of a much larger number of conditions operating over a much longer time. And in fact, if we examine the right kind of individual bits of behaviour at any of the above stages, we may see the beginnings of some next large learning movement, some new struggling little steps onward preparing the way for some new wholesale advance demanded by the unsatisfied pressure of things.

(4) At the back no doubt there remains the limiting factor of learning capacity which finally decides at what rate points shall be seen, lessons taken in, old ways of behaviour revised and new ones learnt, on the smallest and on the largest scale. According to this factor, "obvious" points may be missed, or "difficult" ones seen, and, other things equal, it governs the comparative learning rate. But other things are in fact very unequal. The above point of view displays a sharp contrast again here to the theory of internal development. Since the latter treats the successive beliefs and behaviour of the child as expressions of the deformation or refraction of the world by his specific structural stage, and so obviously as fixed and inaccessible manifestations of inward facts, a barricade is raised against the very thought of planning and controlling the environment in order to help the child on. (At least until maturation is more or less complete.) On my point of view, we have a limit set to possible environmental help, but we have also great opportunities of help. We can in fact only assign a final value to the limiting factor in any particular case when we have provided optimum conditions for it. The learning process depends on the two variables, greater or less capacity for coping with difficulties and greater or less difficulty. This second variable defines the problem for education and for educational control of the environment. This problem becomes of course a very difficult one as soon as we cease to think in terms of verbal information and instruction, and begin to think instead in terms of psychological growth, and the personal experience and learning from experience of which alone the main body of growth can consist. Nor shall we exaggerate the difference which education at the best can make, if we acknowledge, over and above the final internal limiting factor, the difficulty and complexity of the process set out above upon which any *wide* advance depends. But we can reasonably suppose that under rightly-planned control there may be differences worth making in the success, ease and speed with which the child will learn those lessons in security, ability and achievement and their condition of right knowledge, which he has to learn and is trying to learn. And we may look to some prospect of such differences if we make a thorough enough analysis of what in the run of environments known to us helps or hinders, makes or mars, the child's own active learning processes; and if we then plan out and try, in an experimental spirit, an environment which provides the best conditions we can thus discover.

Note 3 (to page 50)

I hope I have made it sufficiently clear that wherever I refer to "epistemic interest", "causal interest", etc. I mean only interest which would be so described *if expressly attended to*. But of course it will only be thus attended to by philosophers, in themselves, or by psychologists, in others (if they do not think it too philosophical). The point, however, is that it can be present, as a distinctive mode of behaviour with characteristic occasions and direction, where its description in the above terms would only be blankly stared at. This is manifest in the case of very young children and their epistemic "why's", but it may easily be lost sight of as soon as it ceases to be self-evident, since we still tend to identify behaviour with formulated awareness of it, and to treat them as standing or falling together. On this tacit assumption, it might be wondered to what strange community of philosophers all the argument about epistemic and causal interests was intended to refer. It might all seem very abstract and remote and unreal, without any relation to the little Toms, Dicks and Harrys of our everyday world.

But the point of my thesis is just that *as psychological descriptions,* these concepts are needed for very concrete and very fundamental facts of ordinary behaviour. The further stage of express attention to them and formulated awareness of them is rare; and even where it occurs, it often adds very little to them. The actual behaviour, at least in some degree, is—and has to be—universal. The degree is a matter, partly of native capacity, partly of trend of interest, but still more of educational and general social environment.

Now that degree tends to remain somewhere near the survival minimum, wherever the environment is completely uninterested in the "cognitive development" of the child, or definitely hostile to it. A certain amount of cognitive development in my behaviouristic sense, goes on willy nilly, as I have endeavoured to show. But some of the natural and habitual associations of the phrase do get in the way when it is applied to such children—e.g. those under the economic and other pressure of our poorer classes; a very large proportion if not the majority of elementary school children—and there seems to be an air almost of mockery about "epistemic" or "causal" interest in their case. Cognitive development remains overlaid in them by all the environmental pressures, and usually gets no chance at all of emerging, beyond the minimum adaptation needed for survival, as an independent, voluntary interest. Unfortunately, elementary education has in the past done little to alter this, and even if it distinguished better than it has done between the living body of knowledge and the empty shell, and administered the former instead of merely the latter, its power would be severely limited by those much more powerful external pressures.

It has to be acknowledged therefore that the ordinary average child under existing conditions drops out of my argument at an early stage. But the question of his education does not. And I remain concerned with the cognitive development of real children, in so far as it does or can occur, not with that of the generalised dummy which has so largely been assumed to be the proper subject matter of psychology, especially the psychology of cognition. I merely postulate a state of affairs in which the environment does at least *mean* to be favourable to the successful development of those modes of behaviour described here as cognitive, and in which it can offer conditions which allow them some scope. This is obviously the case for educated middle class children, who indeed illustrate far better than the helpless poor the incidence of specific unfavourable as well as of favourable conditions, just because in the place of a crushing all round brute pressure, they offer a detailed interplay of helps and hindrances, and a scale of all proportions between them. Here, then, we are on quite concrete ground, where practical application, if desired, follows immediately from theory. But what understanding can be gained in this field becomes available in its turn as at least a broad aim of educational policy even for the great body of children. However little education by itself, unsupported by the easing of the all round environmental pressures, can do for the ordinary average child, it can do more if it does not waste endless effort and opportunity on the outward forms of knowledge, but makes straight for the essential conditions of its real, functional growth.

At this point, however, it may be as well to meet another sort of objection, for which the ground seems to have been more and more prepared. It may appear that I am making everything turn upon cognitive development, as if this were the be-all and end-all of education, and almost of life. But of course I am not trying to state a philosophy of education. I am merely considering the dynamics of cognitive development. I do not indeed profess neutrality in this matter, and think that where valuations are inevitable, declaring them is the best way of keeping them distinct from one's facts. A certain minimum standard of cognitive development seems to me an absolutely essential aim of education, for reasons partly stated, partly implicit in my text; and stress on the case for this standard seems to me essential, because it is far from being generally acknowledged and aimed at yet.

But this is only part—the part which happens to be relevant—of a philosophy of education, not the whole. For the latter this is not the place. Merely by way of correcting the perspective, I add that in common, I suppose, with most of those who have tried to think out a comprehensive educational point of view, I conceive the problem of the right environment to be one of an *optimum combination or balance* (varying with the situation and person) between a number of different, largely competitive and partly conflicting demands. That of cognitive development is only one out of this number. But for each one the first essential is to understand what kind of environment its maximum satisfaction would demand. This knowledge is clearly a condition of any intelligent consideration of the problem of combining the conditions of satisfaction of the different demands as far and as well as possible. And all that I have assumed here is that the demands of cognitive development are among those which have to be taken into account, and so as fully as possible understood, whatever limitations might have to be set upon them in the interest of others. What others we acknowledge, and how we judge their relative importance, is then a matter of our total educational philosophy.

What Is Required of the Nursery-Infant Teacher in This Country Today?*

This paper was read in 1957 at a conference sponsored by the British National Committee of the Organisation Mondiale pour l'Éducation Préscolaire (World Organization for Early Childhood Education) on the subject of education for teachers of young children.

In the British school system, the general term "primary school" refers to a school for children under the age of twelve. Nursery school is for children under the age of five, infant school for children from five to seven or eight, and junior school for those from seven or eight to eleven or twelve.

Isaacs examines the implications, for educational practice, of the belief that human beings have intrinsic value. He outlines the kinds of things that teachers of young children must know, and places special emphasis on their training in psychology.

I

First, a word of personal explanation and at least semi-apology. When I was invited to speak on the present subject, I was very hesitant. I thought it needed someone steeped in practical experience both of the actual work of nursery-infant teachers and of all the aspects and conditions of their training, whilst I could lay no sort of claim to this, but could only talk as a pure, or almost pure, theorist.

However, the title does end with a question mark: I am only asked to discuss a problem. For the most uncompromising formulation of problems,

*First published in *National Froebel Foundation Bulletin*, no. 109 (December, 1957): 2-16. Reprinted with the permission of Mrs. Evelyn Isaacs and the Foundation.

theory and even pure theory can be of real use. Perhaps, therefore, I can turn my very limitations to advantage if I start from this and go on to deduce from it the whole gamut of superhuman demands which the ideal nursery-infant teacher *ought* to be able to meet. That will then certainly lead to a problem, an outsize problem, for which it is very difficult to see any really satisfactory solution. I fear, indeed, that I may find myself in the position of Mark Twain in a story of his which I read many years ago. Surprisingly enough, it turned out to be a super-romantic thriller. It worked up to a tremendous crisis but then, as one turned the page in breathless suspense, there was nothing beyond a blank and a footnote. I cannot recall the exact words, but their substance was that the author was very sorry, but he had got his characters into such a predicament that he just did not know how to get them out again. Perhaps the reader would like to see what he could do.

In spite of this risk, however, I propose to see where the logic of my suggested theoretical approach will take me. If I am right, the point will then be that whatever the difficulties of the predicament, we simply cannot avoid it. For it will then be found to flow directly from the three dominant factors of our present human situation: the principles of progressive education, as we have come to see them—our modern democratic conception of a free, equal and co-operative community—and our vast and ever-growing world of human knowledge and achievement. I shall thus try to perform one service a theorist ought to be able to render, namely to demonstrate the full magnitude of our present problem, without any advance concessions to practice or expediency. This then can at least serve as an unpliable yardstick for measuring (i) what we have already done, (ii) what we are trying to do, and (iii) how far we might have to go if we were resolved to adapt our practice to our problem instead of our problem to our practice.

II

There is, however, an initial difficulty about such an approach. I have spoken of starting from pure theory, as if there were some one framework of theory on which we were all agreed. In fact we must recognise that if we go far enough back towards fundamentals, we are not agreed. When it comes to first principles those of us who would call ourselves progressive educationists may differ all the way from the profoundest Christian or other religious idealism to the complete agnosticism of the scientific humanist.

Yet that in turn is only one side of the story. It remains equally true that in practice progressive education stands for something on which all of us, with the most widely divergent ultimate beliefs, do come together. The interesting and vital question then is: what is it that enables us so to meet? What common ground, in the last analysis, do we all share? Can we after all define some minimum basis of theory which we can all accept? I believe that this *is* the case, and that moreover the principles which we share provide a base broad enough to support virtually the whole structure of what in practice we know as progressive education.

It will accordingly be this basic theory from which I shall set out. I shall try to place it in the clearest relief, because it is intended as the key to all that follows. Indeed, I imagine that step by step as I advance you will see the predicament of what we need to ask from our Nursery-Infant teachers taking ever larger and more formidable shape, even before I come to its final life-size presentation. But let me now turn to our common theory.

III

Our first shared terrain, I suggest, is that of the fundamental right of every person to arrive at his own ultimate beliefs, from his own inward necessity, without let, hindrance or imposition by anyone else. This right is one which progressive educators, whatever their own ultimate point of view, can surely join together in accepting. It has, of course, long been a main cornerstone of our modern political creed. But the important fact is that progressive educators have learnt to construe this principle psychologically and in depth. It is they who are most aware how hollow its mere social proclamation must be, unless the reality of freedom of thought and belief has been built up from within. For the child is father of the man, and the man is shaped by the child, and we have now begun to see what vital conditions must be fulfilled from early childhood onward, if the authentic capacity for freedom is to be achieved.

We certainly do not secure it by simply putting a ring fence round our right to go on with whatever beliefs we happen to hold. Or for that matter even round the right to overthrow or vary them when we feel so impelled. This right indeed we must have, else nothing else is safe, but no mere fence outside turns the state within into one of freedom. If a particular pattern of beliefs has somehow been ingrafted in us, through birthplace or circumstances, the group we are born into, or the pressure of parents or teachers, we may be led to identify ourselves with it emotionally and to fight to the last ditch for our "freedom" to continue within it. Yet that does not transform it into our own free choice, but leaves it the same imposed pattern—decided for us and not freely and inwardly elected by us.

And even if we elect to throw it off and embrace another, the case is not necessarily different. This might be merely a delayed reaction against the original constraint, or may arise from the chance impact on the same inward situation of some potent new influence. Many of us do indeed feel that we have gradually won our way, by successive stages of emancipation, to something like true freedom; but even so we may well realise by what struggles we have had to do so, at what price, and how imperfectly at the end.

And perhaps no few of us have turned to the hopes and possibilities of progressive education precisely because we want to ensure for others what we feel we should have most valued for ourselves: being nurtured in freedom, and truly equipped and educated for it, from the outset.

IV

However, this question of real freedom of belief is, as I see it, only one aspect of a much wider common field. The basic uniting bond, from which everything else follows, is the postulate of the intrinsic value of individual human beings as such. Here again the right to have this value respected is not one that can commence at some set age, such as adolescence or even later, after it has been disregarded during a child's most formative years. The integrity of a human person is one and indivisible, and if we mean to respect it, the time to begin is when he first begins. And that holds all the more because for so long his integrity depends utterly on those in natural authority over him. They claim, indeed, not only the right but the duty to rule and mould him, and up to a point this is quite incontrovertible; but the real question is whether it shall be deliberately restricted to the unavoidable minimum or just left to the free play of the parents' or other adults' native feelings or will. For those who fully accept the principle of respect for each person's integrity the answer is not in doubt. For them the future individuality of every child is a trust, to be honoured to the utmost attainable extent from his earliest years. They feel responsible *to* John (or Jane) Brown as much as *for* them, even at a time when it is hardly possible yet to judge what the new individual is, let alone what he is capable of becoming. It is indeed just this ignorance and this potentiality which so strongly enjoin on us not to impose *our* chosen shape on the child, but to treat him throughout as the trust he is, on behalf of his unknown future self.

But to state the postulate in this way is also to bring into the sharpest focus the problems and even paradoxes to which it gives rise. First, since the trust is on behalf of *every* individual-in-the-making, its exercise is conditioned on all sides by the parallel trust for every other. Secondly, the fact of membership of a community is not a whit less fundamental than the principle of individual integrity itself. Everything we want to secure for the child presupposes the social inheritance in which he is to share and the social membership through which he is to find himself. Without being guided into this, human beings would not even be human, to say nothing of freely choosing individuals. And, thirdly, the particular community nullifies up to a point the very principle with which we began. However much we may want to, we cannot abstain from shaping or moulding him. We cannot avoid imposing a prechosen pattern on him. Everything around him and even his own human nature forces him to grow into the life and the likeness of the society of which he forms a part.

V

From these last paradoxes, I think, all the practical working philosophy of progressive education must spring. Our problem is in fact how to achieve the *optimal reconciliation* of the social steering the child needs and the shaping he cannot escape, with the respect for his integrity as an end in himself which we accept as the very categorical imperative of education. The answer which seems to me to follow is a twofold one. First, we must start in our own minds from the broadest, most inclusive social or cultural pattern within our reach; and we must do all the sifting, balancing and integrating that may be necessary to work out one on which we can bear to take our stand. Secondly, we must seek to open up for each child, as far as ever his and our capacities allow, every avenue of growth into that pattern. And we must do this so that he can, from within, make his own choices, discover his own abilities and bents, and thus genuinely realise himself; but can also, concurrently, take into himself and learn to appreciate that cultural pattern as a whole. It follows straightaway, of course, that he must do his own growing. We cannot do it for him. We can only respect it and provide for it the most conducive conditions, the most effectual guidance, and the freedom of all the roads. It follows equally that we must grasp how the growth of children does take place; by what means and in what conditions. We must understand what may warp it and what can help it; and above all how dependent it is on the child's own positive assimilative and integrative activity; and how much it needs to be continuous and of one piece. And we must also clearly grasp our own part in the process, and our own relation to the growing child. For it is our part that decides how far he merely suffers external imprinting and shaping, and how far he does succeed in growing from within into the reality of our social heritage and communal life.

If this now were agreed, what would our part have to be? First there would be the endeavour, through the utmost encouragement of the child's own interests and activities, to enable him to enter into at least each major aspect of our civilisation. This would mean guiding him to every sort of direct exploration and concrete learning of the variety and scope of the physical and human worlds, present and past—to at least the rudiments of aesthetic appreciation and enjoyment—to the beginnings of diverse active skills, practical, expressive, formative and constructive—to some grasp of the main pattern of the society in which we all live—to a working hold on the ways by which we attain knowledge and our other main achievements and the methods by which we assess these—and, finally, on any assumption, to some sense of what men have thought and felt about their life and experience and world as a whole.

Secondly, all this so far would merely be *equipping* the child to find and choose his own interests, beliefs and way of life; but besides this, he must also be *empowered* to choose effectively, that is steadily and integratively and cumulatively. For that, nothing else will serve than a stable structure of character and personality, in balanced harmony within itself and reciprocal harmony with his community. And for that he needs continual exercise in choice, and experience of its fruits and consequences to integrate with it. And also constant exercise in decision and responsibility, and again experience of their actual outcomes, to integrate with them. But above all his own fullest experience of the conditions and demands of social life. The child must learn to master for himself the lessons of reciprocity and co-operation in all his human relationships. He must come to see—as, given the proper, unconfused chance, he can scarcely avoid doing—that the justice and fairness and understanding and sympathy and consideration and kindness which he so imperatively *needs* from others are something which, by exactly the same token, others equally need and demand from him. And that he can only ask others for all this and hope to receive it, as far as he in turn is willing to grant it. That in fact the two sides, the getting and the giving, hang together as completely interdependent parts of the same thing: each can only flourish if everybody accepts both as their common law or rule.

All this the child, just because of his dependence and need, is particularly fitted to learn; and so to learn by his own lived experience, that it can turn into a very part of himself. He only grows into his community, besides becoming a free individual in his own right, as far as feeling and acting like that becomes automatic for him. But this then must also be the prevailing practice all round him, and he must become aware of the Golden Rule as simply the way everyone has always treated him, as much as the way he is expected to treat everyone. It is here, indeed, that the principle of respect for his integrity becomes so vital, because it is through this respect that the child is enabled to grow into future wholeness. For he can only turn into part of himself what he understands; and he can only understand what in fact is not arbitrary, nor forcibly imposed on him, nor merely pressed on him by words, but such that it can be converted into his own experience and findings and at length reasoned convictions. It is in the measure in which he is from the start treated as a free, equal and potentially rational human being that he may, with due skill and luck, become one.

VI

If the foregoing can serve as the outline of a "common-ground" philosophy of progressive education, what now must be our theoretical demands on the unfortunate nursery-infant teachers who are to turn it into practice? The main headings are, of course, plain enough, and present in all the syllabuses. There is, first of all, the vital understanding of the child and of the teacher herself, which we group together as psychology. With this usually goes some elementary physiology and health care. There is, secondly, the theory or philosophy of education. Thirdly, we have the world around the child—the general knowledge, physical and human, historical and literary and aesthetic, for some aspects of which a place is usually found. And finally, there must be a reasonable assortment of practical skills, from the homely domestic ones to at least some among the handicrafts and arts.

So much for the bare heads of the training: the catch lies in the details to follow. But on the selection side, too, we need a superhuman assemblage of personal qualities. There must be first and foremost a sense of vocation based on a genuine and trial-proof love of children; high stability of character and a steady good temper and balance; endless patience and a great capacity to stand up to frustration, but also quite a firm ability to stand up to the children; immense enthusiasm and zest, enterprise, ingenuity and resourcefulness; and throughout everything else a saving sense of humour, nonsense and fun. It may perhaps be a problem how far those who come nearest to these personal demands will also be the best suited to respond to all the intellectual challenges of the training. But about this we need not necessarily despond— though we may yet have to raise the status and attractions of the nursery-infant teacher's job to a level better related to what we must ask of her.

However, the actual training schedule, when expanded to the full needs of the theory, does seem to present an almost unmanageable predicament. That is the theme I want to develop. True, we have before us the new opportunities of the three years' training, which are the very occasion for our today's conference. Yet the magnitude of the problem seems to me such that not even a whole extra year can make enough difference to it, unless we can also carry through some quite radical re-thinking and re-planning. I am not sure that there might not be room for this, and shall venture to do some extremely tentative thinking aloud about it. I do not know whether or not any progress is possible along these lines; but if not, the problem will remain! And I still hope there is some small value in endeavouring so to formulate it that it really must be faced.

VII

Before I can embark on my expansion I should underline again that on the kind of theory of education I have set out the demands on the nursery-infant teacher are peculiarly heavy. They are indeed far more so than for those concerned with the later years. The further we move up the age-scale, the more the teacher can concentrate on some special subject of his own, whilst the rest, the psychology, the theory of education at large and the general cultivation turn mainly into background. For, as the child grows older, firstly he becomes readier for specialisation without suffering any harm, above all if the earlier work with him has been done well. Secondly, by that time he can only progress by learning how much he must accept the discipline and internal coherence of any specific field of knowledge if he wants to be truly at home in it.

It is true that this hardly begins to apply during the junior school years, so that in theory the teachers of that phase should still be very similarly equipped to those of the nursery-infant stage. Such equipment, however, would be of little use without a radical reconstruction of our whole junior school scheme. And so long as we keep the three R's as our chief aim for these years, we are in fact largely concerned with more or less mechanical training which bears little relation to the main stream of integrative, that is intellectual, social and aesthetic growth.

Thus it is still the nursery-infant teacher who has the widest and most exacting educational demands to meet. During most of that stage the child remains a single, undifferentiated whole person, and the world is still mainly a single indiscriminate whole for him. Thus the teacher must be ready at all times to cope with both these wholes or with any part or element of either in kaleidoscopic succession. On the one hand she must always be prepared for the way in which a small child's attention veers from one theme to another; or he leaps from real-world interest to fantasy and make-believe and then suddenly back again; or his mood changes completely and he becomes querulous or contrary or uninterested, or gets gripped in some other way by forces which he does not understand and which are too strong for him. All this must be expected and handled with as much patience and sympathetic understanding as the teacher can muster. On the other hand, she must be ready at any time to be asked questions, often idly but also often with hard-pressing pertinacity, about almost anything under the sun. Moreover, she herself must always be on the alert to pick up any stir of interest, enquiring or practical or aesthetic, and help it on as far as it will go. She must, in fact, throughout have the sense of what all this means, or can be turned into meaning, educationally. It is during these years that both the child and his world first begin to get compartmented and sorted out. The teacher therefore becomes in a special way the first guardian of continuity and integration. She must understand enough of the workings of the child's mind and simultaneously of the connections and relations of things in the real world to make all his successive changes of interest contribute also to his sense of the cohesion and oneness of that world.

VIII

And so I come to my more detailed blue-print of what the nursery-infant teacher seems strictly to need before she can enter on her work. I can hardly avoid some duplication of the syllabuses, but shall try to bring out what for my theoretical model are the essentials.

First of all, psychology. She must obviously have a clear sense of the dynamics of mental growth in children, intellectual, emotional, aesthetic, practical. And this must not be something merely abstract and categorised. Her children must be living persons for her, interacting with one another, with her, with their own families and with their neighbourhood in a living social context. She must see them as partly shaped by their past history and growth, partly going on with their growth, partly in course of being further shaped, but partly also pressing on with their own personality and progressively—but never more than incompletely—revealing what this is, as they participate in their own shaping. That last essential element, the teacher can only learn as she goes along from each child himself. But this apart, current psychology can have taught her to understand much of the general drama of emotional development in children, with all its successive crises and major adjustments; and also the great epic of their intellectual growth as they build up in their minds larger and more ordered patterns of the world around them and concurrently develop their powers of coordinating these and operating with them, both in purposive action and in their grappling with every sort of problem.

Whilst the nursery-infant teacher must thus envisage the whole panorama of growth up to maturity, she needs, of course, to be specially aware of the stage reached by her three- to seven-year-olds and of the progress she can hope for while they remain with her. But this must go with a reasonably informed sense of the different native capacities, general and specific, of different children, so that she can at least roughly assess what rates and kinds of progress to expect, and not to expect, from each of them.

Furthermore, she must have a clear idea of the distinction between integrative learning on the one hand and of mere training or habit learning on the other. The latter has its significant place in connection with memory-knowledge and many practical skills, but needs to be strictly confined to this; whilst the former is in an important sense growth and development itself.

Again, the teacher needs some notion of the range of difficulties she may meet in her charges and how to deal with the easier ones or when to call in more expert advice. Such difficulties may vary from general or specific backwardness to the most diverse emotional or character troubles or disturbances of normal psychic wellbeing or health. To avoid grave blunders in coping with these, or even to recognise them in good time, the teacher requires a wide background of general psychological understanding and, above all, an informed sensitiveness to early signs.

Beyond all this again, she must have considerable grasp of her own psychology and of her relation to the children, as well as of their relations among themselves. That involves in turn what little we positively know and what more we are trying to learn about the psychology and sociology of group relationships. And though the teacher's ultimate duty of understanding and help is to each child as an individual, we have seen how little she can hope to discharge this duty unless she is also adequately alive to all that his social life means for him.

This, of course, is not yet the whole psychological story, but enough to show how much too much is needed for a bare three years' training course, of which psychology is only one part. If I am right, then besides current orthodox text-books and teaching based on these, a vast deal of careful study is urgently required. To pick out only a few examples, some selected psycho-analytic literature, a representative part of Piaget's work, and perhaps Susan Isaacs' two main volumes on intellectual and social development in young children, would seem to be among the musts. But Piaget alone, until something is done about providing a student's guide to him (which would itself need to be a formidable volume), would demand far more time than any ordinary trainee could hope to give.

Secondly, we have the theory or philosophy of education. This is the groundwork of what the nursery-infant teacher is there to do, and thus the very heart of what she must not merely know but understand. Here she must herself suffer the fullest impact of progressive education. She must carry out her own educative work and progress by her own activity. Above all, she must be stimulated to enquire and probe and think. What is it she is going to try to do? With what aim? For what reason? By what means? And she must end up with some sort of clear picture of the answers to all these questions, a picture that makes sense as a whole and can stand up to criticisms and alternatives. Otherwise she may be a pleasant companion for her children, or even a successful trainer, but she is not a teacher, as the theory of progressive education must interpret this term.

The accepted types of syllabus of the history of educational ideas, the contributions of leading educational reformers, differing current schools or theories of education, etc., will obviously provide the right starting-points. But in the end our teacher has to come to terms with herself, she has to make up her own mind what education is going to *mean for her,* as regards goals, processes, methods and conditions. And for this she must get all the help and time she needs.

Thirdly, there is the illimitable subject of the world into which she is trying to induct her children. We normally assume in her a certain level of general education, and then try to amplify this in a few selected directions. But what major part or aspect of the world, physical or human, present or past, can our teacher afford not to know anything about? She needs at the very least a broad geographical and historical perspective; some elementary knowledge of natural phenomena, optical, electrical, chemical, mechanical; some familiarity with the gamut of living things and their evolution; some reasonable minimum acquaintance with current economic, social and political institutions; a broad idea of the main technological structures of our civilisation, transport, communications, food production, health and amenities; some cultivated sense of the creative achievements of the human mind in literature, the arts, music, architecture, and some grasp of the meaning of religion and philosophy. And, with all this must go an understanding of ways, means and methods, which is so vital both for the teacher herself and for the growing and developing mind of the child. How have we secured all the knowledge, insight and power of control we have now accumulated in so many directions? How are we proceeding to extend these achievements further? How do we assure ourselves that any apparent new knowledge or theory or supposition is true and not false? And by what methods and criteria do we assess success in other—for example, aesthetic—fields? If children are to be equipped to judge for themselves, both the ways by which new knowledge or power come into being, and those by which they are tested are surely even more vital than almost any specific new acquisition? And the teacher cannot begin to help unless she herself has at some time been enabled to grasp these things and can in some degree handle and explain them.

Fourthly, there are the practical skills. These are perhaps the least problem, first because no one is expected to master more than a few; secondly because, thanks to their native appeal, most young people will have gone some way with them prior to the teacher-training stage; and thirdly because in this field specialisation is natural and largely a matter of specific training for both sides. All that need be said is that without some practical or technical skills which the teacher can actually communicate to those children who respond, she would make a poor companion as well as a poor teacher for most of them. The only problem from the present angle is that of yet another claim, or rather array of claims, to the available, or unavailable, time.

IX

This, then, is the almost insoluble problem. The nursery-infant teacher would herself need to be a more or less complete microcosm of all human knowledge, wisdom and skill, in order to cope with those quasi-microcosms, our active, eager, full-living children of three to seven years of age—and steer them along towards the right finished form. Clearly she must fall very, very short of this ideal. But what particular gaps in her armoury, what kinds of failure to understand or blunders in coping with actual situations, do we prefer? Should we aim at the widest range possible and risk producing just a smattering of everything and grasp of nothing? Or if we decide to concentrate mainly on a few selected themes, which of all the equal claimants shall these be? And do we then pick out just a few more for semi-serious attention, or do we now spread ourselves thinly over the whole rest of the ground, because even a smattering of as many topics as possible is better than too many complete blanks?

I can think of no criticism-proof answers to these questions. In practice we have so far got by without too heavy weather and for a while we can no doubt continue in the same way. Nevertheless, our problem is all the time getting more acute. Firstly, both our key-subject, psychology, and our social heritage of knowledge and achievement are constantly expanding; and, secondly, the progressive educational approach with its ever-increasing demands on the understanding and vision of our educators is steadily gaining ground. In the face of these trends, we must surely be brought to a breaking-point sooner or later. The question is whether we might not gain if, without waiting for this, we accepted the challenge to do some radical re-thinking here and now.

Hence the present pondering aloud. Perhaps our right key lies in the broad general fact that a whole view, although often the last stage to be reached, is actually much simpler and easier to take in than any sequence of separate detailed parts. And if it can be provided, it also happens, by good luck, to be far more valuable for our purpose. The right alternative to a smattering is a single, unified figure, or *Gestalt*. Of course that is something we must achieve ourselves before we can transmit it, alike as regards our psychology, our view of education, and our own picture of the world. Perhaps that is where the rub lies and where our real re-thinking is required.

In fact, the problem we are here facing is not peculiar to the nursery-infant teacher, but one she shares, first with every intelligent parent, but also on further analysis with every thoughtful person in our day. This links up directly with a philosophy of education such as I have tried to sketch and is a continuous theme of contemporary discussion. Most of us feel the need for a very much wider vision of the world around us, physical and human, than we can ever hope properly to master. For we know we cannot possibly grasp in any detail more than some minute fractional part. Our only way therefore of securing the wider horizons we seek is through inducing specialists everywhere to work out for us simplified whole views of their special fields. They are, fortunately, in much the same case and have the same need, which, therefore, they can fully understand. For, firstly, each separate scientist is almost as dependent on the sum of his fellows as the non-scientific rest of us. And, secondly, all scientists are dependent in just the same way on the other vital contributors to our civilisation, in the fields of history or law or literature or any of the other humanities.

In effect, in this matter of our interest in something approaching a whole view of our world, we are all in the same boat. And, moreover, that interest, for its own sake, is not all that is involved. There is also an imperative need, on the part of all of us, for some sort of *shared* world-picture. The boat we are all in would soon become a floating tower of Babel which could not even keep afloat, if this need were not satisfied, that is, if we did not manage somehow to rough out with one another's help such a shared whole view. A society in which everyone hugged his own fragment of knowledge and was uninterested and uninformed about the rest would in fact fall to pieces as soon as these fragments became specialised and disparate enough. In practice this trend has so far been held in check not only by the direct struggle of many of us against it, but also by the large body of common traditions, beliefs and assumptions, and even world-views, which we still hold by common inheritance. Nevertheless the trend has in recent years become marked enough to cause wide general concern, and our traditional stock of shared beliefs and assumptions is hardly calculated by its soundness, logic or cohesion to reassure us.

X

Many of us would feel, in fact, that not only should we risk breaking up if we went on pulling further apart, but we are already very unstable because we have failed to draw together in the right way. A reasonably integrated, well-grounded, shared world-picture, at least up to a certain point, is surely a very condition of survival for any would-be co-operative community. It is like a common language, or anyway the only possible basis for one. And, once more, it seems particularly essential for the living together, within one free society, of believers in different ultimate views. The more these diverge, the more vital is it that there should also be a large common terrain in which, without hopeless cross-purposes and incurable clashes, we can all meet. That terrain must, in fact, be both ample enough and very unmistakably defined. Perhaps more problems than we suspect are already due to these conditions not being sufficiently fulfilled.

I cannot pursue this theme here, but do suggest that such a shared world vista, made up of carefully planned whole views of what, with reasonable assurance, we *know* about all major parts or aspects of our world, physical and human, is one of our most urgent social and educational necessities.

And on the nursery-infant teacher falls, once more, a special basic responsibility. For she presides over the years when the first foundations for a future shareable world-view should be taking shape. During that time the child should be building up his first full sense of the variety of things; and we all now believe in encouraging him to question, explore and discover in every direction to the top of his bent. But at the same time, as already suggested, he should also be steered continually towards interconnections and bridges, in such a way that everything will remain for him part of one and the same world. In fact, it should be his single, comprehensive picture of that world that should expand and develop all the time. From that common process in all children a great shared perspective should in the end naturally spring. But to give any real help with this the nursery-infant teacher must have her own clear view of what is to be achieved and why. And for this, of course, she must have been aided to attain the right shareable world-perspective herself.

XI

Here we come back to the whole problem of her training-curriculum and all its simultaneous demands. I have just been considering her as a special, focal case of our general modern problem of an adequate civilised education. This, I have contended, needs to be far more microcosmic for all of us than it has been in the past, because of the world of continually enlarging knowledge and achievement in which we find we live and want to play our free co-operative part. Here, however, the right kind of help is becoming more and more available even for the training-curriculum, just because the need for it has become so plain and universal. Naturally we can see that this microcosmic need is one we can only hope to satisfy, even in modest measure, by going on with it all our lives. What we formally call our education merely lays down the broad groundwork on which, if the work is well done, we shall later want to go on and on building ourselves. That applies to the nursery-infant teacher at least as much as to anyone else; but in her case the groundwork is particularly important, even for the beginnings of her professional task.

However, for her this is only one of the several related parts of her problem. Over and above her general vision of the world around her, she has to achieve some degree of specialised understanding of psychology on the one hand and of the problems and aims of education on the other. But psychology alone covers so vast a field—in truth one which, if properly understood, duplicates the whole rest of the world from its own angle—that here, too, she must to no small extent depend on those large panoramic views which are her key to the wider outside world.

We need, in fact, so to plan all our psychological teaching that a true whole-vision of children as living and unfolding individuals in a living community will emerge. Though intellectual, emotional, moral and practical growth have each their own consecutive story, they must in the end be seen as interacting and integral parts of the one mental life of each one individual. And he in turn must be viewed in the setting not only of his own interacting community but of the larger human society and the still larger human history of which he forms part—in the setting indeed of the entire mystery-play which we call human life.

Our nursery-infant teacher must thus come out of her training with the feeling not that she now knows the "psychology" needed to get her through her exam, but that she now understands children and herself and human beings at large in a way she had not dreamt of before. I believe modern psychology has begun to provide something like this illuminated sense of understanding, together with the reality of knowledge and insight to justify it. I do not know, however, whether our trainees often end up with this sense, or for that matter can be expected to do so, unless our psychological training is expressly designed for it.

Here, of course, a mere theorist must beware both of failing to do justice to what is already being done and of overrating what can possibly be done with the human material and the time at the training college's disposal. Yet one can hardly help being struck by the tenuous relation of some of the psychology acquired by teachers to the actual life and ways of young children. And it has seemed to me that much of our general teaching of psychology everywhere, at least as far as the textbooks reflect it, might be failing in a similar way. It looks somewhat like trying to get across the basic geography, the broad structure and lay-out, of a whole country by going over a long succession of very large-scale sectional maps, say one inch to the mile. Even though carefully joined together, they just do not add up. They do not integrate or fuse into any single whole picture, to say nothing of that of the particular country concerned. The analogy can, I think, be carried right through. What the nursery-infant teacher, above all, needs is a big human-psychological globe; and then a big topographical map of her own continent, the child throughout his growth; and then another large map of her own country, the child from three to seven; but with the stress all the time on the major structural features, relations and proportions which no mere aggregate of separate detailed sections can bring out. I cannot feel that this is the kind of psychological whole-vision and grasp which at present we tend to produce.

What I have just said about the nursery-infant teacher's psychological training applies, of course, also, *mutatis mutandis,* to the other major training demands on her. I have already dealt fairly fully with the vast question of the world around the child into which she, more than anyone else, must strive to guide him—a world which in the longer run is nothing less than the furthest span of present human knowledge, thought and feeling. The third and equally crucial demand is that of the theory and philosophy of education. Here, perhaps, the problem is less difficult once the psychology comes alive for the teacher, and a passably integrated picture of the physical and human world begins to take shape for her; but, nevertheless, once again a final whole-view is vital, and to meet its needs it may well be that both re-thinking of our training programmes and also some provision of newly-written reading would be very much required.

XII

I cannot pursue all this any further now, but should perhaps add one qualifying comment. I have emphasised whole views and wide perspectives as our right answer to the risk of losing everything of value among ever more thinly-spread smatterings. But what of the new risk one may thus be introducing—the risk of losing everything of value in mere vague and empty generalities? These can no more help the teacher in dealing with the all too specific demands of her children than any number of bits and pieces of detailed information without an integrating background. I should certainly feel that as a vital corrective to vagueness there would always have to be a substantial element of detailed study and knowledge, above all in the psychological field, but also in that of general knowledge. But I should also stress the all-importance of ensuring that every teacher learns to link a clear awareness of methods and criteria with the actual results, the knowledge and understanding and achievement, which we gain through them. In the same spirit I should regard it as essential to build up in her a living sense of the bridges that lead from detailed inquiry to those general perspectives which, in so many fields, are alone open to her. Here again, however, nothing will serve but actual detailed study of some given fields, together with direct experience of the way in which the wider perspectives are eventually projected and tested and established.

But it is time to bring this tentative paper to a conclusion. If my schedule of demands on the nursery-infant teacher now sounds just a little less impossible than at first, I fear I have only achieved this by transferring my superhuman demands to the nursery-infant teacher's teachers. I still cannot help feeling, however, that when transferred to the training college arena, the demands need not appear as quite so Utopian. In any case, I have not made any more ambitious claim than to place before you what, on a certain view of the aims of education, does seem to be a real and ever more difficult problem. If as progressive educationists we want to face up to all the implications of our standpoint, what is the minimum that we need from the nursery-infant teacher? How far can we hope to meet this minimum? What do we have to do in order to get as close to it as possible? I hope, anyway, that I have provided some stimulus for thought and discussion.

Early Scientific Trends
in Children*

The following article was originally presented as a lecture in a course on "The Foundations of Scientific Attitudes: Their Development in the Primary School," organized by the University of Reading Institute of Education. Isaacs explores the cognitive abilities of young children, demonstrating the existence of many proto-scientific abilities. He develops the point that it is necessary to regard science as one of the humanities and to view it in its historical perspective in order to help children develop their early scientific abilities.

I

My main aim in this paper is to focus attention on certain trends present in most normal children from three to five years onward which we can, I believe, rightly describe as scientific.

By this I mean no more than tending, in a very real sense, *towards* science, but even so my chief task will be to justify such a description. No one may in fact want to deny the existence of the two related trends which I specially wish to stress. That is, first of all children's natural curiosity and interest in finding out about things, partly by asking questions as to what they are, where they come from, what they are made of, how they work, and so on; but partly, also, if given the chance, by exploring and finding out for themselves. Secondly, their particular interest in grounds and reasons and above all explanations, as expressed in their persistent why questions.

However, before I dwell on these trends in any detail, the issue to be faced is this: can one truly say that they have a bearing on anything we can seriously call "science"? There may be superficial analogies, but could

*First published by the National Froebel Foundation, 1958. Reprinted with the permission of Mrs. Evelyn Isaacs and the Foundation.

anything be further apart than the transient curiosities arising out of children's natural play and fantasies, and those formidable fortresses of highly organised technical knowledge we call the sciences? In fact just because these surface ebullitions of interest seem so familiar and of such small account, we take for granted that they have no real significance for anything that follows after—and long after. And of course least of all for that latest stage of education when young people first become ripe for what are surely among the most specialised and advanced forms of human achievement.

That, however, is the very view I want to try to break down. It serves to perpetuate the gulf it assumes; whilst I wish to suggest a real underlying continuity which we might use for a vital reshaping and quickening of the whole process of education.

I shall in fact seek to show how the apparent gulf can be bridged from both ends. From that of science, we must greatly widen and humanise our ordinary much too narrow view. From the child's end we must penetrate much more deeply into the meaning and latent possibilities of those early drives in children to which I am here referring. We may then begin to discern how far, if really used, they might carry children in the direction of science, anyway in that widened sense which is I believe the rightful one. Till, in the course of the 10 to 12 years minimally available to us, we have brought them to some genuine grasp of what science is, what it signifies in our human story, and what it demands. And a number of them may be ready and eager also to meet those demands fully and become real students of science and eventually scientists.

But let me emphasise at once that my main concern here is not with the ways and means of training professional scientists or increasing our output of them, though this consequence too might follow. The aim I want to serve is, I think, even more essential: namely, to integrate science, in its broadest sense, into its proper place in the education of us all, to the benefit of the whole community. This, of course, is today largely common ground. The air echoes with laments about the great gap which has developed between the humanities and our more and more specialised science, with equal damage to both sides in a world growingly dominated by the latter and its consequences. Various ways of bridging or remedying this gap are in fact constantly being put forward, particularly on the university level, as in a recent announcement from Cambridge and the standing programme of the University College of North Staffordshire.

However, I am suggesting that the true remedy may lie much further back. And anyway, from the standpoint of our society as a whole, a synthesis on the university level, even if it could be made fully effective, would not meet the case. It would at best be limited to a minority, and chiefly of specialists on either side. But what we need is that some sort of integrated outlook which includes science should come within the reach of the community at large: that is, of all those in any way capable of it. And, indeed, no outlook can today be regarded as integrated unless some reasonable appreciation of science—its nature, scope and significance—forms part of it and for that purpose is brought in throughout the process of education. We need to build up towards this the whole time—at least as much as towards whatever else we value beyond the bare rudiments of the three R's, whether history or civics, crafts or arts or letters, or any other humanity. Science *is* a humanity, and indeed for better or worse, that which today most distinctively stamps all our civilisation, as well as shapes our material fate.

This graduated building-process, I suggest, must start from the scientific, or let us say proto-scientific, interests and drives so happily present in most children, and must go on using and developing these all the time. I am not under-rating the length of the way, or the discipline and sustained hard work that simply must come in before competence in even one science can be attained; but that, anyhow, arises later, and for most of us cannot be carried very far. This does not however remotely mean that, as our up-to-date tribute to the importance of science, we should aim at a *smattering* of it for everyone. That would indeed be the sole outcome if we thought our tribute could be discharged by introducing "science" as a "subject" for all during the last two to three years of their education. My case on the contrary is that only by setting out from the young child's own appropriate interests and drives, and working with these right through, can we reach the goal we really want. That is, neither a degree of scientific specialisation which for most of us is not even desirable, nor a mere worthless smattering, but some real broad vision of what science means and—perhaps above all—how it is achieved. What we must in fact seek is to preserve the closest union in the child between ends and means, between methods and results, between enlarging horizons and the ways in which they are enlarged. He should find that each question that is answered or interest that is met takes him further into a scheme of things in which new paths open, new questions arise, and new active curiosities and interests start up. Thus there should grow on him a sense of a number of different directions to be explored, realms to be penetrated and worlds which, if he wishes, he can increasingly make his own; but one and all, whether to do with engines or aeroplanes or animals or plants or burning and melting or rivers and mountains or the ways of different human beings: one and all parts of the same one world, constantly expanding for him, in which he lives and has his being. And simultaneously with this growing picture of that world and its different aspects and provinces, the child should be learning all the time, by his own progressive activities and as it were in his bones, how one builds up and extends this scheme—and also, as we shall see, how one must test and, where necessary, correct it. This sort of concurrent organic growth, carried forward year by year, towards science both as ordered knowledge and as method, is surely the goal we *ought* to want to attain.

The further road into specialisation would then also be open, for anyone who wishes to follow. But it would fall into its limited place within the total perspective of science, which again would remain only a part of each individual's whole view of his world. It would stay duly related to all his other interests and drives and to the larger perspectives to which, if similarly handled and developed, they in turn would lead. We are striving at present to bring together again, at least on the top levels of education, the different parts of a world which we have allowed to get divided and partitioned; but how much better if we merely made up our minds from the outset always to keep it one, since as one for each of us it begins.

This, of course, expresses a familiar wider view of education of which the present approach to science is just one segment. I cannot dwell on it here, but clearly it entails starting everywhere from the native educable forces and drives in the child and learning how to use these to carry him forward in all the chief directions of human growth. The success or failure of education is then measured by the degree of actual achievement of real mental growth. By this radical touchstone many of us feel that traditional schooling does not score very high. But we also realise that neither, if merely left free, will the child educate himself. He must provide the motive force, the interest and drives and the will. We, however, are the pilots, and for our indispensable piloting need a threefold knowledge: first, of the forces available in the child; secondly, of the distant goals we want him to reach; and thirdly, of the main channels which, from where he is, can take him there. And we must find out, if necessary by trial and error and sustained experiment, how he can best be steered aright. The voyage must, however, remain his voyage in every sense. And however poor our actual showing by this measure, any criterion other than the child's own inward mental growth can only be a figment and a sham.

All this, as I have said, is well-known doctrine today, and in spite of many critics and sceptics, a great deal of encouraging work is being done towards realising it. However, it should be seen not as a solution of the problem of education but rather as its radical reopening in a much more difficult and exacting form. And in any case even if the doctrine is accepted in other fields, that of science may well seem peculiarly inappropriate, for the reasons I stated at the outset. And so it may be of special value to show that the doctrine does apply here, too—and that the same problem ensues. The goal is vital; the needed motive forces exist, even in the very young child; and so does the direct road, right up to the proper world of developed science. Something has already been done to utilise these forces and that road, but once we recognise the facts, there remains the challenge how much more still we might yet *learn* to accomplish.

II

Let me turn back now to my bridge from the scientific shore. I argued that we must widen and humanise our view of science. Particularly as educators, we must get it back into its historical context. We must see it as a human enterprise and achievement—but still a very uneven and very unfinished one—within the total pattern of human history. Perhaps I should make plain here that I cannot speak as a professional scientist or even as one trained in any of the physical sciences. I do so as a student of the emergent and struggling science of psychology on the one hand and of the general problem of the meaning and nature of scientific method on the other. I hope, however, that this background may help rather than hinder my particular purpose of trying to restore psychological continuity where we all recognise the drawbacks of division. And though there are still differing views about some fundamental aspects of science and scientific method, what I am proposing to say is, I believe, mainly uncontroversial. It is more likely to be criticised as truistic than as false; yet even truisms may need reaffirming if they go disregarded, or if their task remains undone.

What now is our ordinary conventional view of science? I suggest most of us would think at once of physics and chemistry and then conjure up a notion of laboratories and instruments; a special highly technical language; most often also advanced and intricate mathematics; and of course a vast body of solid, established systematic knowledge, about which no one could possibly entertain any doubt. This would be our standard of reference, and other sciences would very much tend to be assessed by it. Thus astronomy or psysiology would quickly be recognised as equally sciences; geology or zoology would not occur to us so readily, but would be accepted as at least also-rans; but psychology or anthropology or economics would hardly any longer fit in. If pressed we should, of course, have to admit that they were nowadays generally granted the label: but they would not be our idea of science, and our reaction to them would be: "Yes, we suppose they are moving that way; but of course they are not in the class of physics and chemistry; they are not *proper* sciences like these."

This seems to me a not unfair analysis of current habits of thought about science, as evidenced by most of our references to it, our practical treatment of it, our tacit assumptions about it, and so on. We focus on the most developed form, take a static view of this, and treat it as typical. What I feel we need instead is (i) to distinguish more clearly between science as such and the various sciences, (ii) to see these as a range of growing bodies of ordered knowledge, but each at a very different stage of growth, with physics, chemistry and their kin not as typical but as the most advanced models so far, (iii) to view the whole group in terms not only of the achieved knowledge each now represents, but of the processes and methods that have brought all alike into being.

This, then, gives us a relatively simple pattern which can, I think, be briefly summed up as follows:

(1) In various fields of our experience we have found that by proceeding in certain ways we could start off bodies of ordered knowledge which could

then always be built up further and further in breadth, depth and internal structure and cohesion.

(2) When any of these bodies reaches a certain level of breadth, stability and cohesion we begin calling it a science.

(3) Spurred by the successes thus achieved, we have gone on to apply the same procedures in more and more new fields, including much more difficult and complex ones (such as those of the various forms of human behaviour and relations); and usually with at least some degree of success. There is thus now hardly a realm of human experience where we have not made some attempt to build up such an ordered body of "science"; but, as might be expected, our progress has varied widely, partly according to the length of the attempt, partly according to the elusiveness, fluidity, shiftingness or other recalcitrance of the subject matter.

(4) Thus a science is always an aggregate of knowledge existing at a given date. It represents the body of ordered information we possess at that date about some specified field of experience or fact, but generally it is very untidy and ill-defined about the edges, with a broad fringe of half-knowledge and quarter-knowledge, and a great deal of unresolved discussion pending even at the centre. In particular, besides the large main fabric of well-established descriptive facts, there is usually a connecting structure of explanatory theories and hypotheses of differing levels of generality and greatly differing degrees of tested and accepted validity.

It will be seen that the date, say within a decade, is always vital, because everything is in movement and still changing and growing. We should not, of course, be able to talk of sciences at all, and even less of growth, if there were not in each case a massive core of connected knowledge which was both stable and expanding. But dating or historic placing is always needed even as a measure of this main area of growth, and still more in relation to all that is in debate or under trial or half-known or unknown.

(5) If that is what we mean or should mean by a science, then certainly our best examples of what a science can be, will be among the most developed ones. But these must continue to be seen as simply the extreme terms of an advancing series; for what we most need to grasp is the law of advance. And for this we must not only view the series as a whole but pay special attention to its less forward members, and also to some typical beginners and beginnings.

However, before we turn to that law, we must pause to ask what we mean by the term "science", as distinct from the various sciences. Clearly the reason why we can use this collective term—whilst it would make nonsense to join up, for example, all separate animals into one animal—is that the *fields* of the different sciences adjoin and intercommunicate, and are in fact all sections of one field. The same should apply, and largely does, to our various bodies of ordered knowledge, thus allowing us to contemplate them as all one body and each individually as a part of this. But furthermore each has been built up by the same procedures and methods, and they are thus all products of one and the same process. Science at any time is the integral whole of all the ordered knowledge which, by the practice everywhere of certain methods, we have so far built up about the world of our experience as a whole. For a just perspective we must, however, qualify this in some degree; our far-flung totality is at very different levels of growth in different experience-fields, and thus, when taken together, is still a very imperfect whole. One may also think of it as a monster-version of the curate's egg: at any rate it is certainly only *very* good in parts.

(6) But plainly the main key to the wide historical view of science which I am suggesting lies in this matter of procedures and methods. The sciences each and all are the ordered knowledge which emerges when the method we call scientific is consistently applied within a certain field of experience. The very term "scientific" means of course "scientem-ficus", science-*making*. Any true appreciation of science must include the methods which generate it, as much as the realms of ordered knowledge so generated. We must learn to see them together, each as supporting and supported, validating and validated, by the other. And if anyone contends, as I do, that there are genuinely scientific trends present in children from the ages of three to five, and then defines this as meaning trends that make towards science, the test must be whether they make towards its methods no less than towards the knowledge that results from them. This test, as I hope to show, can be passed. It is true that, once more, these are only beginnings which can easily be left unused and may lead no further. But they are so very much the right ones, evincing just the features we most need, that they cry out their challenge to us to use and stimulate and guide them. And thus to study how best to do this, so that the full sense of scientific method, like the vision of scientific knowledge, can become part of the very texture of our minds.

III

What, then, are these crucial features of scientific method? Here I must, I fear, underline the obvious, but my historical approach may perhaps lend it some fresh topical interest. About four centuries ago there set in, as we know, a double re-orientation of human thought which rapidly spread as it prospered. It was this, in effect, which mainly launched the prodigious new expansion of knowledge we now call science, and remains, I believe, the controlling key to it.

First there was the *turning* of thought and inquiry to the actual world of fact. That is, in each case, to the specific concrete field about which further knowledge was being sought. This meant observing and comparing, carefully and methodically; recording what was so observed and trying to arrange it in systematic order; but then being led increasingly to search out from things themselves their own connections and order. That attitude presently brought into being every sort of aid both for extending and for recording observation: magnifying glasses and telescopes and microscopes; barometers and thermometers; graphs, tables and statistics, etc., etc. And, above all, it demonstrated that there was always more and still more to be observed and recorded, investigated and found out; and that each initial factual field was merely a gateway to a new world of fact.

Secondly, there was the *testing* of anything believed or propounded for belief by what was actually found in the relevant field of fact. This was partly complementary to the first attitude, but became an ever more pivotal principle in its own right. For, as observation proceeded, it always brought to light new errors and insufficiencies in previous beliefs, and confirmed the fallibility of almost all beliefs, even if most plausible and apparently compelling. This led to particular emphasis on *selective* observation, and so by a natural extension, to experimental testing. For it now became a vital aim both to track down any possible flaws in existing theories, and to minimise the risks of errors in newly suggested ones. And thus arose also all the elaborate techniques of research, the laboratories, the experimental designs, the repetition and cross-checking of experimental work, and so on.

At the same time, beyond all deliberate testing, a special alertness developed for everything contrary to expectation or in any way anomalous, even where the best established beliefs were involved. For experience showed that these might prove pointers to the most unsuspected elements of falsity or inadequacy, or might even unmask some radically false assumption or fundamental error.

Thus, to sum up, the principle that the one final tribunal for any belief about facts is the actual field of fact concerned, leads directly to constant vigilance for any possible sign of error; to readiness to regard every belief as potentially revisable; and to the most searching techniques of tests for bringing latent errors to light. And it is precisely this attitude which has led to the immensely high reliability of the great mass of our scientific knowledge, on which the whole edifice of our technological civilisation is built.

The foregoing two aspects of scientific method do not, of course, exhaust it. Naturally it took over also the two main tools of thought already in use: inferential logic and mathematics, which are closely related and perhaps at bottom one. Mathematics, in particular, in its basic forms of counting and measuring, grading and ordering, and the related operations, is crucial for all precise observation, comparison and scientific thought. And again its more advanced techniques have alone made possible the widest enlargements of modern science. But mathematics and logic could flourish without a hint of the flood of new knowledge that sprang from the decisive re-orientation of thought to the world of fact. It was this that proved the pregnant novelty, and it was under this new control that mathematics and logic themselves contributed all they did to the further growth of science. And the same control is needed if the early mathematical and early logical interests present in the child are to be used fruitfully in his growth towards science.

IV

If we now turn to our bridge from the child's end, we can see how notably our two proto-scientific trends correspond to the two main aspects of scientific method on which I have dwelt.

First, his natural interest in question-asking, exploring and finding out. Here we have clearly the most direct orientation to the world of fact. He responds to its leads and controls as a matter of course; he need not discover or re-discover them, because he has not yet been turned away from them. That only comes later, when his formal schooling or so-called education begins. He has, indeed, the good fortune, in our society, of being born into a physical environment full of variety, movement, change and challenges, which constantly acts on him and re-stimulates him; and also into a social environment that carries him forward with a continual flow of information and equips him with diverse ready-made question-forms by which he can propel himself further. He picks up in these ways during his first four to six years quite an array of knowledge of the different kinds of things around him—what many of them are made of—where others may be found or come from—what they do, how they behave or work, or what can be done with them—what happenings in what order will occur in different situations and even how various of them are brought about. This knowledge in turn gives meaning to the corresponding question forms which he takes over at an early stage: What is this? What is it made of? Etc., etc. And these questions then surge up almost automatically as new objects and situations are encountered, and lead to further knowledge of the same type.

Concurrently he is keenly interested in similarities and differences, and usually takes pleasure in noting these, and in comparing, sorting and arranging things by kinds, or in regular patterns. That leads readily also to an interest in measuring and counting. Again, he responds quickly to most forms of novelty, and wishes to handle and try out, to pull apart and put together, or more generally to re-produce whatever effects adults or older children can produce. Similarly he wants to explore new places, new set-ups and new activities. And as he grows a little older, but certainly before school age, he becomes particularly interested in how things happen, or are done, or work or have come about. This, too, gets linked to its appropriate question-form, chiefly "What makes . . .?", or else "Why?", in *one* of its main senses. And always the answers mean the more to him, the more concrete they are, and most, if he is actually shown, or still better, helped to find out for himself.

All this, as I began by saying, is familiar ground. But I hope the relation, or potential relation, to the beginnings of science is now also plain. Admittedly nothing much comes of it usually. But we can hardly claim to do much as a rule to keep these interests going and carry them further. Indeed, the conditions and methods imposed on traditional formal schooling, with mass-teaching in schoolrooms and the three R's to be mastered, can hardly do other than to overlay and stifle interests which first of all are essentially individual, and secondly, altogether directed to the real world without. What, however, would happen if we were encouraged to view them all the way through, from the home or the Nursery School to the Infant School, and from this to the Junior, and so right on, as one of the main avenues of education, to be sedulously cultivated and developed?

I believe some material towards an answer exists and gives noteworthy support to the suggestions, and challenges, put forward here. Even with quite young children some very encouraging responses have been obtained. I imagine the records of most progressive Nursery Schools might be cited, but I will only quote the work with which I am personally most familiar. Though going back some thirty years, it remains very much in circulation, and in its kind, I think, unsurpassed. I refer to "Intellectual Growth in Young Children", by the late Susan Isaacs,[1] describing the technique and results of the Malting House School in Cambridge which she organised and ran from 1924 to 1927.

The age-range of the children was mostly between three and five. They were left to choose their own activities, with the adults merely throwing in suggestions, as they arose out of each situation, for acceptance or otherwise. Their time was spread over all the pursuits in which children of those ages delight: physical movement and games; music and song; dramatic make-believe; handwork, drawing and painting; gardening and the care of animals; and even reading, writing, number and measuring in so far as freely taken up and genuinely enjoyed. Nevertheless they chose also to devote no little of their time and interest to the widest range of inquiring, exploring and finding-out discussions and activities, usually initiated by one or the other of them. The following condensed summary will illustrate their scope:—

Attempts, after seeing some wax liquefy on the hot-water pipes, to melt a variety of other things the same way. The burning of different substances in the garden bonfire. Steam versus smoke from this; the smouldering of wet leaves; comparing the amount of soot in the bonfire smoke with that from a burning candle; noticing that a soot-blackened plate seemed burnt, but then proving by washing it that this was not so.

[1] [Susan Isaacs, *Intellectual Growth in Young Children, with an Appendix on Children's "Why" Questions by Nathan Isaacs* (London: Routledge and Kegan Paul, 1930).]

The melting and fusing of glass; movements of mercury in a thermometer in hot and cold water; the behaviour of mercury on its own. The use and construction of a Bunsen burner; the blocking of the pipe and its cleaning; the control of the air-supply, and different sorts of flame. The construction and lighting of the gas-cooker; the bubbling of gas through water and its ignition on the water's surface; the backfiring of the burners on the gas-cookers; the relation of the different control taps of the gas supply; the construction of a gas-fire.

The boiling of water; the small bubbles of air and larger ones of steam. How snow and ice melt under different conditions and the amount of water produced; the making of ice, and watching a small quantity of shallow water freeze more quickly than a larger one; snow and frost and frozen soil; frozen pipes, the gas not working, the unfreezing of the cistern and the lavatory pipes. Water supply generally, and where pipes come from and go to; the construction of the tap and the cistern.

Ice and snow and hail in the garden in winter. The refraction of light by a lump of ice. Reflections in a mirror. The apparent bending of a stick in water. The use of hand lenses and how things look bigger.

What will float in water and what will not. The levels of settling of different soil ingredients in a jar of water; the use of funnels and filters; the behaviour of water poured into a glass U tube. The use of a hosepipe; the moving of a seesaw by the force of its jet. Balancing on sliding-boards. The china-weights on the pulleys of the electric lights; the use of pulleys for hauling up pails.

Aeroplanes circling overhead, the propeller, petrol tank and engine, and the way they work; can the pilot see and hear the children? Aeroplanes spinning and manoeuvring; aerial photographs; maps and map-making; the reading of map symbols; can one go all the way to China by boat? The sizes of steamers and rivers; volcanoes.

Living things, above all animals. The hatching of hen's eggs; their relation to the eggs we eat. The inside of half-hatched eggs, the visible embryonic blood vessels. The differences between wire-worms and earth-worms, and the ways of woodlice. Snails and their spiral shells. Whether a rabbit that had died was really dead. Interest in a human skeleton and comparing its bones with one's own.

And then a real plunge into biology. When a pet mouse died, the children looked interestedly at its body, teeth, tail and fur, and Susan Isaacs suggested "Shall we look inside it?". This led to a close and sustained interest in the dissection of dead animals and every aspect of their anatomy. Dissected crabs, a toad, a snail and a sparrow as compared with mammals. The food in stomach and guts. The cause of death. Rabbit and mouse mothers, babies and fathers, and their behaviour. The formation of a Zoological Club, with three rules: animals not to be teased, to be fed every day, and to be kept clean. A rabbit book and a mouse book for recording observations. And so on.

I feel sure that many of these interests and inquiries could be paralleled not only from other modern Nursery Schools, but also from the experience of most sympathetic parents with their own young children. Let me repeat that we need not overrate their significance. They are not usually kept up for long; either the child's attention shifts, or fact-seeking curiosity turns into make-believe play or carefree fantasying. All we can say is that the varied interests and questions are there, often recur, and can frequently be led on, above all in the atmosphere of a group of eager, live-minded children stimulating one another, towards deeper penetration into the inter-connections and larger schemes of things. And under these conditions the beginnings of both the spirit and the attitude of scientific inquiry can be very clearly discerned. The question is what we can make of them. The framework of school education has in recent years become much more flexible, and enlightened teachers are already demonstrating how much can be done to bring the meaning of science within the reach of children of the primary school years. All such work provides its own support not only for my argument, but also for my recurrent refrain: what *might* we not achieve if we started right from the psychological roots and went all out to develop these throughout the whole period of education?

Before I leave this theme, however, I have still to turn to my second proto-scientific trend, which, at least in part, moves over somewhat less familiar terrain. I have already referred to the broad heading of children's why questions, but now want to explain what has made me divide these from the rest and set them up as a class apart. A difficulty here is that there are at least four main groups which pass continuously into one another, and I really only want to focus on one of them, which I believe to be of particular significance.

There are, first, the why's that inquire for purposes and are fully appropriate only for human actions and artefacts. Children are apt to extend these to almost anything—but gradually learn better, and these why's then become a very limited specialised class. Secondly, there are demands for grounds or reasons, applicable more especially to assertions, and tending more and more towards the arena of argument and logic. Thirdly, we have the quests for causes, with a purposive bias at first but turning quite early into genuine causal inquiries, to find out what has made something happen, or how it has come about. All these are essentially *information*-seeking questions just like: What kind of thing is this? Where does it come from? What is it made of? How does it work? And so on; but of course the causal type comes to be of outstanding scientific importance.

The fourth group, however, even though continuous with the others, falls by its main emphasis into quite another category. It is the group of why's that seeks not merely information but *explanation.* It arises not from a simple blank of ignorance which the questioner wants to have filled in, but from an all-too-positive state of confusion and helplessness which he needs to have removed. It springs typically from a sudden jar, and an onset of surprise and puzzlement in which the subject, not knowing where to turn, appeals in fact for a rescue operation. And it is quite unmistakable in children from about their fourth year onward, when we can pick out from their spate of why's a fair number which clearly belong not to any of the other three groups, but to our present one.

Instead of the mere ignorance which is our natural first condition and needs no explaining, we are faced with a condition of disturbance which is itself a puzzle and a challenge. When does this occur in children, and what causes it?

The reply has, I believe, much light to throw on the child's whole relation to his knowledge, and the nature and extent of his concern with it. But before I pass to this let me quote a few illustrative instances from my study of Children's Why Questions in Susan Isaacs's "Intellectual Growth",[2] all drawn from four-year-olds and under.

Why doesn't the ink run out when you hold up a fountain pen?
Why does it get lighter outside when you put the light out?
Why don't we see two things with our two eyes?
When a building has a corrugated iron roof, why is the corrugated iron always crinkly, and not flat like the other sorts?

And from a small boy to his mother who was lying down and whom he wanted to get up: "You aren't dead, so why don't you get up?"

What I suggest marks out these why's and all their numerous kin is an accompanying "whereas" clause, often explicit but if not, then so plainly implied that we can at once supply it. The child has been struck by an anomaly, or apparent anomaly. He encounters something contrary to what he had expected or, anyway, very unexpected. If used to old-fashioned pens he has probably often blotted his copybook by incautiously holding one over it; but in a fountain pen the ink somehow fails to run out. Putting the light out obviously means darkness, but here it is the opposite. If you close either eye in turn, you see each time a table there: so surely you should see two if you look with both eyes, etc.

And thus we get to the crux of the matter. Puzzlement is a state of disorientation and at-a-lossness. To understand it we must understand the previous state of orientation and implicit confidence. The simple key is that even children down to three to four years have already built up within their minds a quite far-reaching working model of their world, a sort of proto-science of the kinds and constancies of things and the regular rules of their behaviour and relations. This guides them in all their ways about their world, enables them to recognise the objects and happenings they meet, and thus permits them to foresee what to expect and how to respond and plan

---

[2] [*Ibid.*, pp. 291-349.]

and act. But periodically something goes wrong: their proto-science is, after all, still very imperfect and in particular very untested. They are too apt suddenly to find themselves helpless or hurt because some assumption or belief, implicit or explicit, has collapsed on them. And we see the effect of this in their sensitiveness to even small jars—to any observation which clashes with their existing scheme of thought, or for which this has badly failed to prepare them. They then pick up the why question, in our present sense, as the recognised way of expressing their at-a-loss state and invoking the adult's help in coping with it.

What form this help will take, what is the way out from their puzzled impasse, they cannot even try to guess. All they can do is to wait hopefully. The adult may have some simple answer. He may show them where they have gone wrong, either by jumping to a false conclusion or by some misperception or misunderstanding. Or he may demonstrate to them some new distinction they had not met before. Or he may introduce them for the first time to some interfering, deflecting or reversing factor previously unknown to them. Or he may merely tell them that the apparent anomaly is not one at all, but the real rule. Or, of course, he may get into difficulties himself, or just be unsympathetic or uninterested or impatient and fob the child off with some non-answer or simply shut him up. But children go on with their why's of puzzlement, because most often these bring them some measure of help. To the extent to which the adult's reply really meets the point, the child is restored to his previous state of confidence and security, but now on the basis of corrected or extended knowledge, and so on firmer and more stable ground.

Space only permits the lightest sketch of this theme; but what I trust has emerged is how close children come here to the very spirit and attitude of the scientist. Just like the latter, they are specially alert to any experience or finding that challenges their previous beliefs, throws doubt on them, or shows them up as insufficient. They want their scheme of knowledge, or believed knowledge, to be fully reliable both for truth and for at least broad sufficiency in any situation that may test it out. The sanctions behind this in the case of children are, as I have already said, simply the hazards and dangers inherent in anti-expected or very unexpected happenings or findings: the felt collision, the possible sense of helplessness and scare, the demands on them or threats to them for which they are so unprepared. But the lesser jar-effects of merely noticed anomalies or anti-expected, or very unexpected, findings, whatever the background reasons for the attention given to them, become the source of a very real intellectual or scientific interest. The child wants the explanation; he wants to know how to *reconcile* his previous beliefs or assumptions with this or that jarring observation or unprepared-for encounter. Or, if necessary, he wants to have them corrected or amplified, so that henceforth his scheme of beliefs shall provide for this now troubling experience and be prepared for it. There is here something that could lead directly to a keen and interested conscious advance in knowledge as knowledge, in respect both of truth or reliability and of range and scope. The child is, moreover, on the very verge of a testing attitude to beliefs as such, his and others', and it would take little to get him started on the temper of mind and the progressive interest in ways and means of testing that would carry him straight on to what is most distinctively scientific in scientific method.

But here, as everywhere, the differences between the child and the adult practitioner of science are as significant as the likenesses. Firstly, the child's proto-science remains that of a small child's world, narrow, surface-bound and no more than a patchwork. Secondly, he can and always does turn to the adult for a helping hand out of his impasse, where the scientist must do his own groping and searching within the factual world till he can find his own solution. These two factors provide much of the explanation why children's why's rarely take them far and in fact tend to dwindle so rapidly after a mere year or two of real rifeness. Of course those of the main information-seeking types are destined to shrink anyway, since the untenable purposive ones are outgrown, whilst the causal questions, if no puzzlement factor is present, come to be expressed in direct causal form. But even a large number of the why's of puzzlement drop out, since they are progressively cleared up, anyway enough for the child's purposes, as his knowledge of his everyday world grows somewhat more coherent and adequate and meets his limited needs.

Yet there may well be also some more dubious and challengeable influences at work. There may be large losses of keenness and edge, and even much warping and arrest of children's initial interest, through unhelpful adult responses, lack of interest and positive impatience and discouragement. And, perhaps, there is also a more general factor due to our relatively low current standards, well below the scientific level, as regards both explanation and belief-*testing*. Possibly these imperfect standards get reproduced too quickly and completely, in the types of reply to children's why's of puzzlement which are too often deemed sufficient. And perhaps, therefore, the contrast may be at its most extreme here between what actually happens and what could happen if an interest so potentially fruitful were met with the maximum of understanding and resourceful help, instead of something too like the minimum. This is a field which has so far been least explored educationally and is most widely open to experiment and research. We do know, however, that those who wish to get off to the best start in interesting children in scientific experiment and discovery often begin with some surprising, unexpected or anti-expected demonstration. This may, perhaps, help to underline my case, whilst at the same time pointing again to the close relation and mutual support of our two proto-scientific trends, and the value of making all the time the utmost conjoint use of both.

Just one glance, now, before I conclude, at those further potentially scientific trends, which are significant here chiefly as far as we can enrol them as auxiliaries. The most important, as I have already noted, are of course children's proto-mathematical and proto-logical interests and activities, such as comparing, measuring, counting, ordering, arguing and reasoning, so long as they do not become insulated substitutes for factual inquiry, observation and belief-testing.

Next, we have all the technological interests, no doubt most marked in the case of boys, in steam engines, motor cars, and aeroplanes, wireless and telephones, printing machines and lathes, telescopes and microscopes, or well-nigh any human constructions and contrivances, and the way in which they work. Much of this is almost inseparable from the direct interest in natural phenomena and may afford one of the readiest routes to the underlying mechanical, electrical, chemical and other laws, in a connected, near-scientific form. Moreover, anomalies and deviations from what is expected may here again prove particularly stimulating. On the other hand, however, technological interest may either turn more and more into a very limited practical one, or may just exhaust itself. It is not necessarily proto-scientific in its own right.

At a further remove, there is all the child's strong drive towards making, constructing, fashioning, and every sort of planned group enterprise. This may involve at any point the acquisition of new knowhow which, in favouring circumstances, may lead on to a real interest in fuller knowledge, for its own sake, of the field concerned. Here, too, however, the interest may just as easily confine itself to the momentary aim and be left behind with this.

Much more might be said about each of these interests and others that can at times co-operate with the child's more strictly proto-scientific ones. But this would merely take us out into the wider realm of all the child's ways of growth, and their relations to one another. Let me only reiterate that no tribute I have paid to science is meant to detract from any of these other interests. Even as regards knowledge I have not suggested that science is the sole or sole important kind we possess. I need only point to the part assigned in this very paper to a historical approach. And beyond history, or the law, or our social institutions and rules, or other generally recognised forms of knowledge there is ample room for diverse views about what other and more radically different kinds might exist.

That is all outside my scope here. But wherever scientific method has proved applicable, there is no rival to it; and it has certainly generated and is still constantly extending an immense structure of ordered knowledge and understanding which is, at the least, one of the most impressive and exciting achievements of the human mind so far. The argument I want to establish is only this: most children have it in them to attain some share in both sides of this achievement, the epic of the continuing building and the great edifice already built. The road from where they are to this eventual heritage is a direct but long one, and many causes may lead to failure almost at the start. But it seems that most children can be helped to travel it, if the right understanding and endeavour can be brought to bear. The endeavour must be both patient and resourceful; but if a really wide sharing in our scientific heritage can thus be reached, surely few educational enterprises could be more worthwhile.

On a Gap in the Structure of Our General Psychology*

Isaacs contends that inadequacies in the education of children stem primarily from a narrow, fragmentary, and superficial psychology of cognition. He proposes a reconstructed psychology that would have as its central concern the history of the "cognitive map," or world model, that each human being constructs, beginning in infancy. Such a cognitive map grows into a complicated network of beliefs and assumptions, largely unconscious, in terms of which expectations are held and decisions are made throughout one's life. The history of an individual's cognitive life is as dramatic as that of his affective life. A developmental, behavioral approach to cognition, exemplified in the work of Piaget, is needed. However, Isaacs points out that Piaget has concentrated on a very small segment of cognitive history and has overlooked one of its crucial aspects, namely the truth-falsity distinction.

INTRODUCTION

The aim of this article is to suggest a major gap still existing today in the structure of our current psychology.

Any such suggestion must undertake to explain (a) why the gap is still there; (b) why—if it is really major—it fails to show. Thereafter I shall endeavour to sketch out, very summarily, how in my view it should be filled, and what bearings this might have on our cognitive and general psychology. Finally I shall point to some crucial recent work in an allied direction, which I believe has not so far made its full impact, just because of the same gap.

What then is the latter? In the briefest terms, it is the absence from most of our current psychology—as shown by contemporary textbooks—of the whole

*First published in *Journal of Child Psychology and Psychiatry and Allied Disciplines*, 1 (1960-1961): 73-86. Reprinted with the permission of Pergamon Press Ltd., London.

theme of the *psychological* meaning, the meaning for our behaviour and history, of our distinction between *truth and falsity.*

Let me make plain at once that I am not concerned with any *philosophic* problems about truth; these, as we all agree, are no affair of psychologists. My standpoint, in all that follows, will be purely empirical and psychological. I shall only refer to clearly identifiable *happenings and functionings,* and their history, causes and consequences. The argument will be that whatever the philosophic mysteries about truth, we can definitely separate out a *psychological* functional meaning of this notion which plays the most controlling part in all our behaviour-development and history. Here, I shall suggest, is a theme that is vital for any complete psychology of human behaviour; vital but currently left out completely. Various bits and pieces of it do indeed appear in our textbooks, in different chapters and under different headings, but in a way that breaks up their significance and misses their real crux. My contention will be that the *cumulative functioning* of our truth-falsity distinction throughout our lives is the central key to any adequate psychology of cognition; and that everything else in this needs to be organized round it.

WHY THE GAP IS THERE, BUT FAILS TO SHOW

The answer is, of course, all too simple and I have already implied it. Psychologists have long viewed the dangerous notion of "truth", or anything connected with this, as nothing at all to do with them and in fact just a trapdoor into philosophy; whilst safety and science have meant keeping away from the whole philosophic arena. After all, the very establishment of their scientific status had turned on breaking their philosophic bonds, and the one thing to be avoided was to get re-entangled or drawn back. Thus the gap, if it is one, persists because it is in truth a deliberate avoidance. And therefore it also fails to show as a gap.

That, however, is not all. If my case can be made good, it is clear that no picture of our mental life can hold together if its central key is left out. But once the picture is thus disrupted, the missing key is no longer missed. And unfortunately the whole historic "set" of psychology—away from philosophy and towards laboratory science—has deflected us from even seeking a really organic picture of our mental life, or paying attention to its absence. Our official science has mainly settled down on the psychophysiological periphery of our behaviour, or anyway among those simplest, least humanly psychological ways of responding that best lend themselves to laboratory treatment; that is, those that can be most readily tied up with clearly defined, isolable and repeatable stimulus-situations in the physical world. And we have been happiest if we could moor our psychological data to the solid ground of physiological facts (sense-organs, efferent-afferent nervous system, brain, bodily responses), and indeed have strongly tended to seek most of our basic *explanatory theory* there. Thus psychologists seem most at home in the fields most susceptible to this kind of approach: sense-perception, attention, memory, etc., and so-called "learning" theory, i.e. the kind of "learning" which human beings most nearly share with the animal world and which therefore bears least relation to the vast *single and cumulative* learning-process by which we come to behave as human beings. And by the same token, even when psychological experimenters have sought to move "inward" towards motivation, character and personality, the same overall set has led them to seek out the most easily segregable fragments. The result, in the opinion of many of us, has been what was to be expected: too often the worst of both worlds, in the shape of findings apt to be *both* psychologically superficial and scientifically dubious. For in fact our characteristically human behaviour all emerges from a complex cumulative history—and therefore we cannot build it up into stable and worthwhile scientific knowledge unless we take that history into account.

Thus, however cogent-seeming the grounds on which our psychology has come to be as it is, the light which it throws on our human mental life as we actually live it remains bafflingly limited. And it leaves at least room for the question whether, for real penetration into this, some different way of approach is not required by the very nature of the facts. If the more exemplary scientific methods just fail to get to grips with these, must we postpone, perhaps indefinitely, any attempt really to understand them? Or can we find some other objectively controllable and scientific alternative? I suggest that we can, by *reversing* our direction from the psycho-physical periphery, but of course not back via the analysis of consciousness to philosophy, but to the *behavioural study* of our inward psychological *history*. And this is not a self-contradiction, but something perfectly practicable, which is already being done, and done in two quite separate and independent directions.

We have two orders of evidence of what can emerge if we do not break up the psychological context by a premature resort to would-be physiological linkages and explanations, but carry a purely psychological and historical approach right through.[1] The first evidence is that of psychoanalysis, by which invaluable new light has been thrown on the basic dramatic realities of our affective-conative life, even if—owing to the particular difficulty here of bringing the stricter scientific methods to bear—much of the detailed theory remains controversial. The second is that of the work of Professor Piaget and his helpers in the field of our cognitive and intellectual development, which has in fact proved far more amenable to an objectively controlled approach.

---

[1] This would of course be perfectly compatible with our laboratory psychology maintaining and further developing its present field, but now as a borderline study rather than the main structure of the science. And it might well benefit greatly in turn from a more adequate picture of the strictly psychological facts; for *that* is the picture which our very physiological psychology — and in due time perhaps our neurophysiology — must eventually learn to explain.

This has, indeed, already yielded an immense volume of new psychological knowledge and insight, to which I shall return. But what is relevant here is that even in this work there is still missing the one central key which the present article seeks to point to. Hitherto Professor Piaget has not (as far as I am aware) dealt directly with the operation and development of our truth-falsity distinction without which, on my view, our psychological picture cannot make coherent sense. Hence this attempt to exhibit and fill the gap, an attempt which owes to his work much stimulus as well as the strongest existing evidence of its possible value.

THE TRUTH-FALSITY DISTINCTION
AND ITS OPERATION AND CONSEQUENCES

I have argued that we can separate out, from the tangle of philosophic controversies and confusions of this field, a functional psychological meaning of our distinction, which we can then follow through all its potent consequences in the world of observable behavioural facts.

To make this good, I shall have to consider (A) the actual character of the distinction, as we operate it; (B) its effects on our behaviour and history. That will involve me in a mass of truisms, at least for a start. But in psychological matters we can rarely avoid these; our textbooks indeed are full of them; and it seems essential to get the truth-falsity ones spelled out, at any rate once, so that we can then go on from them.

(1) I propose to start with (B) because firstly it is so easy to bring out the clear causal operation of the distinction in our behaviour and lives, and its overwhelming practical importance for us; and secondly, it provides a solid factual basis for turning the flank of all the dismissive objections of philosophers to our normal way of formulating the distinction.

(i) The first banal but crucial point is that each use of the distinction can have either of two quite opposite kinds of effect. In the first place, if we assume or believe or decide that something (I deliberately use the vaguest possible word at this stage) is true, then we shall think it safe to act and build on it. Or if we assume or believe or decide that something is false, then we shall disregard it or act or build on what we loosely call its opposite. But secondly in either kind of instance our assumption, etc., can be either right or wrong; and both what happens to us and our own further behaviour will *diverge completely* according as it proves one or the other. If we are right, we can usually at least go on with our course of action, and often carry it to success. (But every piece of planned or purposive behaviour involves a vast number of such assumptions or beliefs, in *each* of which we must be right if we are to continue to our intended end; of this more presently.) If we are wrong, our course may be brought to a sudden catastrophic halt, or may break up later; at a minimum, if we find out our wrongness in time, we have to stop and alter, or perhaps radically replan, our action.

(ii) And in a very large number of instances there is no room for doubt, either in our minds or in anyone else's, about our rightness or wrongness. Sometimes we merely infer this from final success or failure; but very often we are in no way dependent on such an inference, but have evidence exactly such as our truth-falsity distinction calls for either that we were wrong or that we were right. That is true for almost all our specific expectations or beliefs, once we come into the situation to which they refer.

(iii) We cannot help forming the distinction in our early infancy. That is, as early as we develop our first automatic expectations. We assume that any familiar situation, any situation we recognize, will *go on* in the same way as before. But it soon happens that we suffer a sudden jar or shock because this or that situation in fact turns out differently. That sort of experience sets up in us its own antithesis between things going as we expected and going *otherwise;* and on this antithesis we have never had to go back. It has stayed with us throughout our lives, and has continually determined how we would behave next. It is perhaps the clearest *vera causa* of our history, as well as one of the most important, so that no would-be causal psychology can possibly afford *not* to study it intensively and *not* to present it as the major behaviour-determinant it is.

(iv) In effect, as soon as we give it this kind of attention we can see how the whole build-up of our lives depends on its operation. As we go along from earliest childhood, our behaviour becomes more and more foresightful, purposive and planned. But every step along that road turns on our having learnt to *piece together* more and more information and knowledge about the world around us, that is more and more beliefs, assumptions and expectations which in fact prove to be not wrong but right. Every further extension of each such scheme of beliefs turns on almost every previous part continuing to hold good. By our middle childhood, we carry with us a vast implicit fabric of assumptions, beliefs and expectations, consisting of innumerable interlinked sub-schemes, of which one or another enters into every bit of purposive action that makes up our daily life.

On the other hand, we have also from the start an unending succession of cases where our assumptions, beliefs or expectations prove wrong. They represent only a very small proportion of the total, else we could never build up even our ordinary daily life, to say nothing of greater enterprises; but they make up for their smaller number by the forcefulness of their effects, and anyway there are usually enough of them to keep us well on our toes. From them we progressively learn to distinguish and know better; to pause to consider; to look out for pitfalls and fallacies; to collect and assess evidence; to experiment and test; and to revise and reconstruct no few of our belief-schemes as we go along. So that besides defeating or arresting many of our courses of action and thus changing our immediate conduct, they are also causes of our learning vital *new* forms of behaviour, and indeed of our tending to advance more or less steadily to new and higher levels of cognitive organization.

(2) Having thus sketched, however roughly, the tremendous causal import of our truth-falsity distinction through all our behaviour-history, let me now turn back to (A), the actual character or nature of the distinction, as we normally operate it.

The ordinary intelligent person, if asked about this, would no doubt quickly reply: "Why, something is true if it corresponds to the facts and false if it does not; what else could the distinction be?" Philosophers have riddled this so-called naive correspondence-view of truth with queries and objections, to which the ordinary person might well be at a loss to reply. But perhaps, in the present context, the first thing to be said on his behalf is that he does not have to be committed to any "view" or "theory" at all. He is simply describing what he *means* by truth and falsity, and of this I suggest he is giving a substantially correct description. Here is the distinction as he has actually been operating it, *and as it has been operating on him,* throughout his life. Through this he has learnt everything he can do, and also all the lessons of his failures. These are the facts, which can be followed through and verified by anyone.

Our description, without a doubt, requires more considered and careful formulation. It must be cleared of vaguenesses and possible confusions; we must free it from apparent assumptions or semi-implications through which it could easily slide into a "metaphysical" theory; and it must be enabled to face some genuine though only marginal difficulties. But in its main substance it is just inescapable. The test, I suggest, would be that any proposed alternative would either be found to disregard the actual psychological facts; or else the fuller the account it took of them, the more indistinguishable it would become from a careful "correspondence" description.

Let me then try for this. We can, I think, say with defensible accuracy that our truth-falsity distinction is the distinction between the correspondence or the non-correspondence of a representation in thought (whether believed or disbelieved or just contemplated) with the actual state of affairs which it purports to represent. The very general phrase "state of affairs" is here expressly used to make sure of the widest possible coverage: objects and their qualities and behaviour; substances and their properties; happenings and processes of every kind; situations, occasions, conditions, states; relations and connexions; in short anything we can know, or can believe we know, or can believe. The phrase "purports to represent" is obviously vital in order to pin down *what,* in all our wide world of possible reality, we are thinking *of,* or thinking *about.* The exact psychological meaning of this "pinning down" will be more and more filled in as the argument proceeds, but will also be discussed specifically in a later section. The term "non-correspondence" covers any degree of deviation, from the minutest to the grossest; but for the most ordinary purposes we only talk of "falsity" in cases of material difference.

That is the core, but now for the much-needed clarifications, and the removal of gratuitous stumbling-blocks and difficulties.

(i) First of all, we must keep firmly apart what we *mean* by "true" and what may make us *decide* that a particular belief or proposition[2] is true. That is by no means as easy as it sounds. Very often the two come together and we hold that something thought by us is true, because we have seen that it corresponds; but then by a rebound from this we may be led to say that some other beliefs or propositions (e.g. supposed self-evident "axioms") *must* be true, and therefore correspondence has nothing to do with these cases. But that only signifies that they do not *depend* on found correspondence, not that their truth does not *mean* correspondence; and indeed actual correspondence is just what, if we came into the right situation, we should in these cases most confidently expect to find. (Nowadays, however, we have behind us so many shocks to that sort of absolute confidence that there are not many kinds of cases left where we should deliver ourselves to it. Indeed, the actual finding of correspondence has for the most part become our final *test*—which again confirms how strongly truth *means* correspondence for us, and how vital this meaning is to us.)

(ii) But what of all the host of cases where the very nature of what we think seems to exclude the possibility of comparison and so of correspondence? (Negative or abstract ideas—ideas about the past—concepts like that of the electron or neutron, etc.) In fact, must we not go further and say that the notion of "representation in thought" as such must limit us to the narrow range of visual mental images compared with what they are images of, like portraits with their originals? And what again of all the instances of implicit assumptions or beliefs where by our own hypothesis no explicit thought, let alone representation, is present in our minds at all?

That, of course, is the kind of difficulty which more than any other has caused philosophers (and even psychologists) to dismiss the combined notions of "representation in thought" and "correspondence" as utterly inadequate. But against this we must set the actual facts of our myriad *experiences* of correspondence and non-correspondence, in the most varied contexts, and far beyond the range of visual objects and visual images, or visual perception, or even most forms of specific sensory perception as such. And we must note that experiences of non-correspondence, in particular, seem peculiarly liable to happen to us just in the case of our implicit assumptions or beliefs, of which we were not even aware till we received our non-correspondence shock.

---

[2] Logicians have turned the notion of a proposition into something psychologically very unsatisfactory. Here it is just a representation-in-thought like any other, proposed or put on the table for consideration.

Yet thereafter we have no difficulty in becoming retrospectively aware of them—and even seeing exactly where the non-fit came in!

These irresistible facts must be acknowledged and our apparent theoretical difficulties reconsidered in their light, and not vice versa. I believe indeed that each type of difficulty *can* be met on its own ground (though in some instances not without prior criticism of formulae that have gained quite unmerited currency); but to try to do this here would carry me too far out of my main course. I will only say that beliefs about the past, negative beliefs, unlimited general ones, and those about inaccessible scientific entities all seem to me to come under the above heading. What is, however, important for the further course of my argument is to make two points of principle which are of particularly wide scope:

(a) If we turn to the developmental history of "representation in thought" we can watch how it gradually emerges (of course mainly with the help of language) from automatic anticipation—which is simply, as already noted, the projection ahead, from the recognized part of a familiar experience-pattern, of the rest of the pattern. This is applicable to every kind of experience and indeed later even to internal affective states. What in effect the projection ahead has to correspond to is the experience-pattern which actually comes. Thus in *all* cases of anticipation-beliefs or expectation-beliefs *like is compared with like* and our abstract difficulties about the supposed utter unlikeness of "thoughts" and "facts" or "thoughts" and "things", or the supposed dependence of correspondence on our limited visual experience and imagery, dissolve into thin, very thin, air.

Moreover, though "representation in thought" evolves into something far more sophisticated than any direct-experience pattern, even our most abstract "concepts" usually preserve a double and quite sufficient controlling link with the actual experiences out of which they develop. Firstly, we can mostly recover these as and when we require (and I venture to suggest that something has gone wrong if we cannot). Secondly they are both *acted on* and *tested* through one or another part of their content being *reconverted* in the appropriate situations into specific anticipatory projections[3]: that is, into specific projected experience-patterns to be compared with and judged by the experience-patterns which then actually happen. To all this I shall return.

(b) It is just the types of non-correspondence experience referred to above which force us to re-think the whole relation between thought and consciousness and to make room for the notion of implicit representations-in-thought *actively* functioning in us when we are quite unaware of them. But in fact the whole work of Piaget obliges us to go much further and to think in terms of a vast cognitive organization continually operating in us unawarely, with only this or that fraction emerging into consciousness as and when

---

[3]Most of our "concepts" are, of course, not simple psychic entities, as we loosely tend to view them, but mainly-implicit *complex psychic structures.* See further below.

relevant. We thus have a cognitive "unconscious" comparable with our affective one, but of course the former can usually be made explicit, and moreover we can objectively and experimentally follow through its build-up, in the way Piaget has actually done. Of this, too, more later.

(iii) There remains one more apparent difficulty, which it is not easy to deal with briefly, but which calls for the attempt because it goes down to the fundamentals of all we come to believe or learn. The ordinary person himself may well feel that if his view of truth—falsity as correspondence or non-correspondence of thought with fact is to be reduced to the mere correspondence of finding-experiences with certain represented or pre-represented experience-patterns, this is not good enough. What he means by truth is thought corresponding to things as they actually are, whether we "find" or experience them or not. By that road we can of course all too easily slide into metaphysics, tenable or otherwise. But even here there is no least *need* to do so. For I think we can show, if our genetic-psychological analysis is searching enough, that there is a further *deep organized structure of experience* which the ordinary person is really invoking when he insists that "truth" relates directly to the so-ness of facts, irrespective of whether we happen to perceive them. The contrast really operating in his mind (and that of all of us) can then be seen to be that between immediate perception and a massive psychological world-model, which we believe corresponds as a whole to the world we find ourselves in. This model, however, can in turn be shown to have been progressively built up from experienced elements, and if we follow our human history through from birth, we can recover all these elements.

Thus we can observe how each of us has come to separate out his different main kinds of experience (including that of the relations between the other kinds!); and above all, how we have learnt to segregate, by a most forceful host of concurrent traits, those we later call perceptual from our feelings and desires on the one hand, and from our memories, expectations and beliefs on the other. We can in fact see how the characters and the relations of those experiences to all the rest of our psychic life have fused them together and set them apart in our thought, as a controlling structure-in-depth acknowledged as standing for a "world of fact" or "of reality" precisely in so far as it controls our world of thought. And we can thus grasp what, psychologically speaking, we mainly mean by our "world of fact"—why we believe in it—and how rightly and inevitably we do so.

I cannot do more here than to point to this vital building-up process within our minds, which, to carry full conviction, needs a detailed account of all that enters into it and gives it solidity and depth.[4] It can, however, be safely said

---

[4] For an attempt to offer such a detailed account see Isaacs (1949). [Nathan Isaacs, *The Foundations of Common Sense: A Psychological Preface to the Problems of Knowledge* (London: Routledge and Kegan Paul, 1949).]

that this psychological story must at least be traced through and taken into account *before* we plunge into our supposed metaphysical problems and mysteries. And it is quite able to explain how we can both insist that truth means far more than the correspondence of represented experience-patterns with actual ones, and yet hold on to just that correspondence-comparison as our final scientific test, or court of appeal, for truth.

In effect, each single new comparison now rests for us on a *pre-supposed* world-model in our minds of which every part, as already insisted, has already undergone a myriad correspondence-tests (both involuntary and deliberate) and every new extension or level depends upon the established correspondence of all the prior structure. It is that presupposed world to which our thought has already been found to correspond, which, I suggest, lies behind our feeling that though we may *test* the truth of our beliefs (or hypotheses) by local experiential findings, what we *mean* by truth is their correspondence with something actually there in reality.[5]

SOME BEARINGS OF THE TRUTH-FALSITY FUNCTION ON OUR COGNITIVE AND GENERAL PSYCHOLOGY

The foregoing then represents, if I am right, something like the basic filling-in of the gap from which I began. But, as has emerged, that turns out to be only a starting point for a much more far-reaching reconstruction of our cognitive psychology. This again calls for reassessment of its relation to our affective–conative psychology, and indeed a fresh attempt, as I have indicated, to form a balanced and coherent picture of our behaviour-history and mental life as a whole. Within the limits of the present article, I cannot of course go far into these wider implications, but might perhaps usefully pick out a few further points that seem to me specially interesting or significant.

(1) It has long been a commonplace of many of our textbooks that when we look round us, say in a room or the street, what we actually take in at each moment is only a minute fragment of what we believe we see. The rest is what we usually call "intrepretation". Each new variation in our perceptual field is thus received, or apperceived, into our pre-existing knowledge-scheme or belief-scheme. (These of course link up in turn with feeling-schemes and action-schemes, and we initiate, pursue or vary our active behaviour-courses under the continuing joint control of all these factors.)

So far, good; but that gives only a fraction of the cognitive story, which from the present standpoint needs thereafter to be developed somewhat as follows:

(i) With the apperception or interpretation, there also goes usually an

---

[5] I should agree of course that a residual metaphysical issue or problem always remains. But I suggest this cannot even be properly defined, let alone discussed, till the full psychological story has been brought in.

automatic projection ahead *in time* (just like the infant's, but of course immensely more complex and extensive). Each new feature of perceptual intake tends to activate further "interpretations" which again at once turn into a further range of expectations projected ahead. But this process then means, equally automatically, that each new piece of "interpretation" is *correspondence-tested* by what in fact we "find" (or have happening to us) next. Mostly, as I have emphasized, it corresponds, and if it does, it just fuses into our continuing experience and developing course of action, at the same time generating its own further increment of expectation. This in turn fuses into the next tract of experience which again evokes its own further expectation-pattern, and so on through all the ordinary, mainly smooth round that makes up our daily lives. We do not under these conditions need to be aware at all of the *alternating cycle* between "thought" and "actuality" (the latter always operating as new perceptual intake), which in fact underlies every moment of that round. Only in those cases—*by comparison* almost vanishingly fewer—where we feel uncertain or where something is in dispute, do we pause to formulate some interpretation and expressly look to see whether it is borne out or not. But in just those circumstances the temporal alternating aspect of the ordinary cycle has virtually disappeared from view; and thus we can only too easily miss the element of automatic projection ahead in time which forms such a continuous key part of this cycle as we normally go along.

(ii) However, by these automatic projections ahead we are in fact continually giving hostages to fortune. They are at the mercy of what each next actual moment brings, whether this fits in or clashes. And every so often, there *is* a clash, small or larger. This then thrusts its characteristic threefold awareness on us: the "*clash*" as we feel it; the actual clashing new experience; and the projection it clashes with. The projection is thus forced into our consciousness, and we can by the same token see the silent alternating cycle which is always there, and realize how real and vital the element of temporal forward projection always is, even though silent and unaware.—How any of these clashes, or self-registering errors or weaknesses in our scheme of "interpretative" beliefs, may disrupt and overwhelm our whole behaviour-course, we all know only too well.

(iii) This alternating cycle, as I underlined earlier, has been going on throughout our lives from certainly our first few *weeks* onward (since behavioural preparation, the first stage of expectation, dates back to that time). It has been the daily rhythm, virtually the breathing, of our cognitive life, and has been impressing its cumulative action, affective as well as cognitive, on us all the time. Most of it has gone well enough and served to build up the basis of usable and dependable knowledge needed for all our purposive behaviour; but it has always been punctuated also by cognitive jars, breakdowns, failures, helplessnesses, panics and actual hurts. From these too we have incessantly had to try to learn, and *have* learnt. The alternation, again, between "interpretations" (including beliefs and tacit assumptions) which operated successfully, at least up to a certain point, and interpretations which failed or betrayed us (too often *after* appearing to serve us faithfully for a time) is itself one of the most important affective as well as cognitive rhythms in our life. For it is always taking us by surprise, and so forces us to learn, and to some extent to fear, our chronic liability to be thus taken by surprise. We try to counter this, as we know, in many ways, some very unsuccessful, some increasingly successful. But what of course we can do least against is the fact that so much of our scheme of beliefs consists always of tacit or implicit assumptions, which are only revealed as and when they break down.

Thus our psychology of cognition needs to be an essentially dramatic one; for throughout it there must run the story of that basic alternating cycle between our constantly expanding forward projections and every new actual happening, and all the drama of success and failure that necessarily turns on this cycle. No theory of cognition will hang together or "correspond" to the facts unless it is focused, not merely on our more or less theoretical "learning", but also on all the ways in which we live and act and plan by the forward projection of what we know or believe we know, and thus continually stake ourselves on this, and learn better (or sometimes worse) from it.

(2) As the foregoing makes clear, the "interpretations" which at any time become explicit, either through uncertainty or through breakdown, are usually only a small fraction of a much larger interpretation-scheme which goes on operating implicitly unless some new finding disturbs it. That larger scheme is of course the psychological world-model of which I spoke earlier. It is being pieced together throughout our childhood (its main framework and structure mostly in our first 7-8 years), concurrently with a host of more or less separate local schemes of information and belief to cover the various distinct aspects of our daily life, or our diverse special interests or concerns. Each of these presupposes, as I have said, the whole implicit framework of our developing overall world-model, and thus, in so far as it operates successfully, helps to confirm and consolidate the latter. Normally, in fact, we do not worry about it, and hardly know how much it embraces, how it has taken shape and what it rests on. (It is this indeed that makes us so vulnerable both to philosophic assaults on our basic beliefs and to any irruptions of apparently odd, uncanny or superstition-arousing experiences.) The psychology of cognition, however, must clearly, as a basic part of its task, make that implicit, functional, overall world-model explicit. And that is something it can only hope to do properly, since most of the model is *normally implicit,* by following right through the immensely complex, many-sided, long drawn-out process, beginning from birth, by which the

model actually gets built up. (In some measure, of course, Professor Piaget has now done this.)

(3) All our study and attempted explanation of human behaviour must start from the fact that it is always *dually* controlled. It is not enough to look for the affective or conative motive-springs behind our actions; they are always only one part of the causal complex that determines us. The other, equally important, is the scheme of beliefs and assumptions, partly explicit but mostly implicit right down to its "world" background, which co-directs the entire course of our action. Most of our psychological "world" framework and foundations we can no doubt safely take for granted as we generally do; but the psychologist at least must have its basic directive operation in mind. And, above all, he must take into account that the psychic world-model of each of us, however firm at the core, is usually very vague and wavering about its boundaries, and that this *may* become relevant to the explanation of almost any human action. Psychoanalytic theory, which has so much concentrated on the affective-conative motive-springs of our behaviour, needs nothing more urgently than an equally historical, genetic and dramatic *cognitive* psychology, to correct and complete its general psychological picture; but that is a theme I can only refer to in passing here.

(4) Finally there is the obvious polarity running through all our learning-history which I have not hitherto brought into full relief, and which demands at least some brief comment.

It will be recalled that my formulation of the meaning of "truth" was that it signified the correspondence of a representation in thought with the actual state of affairs *which it purports to represent*. The italicized words were intended to underline the basic double *structure* of virtually all our assumptions and beliefs, a structure that can readily get masked by their usual form, but becomes plain as soon as we try either to apply or to test them. They are beliefs *about* this or that (thing, event, quality, relation, process, etc., whether individual instance or class) and *before* they can be found either true or false, we have to *identify* the case or cases where they are applicable. Throughout the greater part of our world, most of them are just non-applicable.

But in order to identify our cases we must in turn have in our minds a *representation* of them. Thus, strictly speaking, our beliefs or assumptions are not simply "representations in thought" *tout court*, but compound structures of representations *about* something itself represented in thought. In the ordinary course of our active behaviour the primary representation operates indeed quite automatically; particular beliefs get *activated* because something which we meet, or which happens, touches off a recognition, and then through this some particular piece of knowledge or belief linked up with it. That then is the type of process which gives rise to the "projections ahead" already described. These in fact, activated by successive momentary recognitions, generally represent the second part of our belief-structures. And they are the part on which we usually concentrate—as constituting the operative beliefs on which we act. For our psychology of cognition, however, the pervasive *dual* character of these structures is of the utmost importance, precisely because of the different roles of the two parts, one starting up the other and thus controlling where and when it comes into operation. Furthermore, that goes for the *application* of our knowledge or supposed knowledge; but from the angle of its *acquisition* there is another vital point. The first part of the dual structure provides all the *foci* round which we accumulate and organize our knowledge. The second part then makes up the main body of this, that is our scheme of operative beliefs itself.

The pattern is, however, complicated by the fact that we develop considerable constellations of "recognitive" beliefs at the same time as our larger networks of "knowledge" *about* each kind of "object" (or field or subject-matter) recognized. The process starts, as we know, from a mere "click" of familiarity, which at first sets off preparations and expectations without the child even needing to show awareness of what does the setting off. But these clicks develop more and more into structured "recognitive" representations or representation-schemes (however implicitly these may ordinarily function). And the crucial fact is that these schemes must operate separately from and always prior to our body of knowledge or beliefs *about* what the recognition-representation represents, if that larger body is to grow and prosper.

What in effect brings out most clearly both the separate status of these two kinds of knowledge, and the relation between them, is the way in which we learn to distinguish between two sharply contrasted types of error, with the most different consequences. If in applying any of our beliefs something goes wrong, the first question must usually be which kind of mistake we have fallen into. For we may have made a mere error of recognition rather than being wrong in our belief about what we thought we had recognized. And here our further course completely diverges according to the kind of our mistake. False recognitions often show up quickly of their own accord, or else can easily be detected; and once this has happened, the matter commonly ends there. We correct ourselves and go on our now different way. But if we confirm that our recognition was just, then it is our rightly activated belief which comes under fire. We must find out how far it is wrong, and whether we can modify or must discard it; we may discover that other beliefs are implicated and might even have to reopen the whole relevant belief-scheme.

I cannot here pursue the complications that arise insofar as the dividing lines between our recognition-knowledge and, let us say, our substantive knowledge tend always to shift. Nor can I work out the important bearings of all this theme on our theory of language and communication (including some of its worst pitfalls). But it is worth noting that, however much those dividing lines may shift—and particularly during the growth of our systematic sciences—it must always be possible to define them sharply and clearly at any one time. Identification must continue to function before any test of relative belief. And above all it is just the growth of our science that depends most on this. We must be in a position to pin down true cases-in-point—and must be quite sure that we have done so—*before* we can subject any of our scientific theories or hypotheses to decisive experimental test. So that for the very theory of science the dual psychological structure of our beliefs is worth all the attention we can give to it.

THE RELEVANCE OF PROFESSOR PIAGET'S WORK

The foregoing is as far as I can carry the present thumbnail sketch of a very large theme. I have had to limit myself to the barest outline and to rely on this at least to suggest a possible state of affairs that might merit consideration. Let me only add here a further final note regarding the detailed work of Professor Piaget and his collaborators and pupils, to which I have repeatedly referred. This work seems to me of outstanding importance, not merely for child psychology, but for our general psychology of cognition, and so for our psychology as a whole. For by a vast volume of ingenious experiment over a very wide field, Piaget's work has in my view demonstrated the true character of human learning; that is, the single cumulative process which it is, building up level by level a highly structured cognitive organization which operates unawarely in us but can alone explain the ordinary adaptive level of our everyday human behaviour. All this is genuine objective psychology, not philosophy. Yet Piaget has in fact taken some of the main themes which psychologists regard as the typical preserve of the philosophic theory of knowledge and shown first how much there was to be found out about them *psychologically,* and secondly how illuminating this new knowledge is for the understanding not only of "how our minds work", but how they shape our conduct. These themes have chiefly been those of the nature of our so-called "concepts" of space, of objects and the objective world, of causality, time, motion, measure, number and logical relations. Starting from the infant's simplest forms of *action* and remaining all the time within the field of behavioural responses to experimental situations Piaget has exhibited how each of these so-called concepts is in truth a complex psychic structure built up by children over the years by slow stages. And in field after field he demonstrates how, as these structures reach mature foim, they increasingly integrate into a single mobile operational organization which basically controls all the pattern and scope of our active purposive life.

The work of Piaget and his pupils has often been criticized, not without reason, for its insufficient observance of the accepted canons and procedures of scientific research. But that is perhaps a not unnatural fault in a fundamentally new pioneering enterprise. And the consistency and mutual support of his immense body of results, gathered in so many fields over so many years, leaves little room for doubt about their broad general validity; whilst during the last 2 or 3 years his findings have stimulated an increasing number of independent researches by stricter methods, most of which have brought substantial confirmation of his work. Recognition of the full significance of his results has, however, been slow among psychologists at large, just because his whole approach is so contrary to the current set and practice of their science and so easily lends itself to almost automatic discarding as "philosophy".

All this, I suggest, bears a close relation to the "gap" with which I am here concerned. In effect, Piaget's work seems to me to go a long way towards filling it—and thus incidentally indicates how large it has been. Yet, if I am right, it does not go the whole way; there is still a central hiatus, the filling in of which can, I believe, make a quite essential further difference. It is that remaining hiatus which this article has tried to bring into focus.

SUMMARY

Psychologists habitually by-pass the supposed philosphic mysteries of truth and falsity; but they thus also miss out a basic behavioural factor which (a) is open to strictly psychological study; (b) cumulatively determines our whole development and history. By its alternating successes and failures it governs what we do, suffer, learn and achieve from earliest childhood, and is the main key to the far-flung cognitive structure implicit in the growth of all our adaptive conduct, on which Piaget's work has thrown such striking light. The present paper sketches our working truth-falsity distinction in its mostly self-testing operation and chief consequences.

BIBLIOGRAPHY

Isaacs, N. (1949) *The Foundations of Common Sense—A Psychological Preface to the Problems of Knowledge.* *

Piaget, Jean
    (1936—translation 1953) *The Origin of Intelligence in the Child.* *
    (1937—translation 1955) *The Child's Construction of Reality.* *
    (1941—translation 1952) *The Child's Conception of Number* * (with A. Szeminska).
    (1946—untranslated) *Le Développement de la Notion de Temps chez l'Enfant.* Presses Universitaires de France, Paris.
    (1948—translation 1956) *The Child's Conception of Space* * (with B. Inhelder).

*Routledge and Kegan Paul, Ltd., London.

The Case for Bringing Science into the Primary School*

The following essay was originally presented as a lecture in 1961 at a conference sponsored by the British Association for the Advancement of Science and the Association of Teachers in Colleges and Departments of Education. The theme of the conference was "The Place of Science in Primary Education."

Isaacs states his opposition to teaching the general "subject" of science to young children; but if we have an understanding of children's natural cognitive abilities, much can be done to strengthen those that are required by the scientific method. He presents and questions certain aspects of Piaget's developmental findings.

I

The purpose of this introductory talk is to state a broad general case; but it is one which must first of all be guarded against misunderstanding. It is *not* an argument for the introduction of yet another 'subject' into the primary school curiculum, to be duly 'taught' like arithmetic or geography or history, by planned progressive lessons covering a certain syllabus. On the contrary, quite apart from any wider questions of primary school methods, I should hold that even if some subjects called for such teaching, or lent themselves to it, 'science' could not be one of them. For it is not in fact a single subject at all. There are various quite different sciences, and the point about them is that each represents the *intensive, specialised* study of some one particular aspect or section of our world. The outcomes of these specialised studies may be as diverse and disparate in their scope as physics and economics, or botany and anthropology. None of these, in its real *scientific* sense, could have any

*First published in *The Place of Science in Primary Education,* edited by W. H. Perkins (London: British Association for the Advancement of Science, 1962). Reprinted with the permission of W. H. Perkins and the Association.

meaning for children at the primary school stage; and if we try to combine several into a loose whole and then proceed to teach this under some broad title such as 'General Science', we run a double risk. First, if we want to range widely enough to justify the title, we are obliged to spread and dilute our subject-matter till it keeps very little of the character of science. Secondly, even so, we should probably still be implanting in children's minds a far too narrow and restrictive notion of the meaning of science. They would most commonly be led to think of it as essentially rudimentary physics, or at the most this plus nature study. That, in fact, happens too often already, and needs to be counteracted and not reinforced. It is indeed carried to such lengths that I have known teachers themselves classify even 'nature study' as something separate and different from 'science'. Of course, as sometimes interpreted or practised, it bears little relation to what we should normally call science. But the teachers in question had in mind natural history inquiries at least as scientific as the elementary physical ones to which they automatically limited the term. Anything that thus causes us to identify science as such with physics and its near kin, or even with this plus biology, to the exclusion of the whole range of the vital human sciences, is obviously gravely misleading and unsatisfactory.

What I am advocating then is not by any means that primary schools should introduce the regular teaching either of the general subject (or supposed subject) of 'science', or of any specific genuine science. Yet if we are to have neither of these, what is there left to advocate? And why indeed, if the introduction of this kind of knowledge into the primary school is something so difficult and problematic, should we bother with so dubious a task at all?

It is clear, of course, how the issue arises, but we might be urged to keep two very distinct matters apart. In this scientific age of ours there is a strong case for bringing science, at least in some measure, into the education of all of us. And if we start developing that notion, there is much to suggest that since time is short whilst the way to science is long, we ought to begin as early as possible. But how early is really *possible*? This, even if we accept the general case, is a quite separate question. Does it make sense to try to start as early as the primary school? If by that we mean anything that can be formally called teaching 'science', I have already agreed with the doubters. The great majority of children in the primary school age-range are obviously quite unready for either the specialisation or the sustained logical discipline of any genuine specific science. A good many secondary school science teachers feel in fact that the best service which the primary schools can render to the cause of science-education is to leave it alone. They hold that the way in which it has to be 'taught' in order to gain or retain young children's interest too often merely spoils them for later proper learning; it would be much better to start with a clean slate.

II

So much then for the case *against* bringing science into the primary school. I have expressly begun with this because it must, I think, be fully seen and, as far as it goes, accepted. But that I hope now clears the air. The reference so far is to *taught* science, that is, to science as a subject, or supposed subject, for deliberate teaching. The case I wish to put forward concerns something very, very different. I believe that if we are to think usefully about 'science' in the primary school, we must first of all sort out with care the different things we currently mean by this term. When we ordinarily use it in the round, we are too apt to fuse its meanings together into a single vaguely grandiose whole. In fact, of course, *'a'* science always signifies a specific one, but when we talk of 'science' at large, we *ought* to mean one of two quite distinct though connected things. First, we may be referring to the unified sum of our separate sciences; that is, to all of them joined together as continuous parts of a single great structure: the present sum-total, in fact, of all our organised knowledge, understanding and vision of our natural world (including ourselves as members of it). In this sense of science it is self-evidently *not* something that we can dream of 'bringing' either into our primary schools, or our secondary ones, or anywhere else; no one can either 'learn' or be 'taught' more than some minute selective fraction of it.

Secondly, however, we also often want to refer to what *makes* science science; not now the product (so far), but the distinctive set of *processes*, the basic ways and means, which have brought it into being and are still developing it. Science here is the type of knowledge which in fact we achieve by adopting a certain kind of approach; by pursuing certain methods; by accepting certain criteria; and by steadily continuing to focus all these on some particular set of features or subdivision of our world. The different specific sciences are thus the result of the successive application of this same procedure to one sector after another of our world.

Now what I wish to suggest is that here is a sense in which we *can* bring 'science' into the primary school, or rather help it to burgeon and develop there, and with genuinely valuable results. And not only so, but that sense underlies the whole case for incorporating it in *all* our education. When it comes to actual scientific knowledge, even professional scientists must usually be content, as I have said, with some fractional specilised area. Most of the rest of us can hardly hope for more than bare outlines, with perhaps just a section or two partly and sketchily filled in. What, however, we all need—and, as I shall try to show, *can* attain—is some grasp of the common root and core of the sciences, the overall key to what they are, aim at and achieve. This becomes apparent if we glance even in the briefest way at the main reasons why so many of us feel that 'science' has today become a basic form of literacy; why 'scientific illiteracy' is turning into a notorious reproach; why science in some sense now has claims to form part of the very A.B.C. of education.

Thus:

(1) We are all aware of the extent to which the various sciences, through their omnipresent technological creations, now shape and dominate our lives, and our whole human future. At the lowest level, therefore, we all have a strong vested interest in getting some idea of what is hitting us; that is, of securing at least some gleams of understanding of the new force which in these past few centuries has come both to transform and to overshadow human history. But the actual source of that new force lies in the power and fertility of the methods we call scientific, which indeed continue to originate new modes of control almost every day. This, then, is what we need to penetrate into and to grasp, so that we can at least take an intelligent interest in what is happening to us, and perhaps even some time a hand in directing it.

(2) To the same effect, but on a more positive and rewarding level, science constitutes one of the pre-eminent achievements of the human race, in which we should all be enabled to have some sort of share. It represents in fact a most exciting perennial *frontier* story, a continual thrusting of the boundaries of human knowledge further out into the unknown. There is material here which already captures much general interest, but if it is to become something more, for most people, than a series of nine-days-wonder stories, they must have some equipment for following it. This equipment, again, cannot conceivably be a universal grounding in scientific knowledge; but it could be a well-consolidated sense of what *lies behind* all the build-up of science, behind all the detailed insights and large perspectives already won and behind every new extension of these. And that sense could then be used to give body and background to every fresh chapter of the story, or to every sketch of what has gone before, which scientists can offer us from their individual fields.

(3) Our society constantly needs an ever-growing number of specialised scientists, and this creates two distinct problems for educators. First, how to increase the actual supply; secondly, how to cope with the cultural cleavage, of which we have all become more and more aware, between the rapidly increasing scientific community and the non-scientific rest of us. The best way of dealing with both problems is surely that of giving *all* children the fullest help towards active growth in those basic ways of inquiry which point towards science and which, if far enough pursued, generate it. A good many more might then have the chance of discovering that here is the vocation they want to choose. But between them and all those who make other choices or follow other necessities there would always be the bond of their shared basic growth towards science, so that a solid base for future mutual understanding would persist.

(4) Finally, there is a far-reaching moral in the scientific story for many of our other human problems, a moral we have yet to learn to extract for wide enough use. Science represents the vast *growth* of dependable new knowledge which has resulted from our discovering the right way of securing and multiplying just this. That is, knowledge on which, as a general rule, we can with all confidence *build* and *keep building*. By the same token we can also confidently *act* on it, as is shown by the tremendous and ever-expanding technological structure which our scientific knowledge continually supports. Perhaps we should make better progress with our other human affairs and avoid many avoidable failures if we always made a point of creating first of all a basis of *similarly dependable knowledge* for them—in other words, if we always brought to bear on them, as a plain matter of course, the ways of approach and the criteria of judgment which have given us all our sciences. It might greatly help if we merely adopted the elementary scientific rules of (i) always *finding out* the actual facts and (ii) always applying searching fact-tests to our thoughts (suppositions, assumptions or beliefs) about all our affairs. But this again would demand that these rules should not merely be learnt by a limited few as part of the context of a particular science, but should enter into the main stream of mental growth of all of us. In other words, that they should 'pass into our system'.

III

All this, however, still leaves the question whether these various objects, however desirable, can in fact be promoted in the primary school. Prima facie they might appear to demand something not less but more advanced than ordinary scientific teaching—for which the primary school is admittedly not the place. The study and insightful mastery of *method* usually comes not first but last, as a final distillate from a wide field of known applications. The inwardness of scientific method cannot be learnt in a void; it is through long and varied experience of its workings within a particular scientific domain that we come to understand and appreciate it.

This may seem a reasonable objection, but it disregards the psychological key fact. The basic essentials of the methods that build up science (as distinct from all the auxiliary apparatus which they later gather round themselves) are not a late and sophisticated discovery of the human mind, but a crucial part of its initial equipment. They are put to vital use during the earliest years of every infant. They actually build up in his mind, tier upon tier, a first fundamental scheme of knowledge all new to him but *mainly dependable*, precisely in the sense that it can be safely acted upon and further built upon. Only at a subsequent stage, when the basic scheme is already established and in daily working operation, do these fundamental ways of learning tend to get overlaid and largely choked by other influences.

When our children enter the primary school the basic learning drives are as a rule still vigorously active. In other cultures lack of fresh stimuli is no doubt one main cause that leads to their withering away at a relatively early age. With us, however, new stimuli continually surge up all around the child; but all the conditions of formal schooling combine to act as a damping factor. In most children the basic active learning drives are mainly relegated to their out-of-school life, and very often survive only in a very superficial and limited form. In a minority they are later expressly reactivated in the course of a scientific training, but too frequently only within one segregated field.

It follows that if the foregoing is correct, we do not have to *bring* science, as here understood, into the primary school; our first decision has only to be not to shut it out. After that, however, if it is to make the right progress, we must take positive steps to encourage and help it and to bring it on. But before I come to that, let me give my grounds for my unlikely-sounding account of the facts.

Actually there is no difficulty about doing so; most of the *data I* have in mind are accepted commonplaces of child psychology, whilst the significance I want to assign to them has long been underlined by progressive educators (notably in our time by the late Susan Isaacs). It is the present summing up that most needs justifying; here I can largely draw on the very impressive work reported in recent years by the distinguished Swiss genetic psychologist, Professor Jean Piaget. This has in fact provided a novel and arresting unified picture of the fundamental dynamic of individual intellectual development, supported by a great weight of fresh experimental evidence; and this picture seems to me to carry full conviction.

I can, of course, only bring out here the essential pattern; but it will be evident how much this has in common with the characteristic aims and methods of natural science. From the infant's first few weeks onward he begins on his continually expanding course of watching and following, observing and registering. From certainly 3-4 months onward he explores, manipulates, and experiments and goes on to compare, distinguish and sort out. He combines and connects; he learns increasingly by trial, error and assiduous practice to produce and control particular effects; he generalises, falls into error, and learns from his errors how to correct and improve his generalisations; he looks for causes and gropes for explanations. And along all these ways he carries out week by week, month by month, a single cumulative process of finding out and piecing together, till he has built up for himself a usable rough working scheme, or 'cognitive map', of his surrounding world. All this he does during his first 18-21 months, that is almost without help from language, up to a surprising level of accomplishment. It is of course all part of his continuous striving to establish himself in his world. For this he needs to know how to deal with what he encounters; to foresee and adjust, or respond, appropriately; to be able to use and exploit the diverse opportunities around him; and to secure the power of planning his own course and of choosing and realising his own goals in his world. Growing and connected dependable knowledge is what he requires as the basis for all his action and all his own further growth; and on that is concentrated much of his main energy and resources, with impressive success. To get the measure of this, one has only to note the variety and range of foresights and purposive ways of action of which he disposes by 18-21 months.

As language becomes more and more available to the child, from the latter part of the second year onward, we know that the scope of his mental life is further vastly enriched. Speech opens up to him endless new possibilities; but one of them at least is its use as a powerful new tool in the service of all his finding-out, linking-up and organising activities. Most characteristic perhaps is his rapid discovery of the great open-sesame instrument of *question-asking.* Some of our chief types of *finding-out* questions are picked up as early as the third year; others are mastered in the fourth; and by the fifth most children are freely able to use all our main gamut. They then continually want to know: what things are—what they are made of—where they come from—how they began—what makes them happen—what makes one thing different from another—what are the reasons for apparent exceptions and anomalies, and so on. And we find that even as early as their fourth or fifth year they are so clear about what they want or need that they do not necessarily accept *any* answer. They seek one which they can join up with what they already know and understand, and if what they are offered fails by this test, they will press for further information or help, or will even raise queries or objections of a disconcerting appositeness. (All this will be illustrated presently.)

IV

These then are the facts about our typical five-year-olds, at any rate as regards one of the major aspects of their intellectual life. Of course, there are others that loom even larger, more particularly make-believe play and phantasy; but the various interlinked 'finding-out' activities which I have just described continue their dynamic course. In spite of all the working knowledge the child has already built up, our kaleidoscopic world frequently confronts him with new situations, encounters, facts and happenings which he has no means of understanding, does not know how to deal with, and may find either puzzling or just stimulating or challenging. And therefore, if he is given the chance, he will still want to ask questions and thus to secure further knowledge and understanding; and if the opportunity opens up for him, he will continue to be excited and thrilled if he can find out the answers for himself. He is still ready to enjoy exploring, manipulating, experimenting, comparing, trying to discover causes or to think up the right explanations, discussing and arguing and putting to the test. And these precisely are the interests and activities which it is suggested that the primary school should take up and foster; for these are the living roots from which growth towards developed science can spring.

The important point here is of course that, given the wish and the planning, the primary school can use these activities as one main instrument of education. Instead of actually displacing them by the usual school routine of classroom teaching and formal lessons, it can on the contrary set out to organise a large part of school-life *round them.* Children can then not only go on with the vital 'real' learning work they have been accomplishing all along, but can carry it out far more effectively and fruitfully. In their pre-school environment, the opportunities for active exploration and discovery, after the breathless first few years when everything around was new, tend to get fewer and more restricted. And questions addressed to parents who are often either busy or insufficiently equipped will most commonly receive merely verbal answers, sometimes erroneous, frequently perfunctory, in many cases put in terms which the child only half understands. The school, on the other hand, can continually offer fresh stimuli and openings for exploration, in the most various directions; it can provoke questions or expressly invite them; and it can use any that are suitable in order to launch groups of children on their own co-operative quests for the answers. They can be encouraged to consider and discuss, and to put out ideas or suggestions either by way of actual solutions or at least for next steps. They can be guided and steered, helped over difficulties, and offered hints in the right directions or suggestive leading questions. In all these ways each inquiry that has been set in motion can be carried forward through exciting progress to a successful solution, and become an immensely educative experience for all the children who have shared in it. For not only have they thus built up by their own efforts some fresh scheme of connected knowledge and understanding, but they have also experienced for themselves some of the typical ways and methods by which such building up can be achieved.

A varied series of these co-operative group enquiries carried on week by week, term by term and year by year, on a growing scale, in various main fields which thus become progressively better charted and organised, should take children a long way towards a basic understanding of the meaning of scientific inquiry and of scientific knowledge. What they will achieve will, of course, not yet be fully-fledged 'science', but it will serve as the most authentic and the most valuable approach road towards it. And all this is not mere theory, but has been tried out in practice in a number of quarters and found to work. In a recent volume,[1] bearing the same title as that of the present Conference, various teachers in primary schools describe how they have proceeded on just the lines I have sketched out, with results that speak

[1] [Evelyn Lawrence, Nathan Isaacs, and Wyatt Rawson, *Approaches to Science in the Primary School* (London: Educational Supply Association, 1960).]

for themselves. A great deal more material of the same kind is set out by other contributors to the present volume.[2] But these are all merely experimental beginnings. We have yet to test out what can be done on such lines if over a wide range of schools they are adopted from the outset with the five-year-olds and carried right through to the end of the junior school. We know that a number of infant schools have done very good work on just these lines and produced surprising team results, in the form of 'finding out' activities as well as of sustained construction. If all these children had the opportunity of continuing in the same way, whilst naturally always moving on to larger fields to conquer, we should be gathering an ever greater body of experience for the further improvement of our own planning and methods. And we might then hope to demonstrate irresistibly that we had indeed found the right road for turning science into an integral and invaluable part of all our education.

Of course, what could be done in the primary school would still only be introductory to the more deliberate 'scientific' work of the secondary school, but it would provide the right introduction. Children would be ripe for this work as a *meaningful* next stage. Those who did not feel specially drawn in that direction would at least be well prepared to take in the broad general scope of science as a major human achievement, together perhaps with some closer study of a specific field—physical or biological or human, according to their individual trend of interest. That field would then, in effect, be seen as *representative* of the specialised work of science, with particular stress always on methods and criteria at the same time as on results. On the other hand, those children who were keen to go on with some particular set of inquiries, or to get to know and understand much more about some larger scientific field of their own choice, could be carried fairly quickly into the fully systematic study of all that had already been 'found out' on that theme.

Even here, however, the aim would always be to ensure the utmost continuity with what the children had already done. The first endeavour would be to establish a sense of the *questions and problems* which the chosen special field presented to those who wanted to build up 'science' about it. An effort would be made to project the pupils into the living history of the science. Particular attention would also be paid to the way in which the basic initial 'finding out' approach has everywhere come to be enriched and refined by an ever-growing body of special aids. Thus the vital contributions of all our specific instruments and techniques, of our controlled technical languages, and of that great universal tool of human thought, mathematics, would get their due weight—but would yet be seen as remaining dependent on the fundamental orientation which the pupils had already so long been experiencing for themselves. That is, the attitude of setting out to learn about

---

[2] [W. H. Perkins, ed., *The Place of Science in Primary Education* (London: The British Association for the Advancement of Science, 1962).]

the world from the world itself; a process always of thinking as well as looking, but with the looking in final control, and the thinking ever subject to the test of further looking of the most searching kind. Thus as the pupils took into their minds the full present structure of their chosen science, they would at the same time keep it firmly linked with the processes of sustained factual inquiry, imaginative yet also critical thinking, and rigorous factual testing, of which it represented the outcome *so far.* And the final result should be to give them the sense of themselves joining in something living and growing— the further building up of a great structure of which the end is nowhere in sight and which remains always open to fresh transformations and revaluations in the light of new horizons yet to be reached.

V

Up to a point the case I have now stated might be regarded as complete. It could be briefly summed up as based on these two premises: (1) at this time in our civilised history, we all need some understanding both of what science means and how it comes into being; (2) we all have the roots of this understanding within us, since throughout our first years we are busily building up our own first fabric of mainly dependable knowledge in just the ways by which each individual science has begun. By the age of five we have already advanced a long way, and are still wanting to thrust forward further, if only we are given the facilities and help which we need for going on.

Therefore, it follows that the primary school could provide the great opportunity of taking up these drives, giving them guidance and scope, and carrying them to the very threshold of our developed sciences. However, since for the second of the above premises I have particularly invoked the work of Professor Piaget, I am bound to note that there are parts of his work which seem to suggest somewhat narrow limits to what children can actually accomplish during the primary school period. His investigations of intellectual development during the first two years had brought out all the cumulative active learning and psychic building up which children carry through in that time in terms of *behavioural* achievement. But he also holds that thereafter, when they go on to *verbal thinking,* they are in a sense obliged to start their learning all over again; and that then must come a long period of slow and laborious growth before they can attain any kind of *ordered conceptual and logical thought.* Moreover, this in turn only evolves very gradually from its first beginnings to the level required for even elementary science.

Thus Piaget sets out a wide range of experiments to show how at the age of 4-5 the thought of average children is still in a state of wholesale logical confusion and incapacity; and how it is only towards 7-8 that they attain their first structured and stable concepts in such rudimentary fields as number, or spatial notions like length or distance, or some of the basic logical relations. Even when by 7-8 they do achieve these concepts, their range is found to be very limited, and at around 11 a majority is still not able to handle freely the more abstract logical relations needed for most kinds of sustained reasoning, whether scientific or of any other kind. It is not until some time between 11 and 14 that average children become capable of operating (or understanding) the logical processes needed for solving fairly simple scientific problems. It would therefore seem to follow that no real scientific approach can even begin before about 7-8, and that it must stay very sketchy indeed till some time *after* 11; which would perhaps not fit in too badly with what many teachers of science already believe.

However, there are, I think, good reasons for holding that the foregoing represents only one side of a picture which in fact has two faces. I cannot discuss this in any detail here, but Piaget's own account of the basic forces of intellectual growth as they emerge during the first two years makes clear, in my view, that his later negative findings cannot constitute more than part of the story. Obviously all the cumulative learning, building up and growth which can be noted in the pre-verbal phase goes on in just the same way after the mastery of language, and indeed in increased measure. It is true that language also ushers in a new era of assiduous and absorbed verbal *phantasying,* and at the same time engenders a whole new world of vague and confused verbal ideas which are apt at any moment to pass over into pure phantasy forms. Nevertheless, the child equally continues all the time to expand his experiences and activities, his knowledge and powers, in the real world, and here too he derives immense new help from language—above all through those organised question-forms to which I have already referred.

Thus verbal thinking tends to develop on two largely separate levels: one on which it remains closely linked with children's own active experience and learning processes, is fully controlled by these and advances turn by turn with them; and another level where for lack of experience, knowledge or direct active interest, it lags far behind and long remains unorganised, vague and fluid. Piaget's experiments tend to test children's capacity for ordered concepts and logical thinking in situations in which their own drives and inquiring interests are *not* actively engaged: that is, where they do not start from questions to which their own course has brought them and for which they themselves want to find the answers, but are plunged into alien problems from without. Almost all of these are moreover concerned with the formal world of number, space, time, etc., and their abstract relationships, which are fundamentally *uninteresting* to most young children. Therefore, Piaget's findings generally register a level of performance well below the best which they can achieve, within the living context of their own learning, thinking and growth. And furthermore, those findings refer typically to children in current educational settings and must therefore to some extent reflect any basic limitations inherent in these. Thus they cannot, above all, be used to rebut the possibility of quite other results if we drew the right moral from Piaget's own fundamental work and provided the utmost scope and help for truly constructive learning and thinking—even in those fields where he finds growth *under current conditions* so slow.

For all these reasons I suggest that his more negative conclusions regarding the primary school age-range need only be kept in mind as partial ceilings applying under present circumstances and in certain limited directions—ceilings therefore that have yet to be re-tested after more helpful conditions have been fully tried out. Moreover, even on the most rigid interpretation, they would leave useful scope for *approach*-work of the type here outlined—from 7-8 years onward for the average run of children, and a good deal earlier for the brighter ones. In fact, however, there is little ground for thinking that the ceilings would apply *at all* to children's powers of active constructive learning in the situations here contemplated: namely, those of their own pooled efforts to find their own answers, under skilled guidance, to many of their own questions about the concrete world around them. Here again I can refer to the very successful work already recorded.

By way, moreover, of clinching this thesis let me now give some illustrative examples of the kind of intellectual performance of which even children as young as 3-5 are capable under the right conditions. For the sake of convenience I have taken these partly from Susan Isaac's *Intellectual Growth in Young Children,*[3] and partly from Professor Valentine's *Psychology of Early Childhood,*[4] but I am sure that everyone in touch with children in a reasonably free setting could multiply them many times. I have placed the material under [six] sub-headings which I hope will bring out the continuous momentum towards 'science'—the drive towards trying to find out, to explain and understand—the impetus towards logical thinking and reasoning, which seems to me so real and significant:

Generalising, comparing and contrasting

Age 2 years and 4 months: 'That too big for B, not too big for Daddy.'
    3:7 Hearing someone say 'By the light of the silvery moon' a child remarks: 'All light is silvery, isn't it, mummy?' Asking, in Kew Gardens, what each tree in bloom was 'going to be' and being told about several in succession [being] 'cherry trees', a child says, 'Oh, I see, all white trees are cherry trees'. (The kind of beginning in *explicit* generalisation which leads to the discovery of error, and of the need to generalise more slowly and cautiously.)

[3] [Susan Isaacs, *Intellectual Growth in Young Children with an Appendix on Children's "Why" Questions by Nathan Isaacs* (London: Routledge and Kegan Paul, 1930): *passim.*]

[4] [C. W. Valentine, *Psychology of Early Childhood* (London: Methuen, 1942). pp. 462, 472-481.]

3:8   Another child: 'I'd like to see dogs' teef and cats' teef and cows' teef
      and horses' teef and frogs' teef and camels' teef and mice's teef.'
      Asked why, the child says, 'To see if they're like ours'.

3:10 In a car: 'People like driving downhill and don't like driving uphill. I
      don't like pushing my pram uphill.'

4:2   A child talking about his dog Snowball: 'Has Snowball got a tongue
      right back to his chest like us?'–'*Yes*'–'Have all dogs?'–'*Yes*'–'And
      cats and cows?'–'*Yes*'.

4:2   The same child, in the garden, where he had seen a worm with an
      egg band three days previously: 'Why do worms have eggs?'–'*To
      make new little worms.*'–'Ants have eggs. Do they make little
      ants?'–'*Yes*'–Then similar questions about spiders and flies. Then
      'Do cats have eggs?'–'*Yes, but we don't usually call them eggs. We
      don't see them.*'–A few minutes later: 'All kinds of things have eggs
      then?'

4:9   'Will water go through cloth?'–'Through wood?'–'Through soil?'

Causal inquiries

4:0   'What keeps the moon up?' . . . 'What keeps the stars up?'

4:1   Looking at a clock: 'What makes the wheels go round?'

4:5   'How does the water get up in the sky? How does it get down
      again?'

4:7   'How does the water get up the pipe?'

4:8   'What makes the sky blue?'

4:8   'What makes the colour at sunset?'

4:8   Playing with a toy balloon: 'What keeps it up?'

4:9   Told that the clouds bring rain: 'What makes the rain stop? There
      are still some clouds.'

4:11 In the garden: 'What happens if a wasp stings a wasp?'–'*What do
      you think?*'–'I think it would be all right; he'd just have some more
      sting.'

Demands for explanations

3:0   'Why does the holding end of a spoon get hot?'

4:1   'Why does it get lighter outside when you put the light out?'

4:1   Watching a fountain pen being filled: 'Why doesn't the ink run out
      when you hold up a fountain pen?'

4:1   Told that a building has a corrugated iron roof: 'Why is the
      corrugated iron always crinkly and not flat like the other sorts?'

4:5   In the bath: 'Why does the water spread out flat? Why will it not
      keep up in the middle?'

5:0   'Why does water go out of the way when anything goes in?'

Explanation challenged

3:8 'Why don't we milk pigs?'—'*Because they have little ones of their own to feed.*'—'So do cows have calves.'

4:4 'What are seals killed for?'—'*For the sake of their skins and oil.*'—'Why do they kill the stags? They don't want their skins, do they?'—'*No, they kill them because they like to chase them.*'—'Why don't policemen stop them?'—'*They can't do that because people are allowed to kill them.*'—'People are not allowed to take other people and kill them.'—'*People think there is a difference between killing men and killing animals.*'—And then the exclamation: 'You don't understand me.'

4:6 'Why is the water bottle cold in the morning? Does the heat go into me?'—'*Yes*'—'Then why am I not as hot as the bottle was?'

4:9 A child whose father is a professor at the university asks what he does there, and he tries to give reasons which the child can understand: '*I talk to people who teach children and tell them how to teach children.*'—'How do you know how to teach children?'—'*Some time ago I used to teach children myself.*'—'How do *you* know how to teach children, and not those people who teach children?'

Other challenges of reasons and reasoning

3:3 Being told that he must not lick the butter off the toast: 'Why can't I?'—'*It is bad manners to lick. We don't lick things*'—After a pause, 'But we lick ice cream.'

4:1, 'Why do we have to pick up things that we put on the floor?'—'*If we were running and trod on them, we might break them, mightn't we?*'—'We shouldn't break those big bricks, should we?' [I.e., 'We wouldn't . . . , would we?']

4:2 Told: '*Don't suck your fingers. Only babies do that.*'—'Babies don't. Barbara doesn't.'—'*Oh yes, babies do.*'—'Barbara doesn't. One baby doesn't.'

4:0 A girl called Rose Marsh is told: '*People don't eat red black-berries.*'—'Marsh's do, and I'm a Marsh.'

4:3 Nurse to feverish child: '*If you take this powder it will put you to sleep and that will make you better.*'—'But I went to sleep last night and it did not make me better.'

Other reasoning and theorising

3:7 Talks of 'Fairies going up in the air". Father asks how they are able to fly. 'They had wings, you know. Angels have wings like birds, and fairies are like angels; and so you see fairies are like birds.'

5:5 'If Helen caught my whooping cough, and I caught mine from Billie, how did the first girl in the world to get whooping cough get it?'

5:5 Grown-up: '*You did find your way then?*'—'I shouldn't be here if I hadn't, should I?'

5:1 Child talks about the size of an aeroplane as if he were confusing size with height above the ground. Adult asks: '*Are you referring to the height the aeroplane seems when it is in the air or the size of the aeroplane when it is on the ground?*'—After a pause: 'No, I mean the size it is all the time.'

These examples should leave little doubt about the main point at issue. However, it may be worth while to supplement them by quoting a notable experiment from Piaget's own work. He has carried out an elaborate and very interesting study on the growth of the idea of classification, but in my view his conclusions may again be leaning too heavily on children's mere ability or inability to handle the *formal* logical relationships between sub-classes, classes and higher classes. Young children's minds just balk at this kind of problem as fundamentally non-meaningful for them. Piaget thus gets mainly negative results from 5-6 year olds. He is, however, himself aware how little there is in these formal relations for their minds to grip on, and by way of making things more interesting, he turns one of his questions from being one of pure classification into a problem of *causal explanation.* As soon as he does so, he gets notably improved results: as many as 18 out of 31 of his 5-6 year olds now produce the right answer.

The experiment consists in presenting to the children a scale which has attached to it a ball inside a case with a slot, so that when a certain weight is placed on the scale, the ball comes out of the slot. The children are then offered a number of boxes, varying in weight, colour and size. They are asked to say which box they think will make the ball come out and why, and then to see whether they are right. After that, they are allowed to experiment until they arrive at a settled conclusion. The 18 children who reach the right answer reason correctly that it cannot be the colour that counts because some boxes of the same colour do not bring out the ball; and it cannot be the size, on the same kind of ground. It must be the weight, because the heavy boxes, whatever their size and colour, do bring out the ball.

This is an admirable example of quite young children having a scientific causal question put to them, and showing how they can rise to it. For they have a constant natural interest in finding out the controlling causes of things (they have been trying hard to learn about them almost from birth). They are therefore very easily aroused into actively thinking about them, looking for the answers, and trying to cut out wrong ones. In these circumstances we readily get a type of performance which is quite unhampered by the logical incapacity found by Piaget in so many of his more formal situations. There it is undoubtedly present, and we must both allow for it and see if we can find the right ways of overcoming it; but children can far better learn to cope with the logic of real concrete problem situations arising directly out of their own experiences and activities, and this indeed is our right cue for helping them even in the more formal domains. Causal explanations, in particular, are for them, as for scientists, close to the very centre of all their finding-out interests. They are our main high road to foresight, the sense of understanding, and the kind of knowledge which is power. But of course they must be the *right* causal explanations; else they become traps into failure and danger. All children have had ample experience of this; and they have therefore a strong vested interest in avoiding it, if they can. Their eagerness to learn causes, and to learn the right or true causes, is thus among the most powerful of their natural learning drives, and one which is constantly and freely available for our educational use, if only we would make up our minds to use it.

VI

In conclusion, then, I have been arguing essentially that we should use the primary school years for the deliberate and sustained fostering of those 'finding-out' activities (and everything that goes with them) which are the common core and first root of all our sciences. My thesis has been that we can turn them into progressive approaches *towards* science, which will greatly help both the majority of eventual non-scientists and the minority of future scientists. The first will gain some real power of appreciation and understanding of the work of science as a whole. The second will have the right foundation for the most fruitful study of any one specialised science: a sense of the distinctive methods and criteria which achieve science as such.

Moreover, as already brought out, we should thus eliminate what may well be the main cause of the present marked division between science and the rest of our current world. I have suggested that we ourselves largely create this by the normal working of our educational scheme. The latter, in the first place, switches children right away from their natural, spontaneous, active, inquiring and finding-out processes (which might carry them closer and closer to science) and replaces all these by something altogether different—different in setting, in subject-matter, and, above all in the way of learning now called for; that is, learning by being taught. Then, a number of years later, we start teaching to a relatively small body of pupils one or two selected sciences (most often physics and chemistry) as separate and self-contained intellectual systems or worlds. For everybody else these sciences, or the few others that might be similarly picked upon, remain closed books. And there develops the general tendency already described, for physics and chemistry to become the main normal image of 'science', and for physicists and chemists themselves to share this view, with the most closely analogous other sciences as an outer fringe, and everything else relegated to the non-scientific world. This, then, leads to a far too narrow and far too static notion of science as such, which helps in turn to regenerate the same educational circle.

In fact, of course, physics and its kin simply happen to represent our most advanced and developed sciences, now segregated in a very elaborate world of their own, a world of laboratories, physical instruments, technical language and mathematical tools. But though we do have here the present highest level of scientific achievement, it simply constitutes the current summit of a slope on which a number of other sciences are struggling at various points, each as truly a science in virtue of its aims, methods and criteria as physics itself. It is these that have launched physics and its kin on their course; and they equally constitute the motive force of such human sciences as psychology, anthropology or economics, even if for various reasons of later start and more complex and fluid subject-matter, these sciences are still in a less developed phase as regards their results.

Once this much more comprehensive and dynamic view of science is adopted, we can easily see how it joins up with the educational approach here put forward, and how our existing division into two cultures, scientific and lay, disappears. Whether children eventually grow into physics or chemistry, or into biology or geology, or into psychology or archaeology, or into the law or letters, or into some art or craft or technical skill, or into any other of our thousand and one human occupations, they will have in common a vital, unifying groundwork of experience and constructive learning. They will share the same developed sense of how we have come by all our most dependable organised knowledge of our world, and the same ensuing power of entering in at least some degree into the visions and perspectives which that knowledge has to offer. Here surely lies the most valuable contribution of science to the education of all of us. But that contribution depends first of all on our making the right use of the interests, drives and capacity for personal active 'finding out' with which most children enter our primary schools.

Piaget: Some Answers to Teachers' Questions*

Isaacs had been concerned with the psychology and education of young children for approximately forty years when he was asked by the editor of *Teaching Arithmetic* to respond to a series of questions exploring the meaning of Piaget's discoveries for teachers. By this time Isaacs had become well known in England for his interpretations of Piaget's findings and their implications for educational practice. His responses to the questions became the occasion for a summary of Piaget's work and for a more complete critical analysis of that work, together with its implications for teachers.

AUTHOR'S FOREWORD

This pamphlet owes its existence to the initiative of the Editor of *Teaching Arithmetic,* Mr. G. Price of Chorley Day College. He sent me some time ago the set of questions which appears [below] and suggested that if I cared to answer them, he would publish the questions-and-answers in his journal as a kind of "interview". That seemed very simple and easy: most of the issues he was raising were always cropping up, particularly in lectures or talks to teachers, and some I had already dealt with, up to a point, in various of my own publications.

However, when I got down to trying to cope with the questions, in the order in which they were set out, and in their proper relation to one another, I found myself led a good deal further afield than I had foreseen. The "interview" in fact built up into something like a brief overall presentation of Piaget's work as a whole, together with its significance for education—but also with a critical side to my survey which I had not developed so fully before.

*First published in three parts under the title "Psychology, Piaget and Practice" in *Teaching Arithmetic,* 2 (Summer, 1964): 3-10: 2 (Autumn, 1964): 2-9; 3 (Spring, 1965): 11-16. Reproduced by the National Froebel Foundation, 1965. Reprinted with permission of Mrs. Evelyn Isaacs; National Froebel Foundation; G. Price, former editor of *Teaching Arithmetic;* and Wynn Williams, Ltd., publisher of *Primary Mathematics* (formerly *Teaching Arithmetic*).

My study has duly been published, by instalments, in *Teaching Arithmetic*. But as it went far beyond the arithmetical field, and Mr. Price's searching questions are so very much of the kind which working teachers continually ask, it seemed that it might prove of interest and help to a broader teacher audience. Both Mr. Price and the publishers of his Journal, the Pergamon Press, Ltd., have kindly given permission for the study to be reproduced as a National Froebel Foundation pamphlet, and we are glad to acknowledge this with our best thanks. But particular gratitude is due from me to Mr. Price, if the task which he set me should have led to a widely useful result.

The text is substantially as published in *Teaching Arithmetic,* apart from a few slight verbal changes and the addition of a short bibliography.

THE QUESTIONS

I. Why has Piaget become so well known only in recent years, throughout education?

II. What are the most important implications of his work for the practice of teachers at Primary level?

III. Can it be said that Piaget's work gives theoretical support to the kind of practices in education coming under the heading of "activity methods"?

IV. Are there real dangers that his ideas will be misinterpreted by teachers, and in which way?

V. How would you recommend that we avoid such dangers?

VI. Turning to Piaget's work in number: what are the specific implications of his discoveries for the approach to mathematics at Primary level?

VII. Do you see any contradiction between the use of structural apparatus in mathematics and Piaget's principles?

VIII. Our system of decimal numeration, place-value, etc., which forms the structure of arithmetic is obviously man-made. How could the child at any given age-level gain the concepts of this artificial structure without the use of special apparatus?

IX. Finally, in the light of Piaget's work, at what age level would you expect a pupil to benefit from the kind of teaching—or instruction, if you prefer—in which the conventional "chalk and talk" method is used rather than the discovery of knowledge by the pupil?

THE SUGGESTED ANSWERS

SECTION 1 [BACKGROUND AND BASIC ISSUES]

I: Why has Piaget become so well known only in recent years, throughout education?

His early books, translated between 1926 and 1930, created a considerable stir, but met with a good deal of criticism. After that, there was a pause in his writing, but a much longer gap in the flow of translations, due largely to the intervening war period, and it was not until 1950 that the flow recommenced.

Moreover the new translations, based on Piaget's publications from 1936 onward, broke quite fresh ground, and it took some time before people began to see their significance. This was almost inevitable since (i) many psychologists still had question-marks in their minds about the earlier books; (ii) the most striking of the new translations—in 1952—was "The Child's Conception of Number" which proved very difficult in its theory and far too surprising in its results to find ready acceptance; whilst finally (iii) the new translations came out in quite haphazard sequence, without regard to either their logical connections or the order in which the original books were written—and, one after another, again proved a great labour to read.[1]

Thus before the full portents of Piaget's later work could be taken in, two things had to happen. (1) The random flow of translations had gradually to get joined up into something like a single coherent picture. (2) A sufficient number of his astonishing findings had to be verified by independent experimenters in this country, under conditions that carried firm conviction. Both these processes needed quite a lot of time, and it is only during the last few years that everything has begun to converge. On the one hand various workers who repeated many of Piaget's experiments have substantially confirmed his results, not only about number, but also about space, time, measurement, volume, etc.,[2] and this has become more and more widely known. On the other hand the psychological "grand design" which runs through all the later work has come to be seen and discussed as a connected whole. And the great potential significance of this work for education has been recognised in principle, though the concrete implications still largely remain to be worked out.

Perhaps in all the circumstances a total of some 10-12 years since the Number volume first presented its challenge is not so very long for the above position to have been reached.

II: What are the most important implications of Piaget's work for the practice of teachers at primary level?

---

[1] See Bibliography [end of chapter (pp. 157-158)].

[2] See in particular ([chapter] Bibliography) K. Lovell 1962.

III: Can it be said that this work gives theoretical support to the kind of
*   practices in education coming under the heading of "activity methods"?*

(II) (i) As might be expected from the above course of events, the first large
issue to arise in practice was that of the implications of Piaget's work in the
"number" field. But that issue cannot be dealt with in isolation, for a double
reason. First, the "number" inquiry forms only one section of a greater
whole; and, secondly, this is itself part of a still larger one. Therefore if we
want to get the educational implications right, we must really *start* from the
basic overall canvas—then go on to the more limited scheme within which the
"number" study falls—and only thereafter turn to "number" itself, in due
relation with the various other themes with which Piaget links it up.

(ii) Perhaps, however, the best way of making all this clear is to proceed
first of all in the reverse order. The "number" research forms one part of a
whole that also covers the growth of (a) children's spatial and geometrical
concepts; (b) their ideas of motion, speed and time; (c) those of mass, weight
and volume; (d) those concerned with the most basic logical relations, such as
whole and part, classification and serial order; and finally (e) the most
advanced types of logical concepts and operations, usually only reached at
adolescence and needed, for example, for the solution of complex scientific
problems. In fact what Piaget really aims at is to trace through the successive
stages of development children's *powers of logical thought* as such. These
stages should, in his view, show up most clearly in the progress of the above
notions, since all of them (including that of number) are either of a directly
logical nature, or else particularly dependent on our logical powers.

(iii) He duly brings out the various cross-connections of these concepts,
and shows how important it is to see them all as elements of one organic
whole. But that is a large theme on which I can barely touch now—though it
will briefly recur later on. The point to be noted here is that all this set of
investigations only begins from an average age of 4-5.

That serves as Piaget's zero-point, at which in most children the
growth-process concerned has not started yet. (This defines his "stage 1",
where the above ideas are still wholly lacking, whilst his "stage 2", really
showing the *first* gropings forward, does not usually come till 5½-6½). thus
we have here an evolution which only sets in relatively late, when a long and
complex *prior* history of intellectual development has already taken place.
Yet this latter must clearly furnish the basic framework into which the whole
later evolution has somehow to be fitted. The first question to be asked is
therefore how Piaget conceives that basic framework. And his answer to this
constitutes, I suggest, the real foundation from which our study of Piaget
must begin.

(iv) The book on Number and all the others which only start after five
should accordingly be left till later. We must turn first of all to quite another
part of his work, where he is concerned with the prime motors of mental

growth as such. He has carried through a minutely detailed study (supported by a host of revealing experiments) of the learning progress of his own three children, from birth till around 18-21 months. From this he builds up a most illuminating new picture of the underlying dynamics of intellectual growth. He shows in effect how during the above fateful period the whole ground plan is laid for everything that follows. This work is fully set out in two complementary volumes: "The Origin of Intelligence in the Child" (French original 1936; translation 1953) and "The Child's Construction of Reality" (1937 & 1954).

The basic principles involved are further discussed in a third volume, first planned at about the same time, but only completed much later: "Play, Dreams and Imitation in Childhood" (literal translation of French title: "Symbol Formation in the Child. Imitation, play and dream. Image and representation" 1945; translation 1951). This also is of very great interest and value, though in some parts more open to debate. It carries the early psychological story a good deal further, but mainly from the special angle made clear by the French title; so that it is *not* a full continuation of the earlier two books. It is these that should in my view be regarded as the fundamental starting-points for all Piagetian studies, whilst the third volume should then follow as an important but only partial complement. And it is the first two books that point most plainly to the crucial educational implications of Piaget, as I shall try to show.

The position then, as I see it, is this: The process of *logical* growth which he studies only begins after five; he deals searchingly with overall intellectual growth during the first 18-21 months; but he does not follow through the *full* growth process during the vital intervening years. Here there remains a very material gap. And that is not all. We must, I think, note most carefully that in taking up the study of how a child's powers of logical manipulation develop, Piaget has *switched over* to a much narrower theme than that of his first basic work. He is now solely dealing with a single aspect of intellectual growth, viz. the growth of the child's formal logical equipment. Even this, in my opinion, is viewed from a somewhat limiting angle; but that is a point to which I shall return later.

(III) Meanwhile let me sum up the educational implications which I regard as most crucial. These bring us to the question of "activity" methods. It can, I think, be fairly said that Piaget's fundamental psychology of mental growth not merely supports such methods, but decisively demands them. A radical "activity" approach over virtually the whole front of education is in fact now shown to be the only one that *makes psychological sense*–at least for all the primary period, and even well into the secondary.

The section that follows will briefly set out the argument, which goes down to the very roots of the theory of intellectual education.

SECTION 2 [PSYCHOLOGY AND PRACTICE]

[Theoretical Foundations]

A: [*Living Learning*]: The psychological basis of the above implications is
that Piaget's work leads to a concept of *living* learning such that traditional
school "learning" appears almost as its negation.

Thus:

(a) True or living learning originates from the child, and indeed directly
from some of his strongest interests and drives.

(b) It is pivoted on his own active relations to the world around him: what
he *does* and what experiences, and learning, this brings to him. It starts soon
after birth and operates mainly through his power of applying to his world an
ever-growing range of activities—above all exploratory, experimental and
effect-achieving.

(c) Most of the latter, but especially the exploratory ones, have a built-in
self-extending character, since they frequently lead to results which (i)
re-stimulate them, and (ii) enlarge their field. At the same time they also
develop further from within, and increasingly combine with one another to
form larger and larger wholes. By all these processes the child's learning
powers are continually expanded. Thus he watches and finds more to watch;
follows and finds more to follow; turns towards sounds and sees as well as
hears; comes to look at what he grasps and to guide grasping through looking;
manipulates and produces effects which then prompt him to repeat his action
till he can produce them at will. And as fast as he learns to walk, he is able to
extend and multiply these situations almost indefinitely.

(d) There are thus set in motion great numbers of *spiral* progressions by
which the child's actions generate fresh experience and knowledge—which
then enlarge his range of action—which then generates yet more experience
and knowledge and further enlarge his range—and so right on. Living learning
is in effect a cumulative process that goes on throughout earlier childhood,
continues (though chiefly outside our schools and formal education) during
later childhood and youth, and usually operates in some degree over all the
rest of our lives. This cumulative learning has from the outset behind it (i) an
intrinsic interest and pleasure in the self-extending activities of exploring,
experimenting and discovering, producing effects, using familiar means for
fresh ends and finding fresh means for familiar ends, etc.; (ii) the constant
need for the *felt* security that comes from *knowing what to expect* and *being
prepared for it;* and (iii) all our drives for increased grasp and practical
powers, as the keys to every success, advance and achievement in our world.

B: [*Before Language*]: Piaget's study of the first 18-21 months demonstrates,
step by step, all that children accomplish by the above cumulative learning
processes during that time. That is, before the child's own use of language

plays an important part, and above all, before word-borne thinking comes at all into the story. Over that relatively brief period Piaget shows the infant building up, stage by stage, a working psychic schema of (i) a host of different *objects,* persisting and moving independently of him, in a rudimentary spatial order; (ii) sets of actions and happenings pivoted on those objects, in a rudimentary time order; and (iii) particular kinds of actions bringing on particular happenings, in a rudimentary causal order. This of course is all evidenced by the infant's actual behaviour, in the shape of appropriate changes and developments as more and more elements of the schema come to be at his disposal. By the time he reaches about 18-21 months, we have only to work out what is implied by the wide variety of action-sequences he can successfully carry through to *verify* his command of the foregoing full pattern.

In effect, by that age he has already achieved the most fundamental learning of his life. For the above schema reflects so faithfully the actual main structure of the world around us that he will not need to alter it, but only to keep on developing it, for the rest of his days. The main burden of his later learning can in fact be summed up as: (a) steadily extending the schema's range; (b) going on with every sort of filling-in activity; (c) more and more fully organising it, to correspond with the relations and connections which he finds in his world. The basic psychic structure, once it has been built up, is just taken for granted, whilst the same processes of living learning that first pieced it together continue to build it up ever further.

C: The Part Played by Language: The above facts and their implications need to be underlined because so much happens later to obscure the true picture. What the infant can pick up in his first 18-21 months is usually held just to prepare the ground for the true mental progress that only language and language-borne thought can bring. These we regard as the real keys to human intellectual development. And such they unquestionably are; without them all the child's exploratory and other schema-forming activities would not get him beyond coping with the order of things immediately around him. But the point here is that whatever more these keys can do for the child, they can do only on certain definite conditions. They are not independent of his living learning activities or able to advance him in separation from these. On the contrary, both are instruments that can only operate with success *if* (a) they habitually start from these activities; (b) they are continually kept linked with them; and (c) they remain in fact, up to a very advanced point, under their firm control. Where these conditions are fulfilled, language and thought do vastly enrich and multiply the child's living learning itself. Where they are disregarded, both are apt to trail off rapidly into mere verbalism and vacuity.

This controlling relation of our active learning processes to both language and thought is, I believe, one of the most vital implications to be drawn from

Piaget's basic work. But it differs so radically from the assumptions on which our educational practice commonly proceeds that it needs rather closer discussion.

1. [Language as Sound-Patterns].—In the case of language viewed as the vehicle through which we constantly try to bring new information or "knowledge" to children, the facts are plain enough. What actually comes to them is just a series of sound patterns; it is *they* who have to understand or interpret these, that is, to provide them with *meanings* out of their own built-up store. And these can no more have been generated earlier by mere sound-sequences than they can be now. The normal first sources for most of them are each child's own experiences. Grownups, when first supplying any particular sound-label, try of course to identify the right experience for the child; e.g. they point to particular objects, repeat the sounds in conjunction with given actions or happenings, and so on. But it is what these signify to *him* that provides him with a meaning for the sound-label; and the substance of this is naturally built up from all his encounters and interactions with the objects, happenings, etc. themselves.

Subsequently, as sequences of familiar words reach him, he is able to link up their meanings as he goes along and thus to combine these into some freshly imagined or conceived whole. Even so, however, if we specially want to introduce him to anything very different from his past experience, we shall usually know better than to trust to language alone. Really new meanings can only be generated through new actual experiences, or at least fair likenesses to these. But in the latter case the communication is liable to remain very imperfect, unless we can also closely relate it to something actively worked over and forming part of what the child has already made his own.

Communication that takes all this into account is, however, for most small children the exception rather than the rule. Normally there impinge on them day by day a host of statements, information, etc. which they cannot possibly translate fully into their own experience. In the case of many words they are just left to pick up the meanings for themselves, as best they can, from either the real context or the verbal one. If they ask express questions, they are given "explanations", but often very perfunctorily and only in the form of other words. In many fairly clear instances the picking-up process works well enough for ordinary practical purposes; a good deal of most children's vocabulary has been arrived at in this way and certainly enables them to get by. On the other hand, however, the great spate of purely verbal impacts does mean that round their limited core of actively-worked-over experience and real living learning there gathers a large world of vague and shifting verbal "ideas". That is, words of all kinds with only the most shadowy quasi-meanings or half-meanings attached to them.

Our schools try hard, of course, to remedy this state of affairs, at least in relation to what they expressly set out to teach. But the remedies are rarely adequate, partly for reasons to be further discussed later on, partly because so much of the vocabulary apparently understood by children belongs in fact to the verbal twilight world described above. Teachers cannot usually avoid largely drawing on that world. They can only provide "specimens", pictures, etc. in relation to some *few* selected key-words that happen to lend themselves to this.

In effect, the assumption that language can of itself communicate knowledge—provided only that most of the words used are "known" and some few are illustrated or "explained"—can constantly be seen to break down. The crude and often total misconceptions so often formed by young children are familiar ground; but they can frequently be paralleled right through the school years. And if crude error is avoided, this is apt to be only through sheer vagueness or fuzziness. The only real remedy is to grasp very clearly how little words by themselves can communicate during the earlier years; and to combine them wherever possible with a maximum of the activities and experiences that can generate living learning. We do in fact find—as early even as the four year age-level—that where children ask questions springing directly from their own experiences and have the chance of freely discussing the answers offered and actively trying them out, language will not fail either them or us. It will not only do its vital work of quickening living learning, but will itself become charged with meanings on which it is possible thereafter to build.

On the other hand, where verbal "telling" or "explanation" is chiefly relied upon, we need not do much testing to establish how little young children have usually taken in.

Verbal communication can only become a source of real knowledge and understanding where children have already done so much living learning that they can meet verbal explanations three-quarters of the way. This is a condition which is not at present often fulfilled.

2. Thought as Internalised Action.—Our second great key to intellectual advance is of course the directed, purposive thinking which only becomes possible through language. But, once more, it only becomes possible on the right terms. If these are met, thought can become the instrument by which we turn our experience into knowledge, use this to solve problems, start from it as a springboard for gaining further knowledge, learn the lessons of errors and failures, etc. etc. It is, however, obvious that what we depend on here is the support, at every step, not just of word-counters as such, but of their right meaningfulness. That is, of authentic, clear and stable ideas linked with these counters. The jumbles or half-meanings of vague and shifting meaning-phantoms referred to earlier, which make up so much of children's verbal world, are no use for any of the real work of thought. Effective thinking (and growing progress in this) needs the kinds of full-bodied meanings and ideas which can only emerge from the activities of living learning, worked over themselves with the help of language.

That, however, is not the whole story. There is more involved than merely this relation of dependence. On Piaget's view, which all the data strongly support, the activity of thinking is itself derived from the child's outward action. Indeed, it *is* such action, continued in another form: carried on internally and then gradually refined and developed up to the final level which Piaget calls operational. Even the most abstruse logical or mathematical operation remains for him a form of action, organically evolved from the child's first directed behaviour. The evolution is clearly traceable, although, as already noted, Piaget himself does not follow it through fully. But at any rate the earlier stages, and thereafter the constant cross-links with the child's world of outward action, are made plain.

The process of "internalisation" may well begin when with the help of word-counters (now themselves internalised) the child first *enacts in imagination* what he is going to do, before he actually does it. (He often in fact announces this aloud). But where he finds himself prevented from acting, or anyway held up, something more also starts happening. He will then struggle to imagine other ways of acting, perhaps drawn from similar or partly similar situations, and try these out. Or he may keep worrying at what is actually in front of him, in case this of itself should throw up some fresh idea of what to do.

Such processes of mental enactment in advance (particularly experimental) are probably among the main leads-in to the new activity of directed thought. But once this is launched, it quickly spreads and multiplies in the most varied directions. In fact it soon gets drawn in to help with every sort of purposive or goal-pursuing behaviour. By means of word-borne thinking the child can prepare for what is going to come, "think of" what *may* be coming, or "think again" if something different comes. He can also make mental comparisons, draw contrasts, develop ordering schemes, etc. Similarly he can now continually diversify and enrich his exploratory activities, and of course also retain their outcomes, connect these up and organise them. Or he can mentally reconstruct some past situation or course of happenings. Or something vividly remembered may start him on a trail of make-believe play which he carries forward by a continual alternation of outward and inward language, action and thought. Free phantasy naturally plays a large part here; but this is also one of the chief ways in which the child works over all the more stirring situations and happenings of his real life and turns them into an organic part of his world of thought.

All these are roads by which he moves forward from his first plane of mental growth in terms of working schemas to the later one of explicit (word-borne) *ideas*. With the help of the right opportunities for active living learning, his incipient ideas will develop more and more substance, will link up with one another in connected groupings, and may at length evolve into organised structures of conceptual knowledge. This of course comes about turn-by-turn with the development of his thinking processes themselves, as these gradually grow into the disciplined scheme of thought-*operations* already referred to.

That is merely the sketchiest indication of a long and complex story, of which the main point here is just this: it is conditioned on all sides by the world in which we live and act, explore and question, experiment and test, plan and construct—and in all these ways cumulatively learn. The growth of our thought depends on this world for its material, its stimuli, its motive forces and above all its tests. It takes place in effect through a continual shuttle movement of our minds between the two worlds of outward and of inward action. In the measure in which the shuttle movement is maintained our thinking prospers. Where this gets severed from its sources and controls, we can constantly watch it losing itself in vagueness and confusion (with the exception only of logic and mathematics, where however it is merely concerned with its own workings). On the other side, in diametrical contrast, we can note its most spectacular successes precisely where, as in the world of science, its relation to its sources and controls is most intimate and continuous.

Bearings on the Schools

The foregoing section [Theoretical Foundations] has set out the framework for education to which the Piagetian psychology of active learning and mental growth points. If it is in truth valid, what is the moral for our schools?

(1) First we now have the full measure of the psychological gulf between this framework and our traditional views. These are based on assumptions about teaching and learning, language and knowledge which work in with one another to form a single, seemingly self-evident whole. Putting it very schematically, learning is what happens with normal children if they are properly *taught*. Teaching must mainly be through language (whatever supplementary aids we may also bring in), since most human knowledge is embodied in this and can only, in the end, be conveyed by its means. The chief aim of education is in fact this conveyance, by methods and under conditions that will make it as effective as possible; i.e. that will successfully transfer to children the same kind of knowledge, embodied in language, as is possessed by the teacher.

Now from the present angle what these assumptions mean in practice is this: the teaching situation so conceived involves lifting the child right out of the context of his living learning—with its own motive-springs and starting-points, its active stretching-out and all its rewarding own achievements—and setting him down in a sort of "looking-glass" world where things virtually go by opposites. Here he must acquire a new way of life (oddly known as "learning"), which is essentially behaving to order, under continuous verbal direction. Nowadays, of course, this no longer starts abruptly and in full force; most children are allowed quite a long period of transition. But in the end they must fall in with the *real* aims and rules for which they are being sent to school.

For they are in effect put there to be taught; which means expressly clearing out of their minds all that ordinarily fills these and handing them over to the teacher with, as it were, "vacant possession". Their task is to co-operate faithfully with his attempt to furnish their minds, compartment by compartment, as they ought to be furnished. They must make every effort to *take in* what he offers, as he offers it; they must listen as directed, look where directed, act when directed. Of these various demands on them, listening is the most crucial, because it is both so difficult to keep up, and so essential. For language can alone provide the necessary connecting links, give the teaching continuity and cohesion, and build up organisation. Therefore, children must above all follow the spoken word, lesson by lesson—and thus allow themselves to be slowly led, according to some master plan of which they know nothing, to various labelled but otherwise unknown destinations. These they must patiently wait to learn more about when they begin to get there.

Naturally most children will obediently try, as far as in them lies, to comply with what is expected of them. In their varying degrees they will endeavour to "learn" at least some part of what they are taught. A number of them will indeed get fired with real interest in this or that "subject" and put active energy into mastering it. But even then it will often only remain a "school" interest, and a transitory one. Whilst in far too many cases no spark will pass at all. Something will be "learnt", but it will not begin to *mean* anything to the child, and most of his own dutiful efforts as well as those of the teacher will in the long run just go to waste. In other words, the foregoing account of the way the teaching situation operates is not the travesty it might look, but a description of the way it actually works out, psychologically, for quite a large proportion of children. Thus we know only too well in how many cases school geography or history or English never become more than what the children were "made to do in school" (very much as I have put it)—and get almost immediately forgotten or discarded.

We tend to treat most of this wastage as inherent in the nature of things (or anyway in that of many children); but it will be clear that on the present view much of it could merely be the effect of a misconceived psychology of "learning". What can we expect if our teaching situation basically *shuts out* the very forces needed to generate real living learning? That is, the very forces which have already brought even the most ordinary children quite a long way and which our schools should be trying hard to take over and strengthen—so that they might carry the same good work further and further.

(2) It follows therefore that our traditional approach needs to be virtually reversed. We must seek out children's own active interests in the world around them—stir them into asking questions—and then encourage

them in every possible way to search out their own answers and make their own progressive discoveries. Where home environments have been favourable, we shall merely need to continue what has already been well begun and to provide the right conditions for taking it very much further. For the school can bring to bear a combination of helpful factors which no home can emulate: frequent planned opportunities for interest-arousing experiences—the strong mutual stimulation of children working on something together and freely discussing it among themselves as well as with the teacher—the constant availability of a wide range of material and equipment—the ability to go on with a particular project for some time and to continue the overall momentum of the learning process over a whole span of years—but above all the continual presence of grown-ups who are there to give judicious help. That is, to suggest, hint, raise questions, offer comments, give a hand, encourage, and generally guide or steer children's activities along lines which will restimulate as well as reward them, and always incite them to take some further step forward. Here of course it is vital that the teachers themselves should have had every chance of understanding both the processes they are seeking to foster, and the most fruitful ways of co-operating with them.

Where home conditions have discouraged mental growth, it may be important to start with some extra effort in order to get the channels of living learning cleared again. Above all, the impulses towards active stretching out may need to be revived. In most normal children some measure of success can be hoped for, since without some native drive towards active growth normality would not have been achieved at all. Naturally in any group of children some will contribute more and some less to most enterprises; but even the less responsive will tend to get something out of the momentum of the whole group—and to advance further in this way than they would be likely to do under conventional teaching.

(3) On the present view children's own explorations and discoveries, spread over a wide area of interests and gradually expanding in scope, would form the main way of learning at least during all the Primary School years. Over that time they should build up a broad basis of diversified experience; some solid beginnings of connected knowledge; and above all much first-hand familiarity with the typical ways and means of going forward in a number of different fields. Furthermore, as the result precisely of this kind of learning, they should themselves discover two things. First, where their greatest personal interest lies; that is, what they most want to know more about. But secondly also, how much more *preparation and help* they need for finding the proper answers to most of their own questions. They would thus be brought to the stage where they should welcome the chance of learning far more in a fresh, planned way about anything that keenly interested them. And they would in fact now be in a position, at least in their own chosen field, to profit by being verbally taught. For not only would what they had already done

now equip them for rightly *interpreting* verbal teaching, but this would get transferred to it just that active interest which had generated the previous living learning in the same field.

(4) The foregoing has been focused on the main intellectual substance of education: viz. the building up of authentic knowledge and understanding about the real world around us (physical, living and human). It has thus been concerned with the themes of "subjects" like geography and history, nature study, elementary physical science, number and measurement, and the main aspects of human affairs. Obviously, however, schools have also to cope with some very different types of tasks—in particular, equipping children with the indispensable tools of reading and writing. Mastery of the arbitrary conventions on which these depend does seem to call for "learning" of the traditional kind, and this has no doubt helped to establish the latter's entrenched status. But even here all the psychological objections to traditional teaching remain—and are confirmed by the many children whom learning to read leaves with a permanent *dislike* for reading. The right solution here again is to avoid all the traditional hurry, and to aim rather at building up a state of mind in which children themselves will want these skills. Prior to this, we should rely on their active interests directly leading to a good deal of picking up as they went along. But there would also be much which perforce they would miss, and that should bring about growing pressure from within really to get hold of these keys, for lack of which they were so often badly handicapped. Thus there should emerge the right combination of active will to learn with some groundings of knowledge to make teaching both welcome and effective. Children might then be as eager to master these skills as, for example, those of games in which they badly want to take part.

(5) It could be further urged that schools are concerned not only with knowledge and understanding, but just as much with imagination and expression. There is, however, nothing here to conflict with the present approach. On the contrary, as we well know, just this further realm has always proved the most resistant and rebellious against conventional "teaching". In effect, it flourishes and grows in very much the same mental climate as the real learning which leads to living knowledge; that is, wherever there is full scope for children's own strong interests and stretchings out, free activities and discussion, constant fresh explorations, experiments and discoveries. Indeed, the two worlds have such large areas of overlap that each will often directly start up new surges of enterprise and advance in the other. There are naturally also important differences, which cannot be pursued here; but the main fact is that the world of imagination and expression demands just the same educational attitude as that of knowledge and understanding.

(6) Finally, although I have made so much of the contrast between the "activity" approach, as here developed, and certain *traditional* educational

assumptions, it is of course clear that our actual practice has moved some way ahead of these. But the basic contrast in principle needs bringing out all the same. The advance in our practice has been largely due to the growing influence, direct and indirect, of "activity" doctrines. Most of this influence has not, however, gone very deep—that is, not down to the level of fundamental re-thinking. Apart from a number of dedicated Infant Schools (widely regarded as representing a pre-teaching stage anyway) and some Junior ones ready to risk their more expendable first years, teachers at large still treat progress in methods as one thing, but fundamental principles as another. The latter remain unquestioned, and often even unformulated, in the background. Yet it is just such tacit background assumptions that most need to be brought into the open, to face their present new challenge. If Piaget's work is valid, we must revise our very idea of learning. Above all, we must emancipate it from that of teaching, and think in terms not of "aids to teaching", but of help in real, living learning, at least over the whole vital period of the foundation-building primary years.

SECTION 3 [DANGERS OF MISINTERPRETATION]

IV:Are there real dangers that Piaget's ideas will be misinterpreted by teachers, and in which way?

V: How would you recommend that we avoid such dangers?

(IV) The dangers certainly exist. I have already indicated on broad lines where they lie, but can now develop this theme somewhat further. There are, I believe, two main pitfalls. The first arises if the studies of children's mathematical and logical ideas are viewed in isolation. The second awaits us even if we rightly join up these studies with Piaget's work on early development—but then treat them as a full continuation of this, instead of representing only one sector of further growth.

(1) The first pitfall is best illustrated in terms of the volume on "Number". Its thesis is commonly taken to be that this idea *slowly develops from within* and only matures in most children some time between 6½ and 8 years. The evidence of all the experiments seems to converge on just that conclusion. What therefore appears to follow is that it is a complete mistake to try to teach number to most children before the above age. (And similarly with such other topics as length, measurement, distance, etc.)

Such a reading is almost unescapable, and all the more so since work on so many children in other countries has led to parallel findings. Nevertheless there is a catch present. Piaget is seeking to analyse the *nature* of the inward process by which certain ideas develop, and not really studying the *rate* at which they develop—or what might or might not influence that rate. He finds that the process shows a definite succession of stages, and his evidence for this can of course only be that these stages always manifest themselves in the same time-order. That therefore is what he sets out to test, and the clear progression in the average age-range at which each stage appears is his proof that his analysis of the inward succession is correct.

But he himself takes care to keep his average age-ranges fairly wide, so as to leave ample room for his own found variations—and even so he quotes quite a number of cases of actual age-overlap. As he has emphasised, he is not in fact concerned with the ages he reports as such, but only with their manifest successiveness. It is true, of course, that the similarity of those age-ranges in different groups of children from different environments (and even countries) lends colour to the inference that we are here dealing with something at least broadly maturational. Yet Piaget himself would reject this inference if it were thought to establish that no outward influence, or change of conditions, could affect children's *rate* of growth, that is, the actual ages at which the successive inward stages are reached. Indeed, most of the similar age-findings come from environments which share the same general (Western) educational assumptions—and therefore cannot be evidence of what *radical* changes in these (based for example on all the deeper understanding which Piaget's own work has brought us) could achieve.

We have only in effect to turn back now to his basic conception of human mental growth. If this springs essentially out of the interactions between the child and the world he finds around him, the character of that world must be constantly affecting his growth. The basic *quality* of the latter may well be firmly laid down in our human and personal make-up; but we must expect that at the least our *rate* of growth—above all in the main growing years—will to some extent turn on the helping or hindering features of the world on which we so fundamentally depend. And the better we understand the processes and the dynamics of intellectual growth, the better we should be able to provide the conditions in which this can proceed most freely and abundantly. That is, up to its maximum powers, instead of perhaps only some gratuitous limits far below these.

The bearing of that standpoint on the use of Piaget's work on number is further commented on below. Here I pass on to:

(2) The sharp narrowing of scope which, as already remarked, takes place when Piaget passes from his basic study of the first years to the work on children's logical and mathematical development. The former deals with the full process of their interactive learning from the world around them; but the latter only with certain slow-growing inward contributions to this. Logic and mathematics sum up for Piaget the most advanced ways in which our *thinking powers as such* can operate. Their growth, as he traces it, is not usually completed till around 14-15; whilst at 6½-8, when most children have come to grasp basic ideas like that of number, length, logical class-relations, etc., we are only just at the earliest level of genuine logic. In fact some 3-4 years more are commonly needed for the mastery of more difficult ideas on the same

level. Thus on Piaget's showing it is not till about 11 that most children begin the long-drawn-out second part of their journey towards full logical and mathematical reasoning. (Note that the main emphasis, once again, is on the order of succession, not the actual ages. The latter merely represent a broad present-day guide, and are subject to all the qualifications already set out. But that Piaget sees the evolution as an inherently protracted one, bound to stretch over a number of years, is hardly open to doubt.)

All this, however, deals only with our internal powers of formal logical manipulation of ideas. It is not a picture of intellectual development as a whole, but solely refers to one of its instruments, even if a very important one. And I think it does not even reflect the full development of this instrument, but merely that of its most refined and slowest-growing forms. Here in fact we must supplement findings concerned only with one selected field by turning back to Piaget's own full account of the character of mental growth as shown during the first 18-21 months, and going on from there. (In "Play, Dreams and Imitation" he has taken the story somewhat further but, as previously remarked with a certain shift in direction.) What, I believe, needs special underlining is that the self-same processes of living learning— through exploring and experimenting, goal-pursuing and goal-achieving—must clearly *continue* to extend and enrich the child's connected knowledge of his world. And moreover through his growing mastery of language during the third and fourth year, together with the development of language-borne thought, his progress constantly gains in range and power—though only where these fresh resources are kept in living relation to concrete activities and experiences, as already noted.

However, to a considerable extent things do work out like that. We all know the immense intellectual advances which most children exhibit between say 2 and 5½, but particularly from about three onward, when they have sufficiently mastered language to make free use of it, both for communication and as an instrument of thought. There are indeed ample facts to show that during this latter period the child's living learning generates from within the beginnings of an authentic working logic which he is quite able to express in words. Under suitable conditions most children from their fourth or fifth year onward use a variety of organised question-forms: (What? Where? When? How? What makes? Why? etc.), and many can offer logically significant comments or retorts, bring up logically valid objections, and carry through their own independent trains of reasoning.[3]

This, however, occurs only in the context of their own active interest and questionings, their eager pursuit of self-set goals, and their efforts to overcome obstacles, find new ways, avoid mistakes and failures. On the other side, much else is happening at the same time, and can easily confuse the

---

[3] See [chapter] Bibliography – S. Isaacs (1930) and Wann, Dorn and Liddle (1962).

above picture or even overshadow it altogether. Language serves to expand not only the child's active learning, but also all his phantasy life. And furthermore there is the continual stream of ill-assimilated verbal information, explanations, stories, etc. which flows in on the child and sets up in his mind the ever-growing world of shifting verbal shadow-ideas to which I referred earlier. This moreover merges readily with his vaguer phantasies and together with these forms a confused floating background-world which we frequently come up against in our 4-5 year olds.

In Piaget's earliest studies he particularly noted this fluid background-world, which indeed he did much to probe. He was also struck by the contrast between that world and the levels of effective practical thinking which children of that age had already attained in their life of action. That led him in fact to develop the view that as they move from the closely penned-in practical plane to that of free verbal thought, they somehow lose their hold, drop down to an earlier level, and now have to do much of their previous learning over again in the new verbal medium. They have in effect to find a fresh means by which they can *order and control* this new mode of verbal thinking. Hence for Piaget it is in the natural order of things that the new form of control should take some considerable time to build up, and that a series of soundings made as early as 4-5 should show no signs of it yet. Everything indeed seems to fit together. His tests on such elementary ideas as those of number, length, distance, the simplest logical relationships, etc. all confirm one another and show that at first there is just no sort of logical grasp or control at all, but that this then emerges by degrees and develops concurrently over the whole field.

However, in spite of the apparent force of such a view, I have suggested that it represents only a very partial picture of children's intellectual development. The world of amorphous confusion into which they so readily slide back in their unsupported verbal thinking constitutes only one side of their mental life. There is also that other one referred to above to which Piaget's own fundamental psychology points and in which the child, under the close control of his living learning activities, evolves a very real capacity even for logical *verbal* thought. Yet even if this can be factually demonstrated, as early as in children's fifth year, there remains a real problem. What are we to make of the apparent complete contradiction between these facts and all the great body of Piaget's actual experimental results?

The main pattern of these results cannot, in my view, be questioned and indeed, as I began by stressing, has been repeatedly confirmed by other workers. But the other facts are just as undeniable and moreover have the support of Piaget's own most penetrating psychological work. Therefore the two sets of data must somehow be reconcilable. And in my view this can indeed be done but only on the lines already foreshadowed, namely by interpreting Piaget's experimental findings about the growth of logical thinking rather more narrowly than he himself does (though still very widely!)

The grounds on which such a narrower interpretation appears justified are twofold. Very summarily:

(A) The fields which Piaget has chosen for investigating the beginnings of logical thinking (particularly arithmetic, geometry and purely logical relations) are all closely connected and depend from the start on a *developed* level of logical thought.

(B) They are altogether lacking in just the features that contribute most towards *bringing about* such a level.

As regards (A): The ideas which Piaget finds so completely absent in most children of 4-5, (such as "conserved"–and properly structured–notions of number, length, distance, logical class-relations etc., etc.) are themselves synthetic products of our logical powers. Therefore the child cannot begin to form them till he already has these powers. Yet until the ideas are basically there, he has nothing to grip on in order to help him in more fully mastering them. This circle eventually gets broken; but the early stages of logical progress come far more easily where a child can start from ideas of concrete things or happenings, about which he has already built up a good deal of connected experience in the real world. (B) Furthermore, most often, these *constructed concepts* and the artificial world of the relations between them are devoid of all natural interest for young children. They are right outside the main stream of a child's living learning, and there is nothing in them that arouses spontaneous questioning, presents meaningful challenges or demands, or stimulates him to do real thinking of his own. Usually he only enters into the world in question because he is made to do so, and it gets no more than an external and enforced kind of attention, without any inward learning interest or drive.

On both the above grounds children's logical grasp and powers in that kind of world should be expected to *lag well behind* the growth of these same capacities elsewhere. This lagging progress cannot therefore be used as a measure of anything else. The time-lag might indeed be partly remedied if the fields of number, etc. were brought into closer relation with the mainstream of children's living learning. (See further below–under VI). But that is only to say again that the real key to logical development must be sought in that stream, where everything conspires to *help* rather than to hamper.

The foregoing does not, however, diminish the outstanding importance and value of Piaget's findings within their own realm. The latter remains both far-reaching and vital. The working logic which children evolve out of their own living learning can serve them well over a large area of further concrete learning; but it cannot take the place of pure mathematics, in all its forms, or of its instrumental applications to virtually every field of science, or of the most advanced and complex kinds of *logical* operation. In all these various fields Piaget's demonstration of the many stages which must be passed through before complete control of our logical resources is achieved retains its full force. It needs therefore to be kept closely in mind in any educational plans that look at all far ahead. The process may not indeed have to spread over the length of time which, under present educational conditions, Piaget registers. But his work does show, at the least, how much has to be accomplished, and indicates that even at the best the road can hardly be very short.

On the other hand, on no account must his negative findings about the earlier ages lead to any disregard of the positive facts insisted upon above. In their own fields of living interest children are capable, from 3-5 onward, of a large range of explicit logical activities: they can compare and contrast; distinguish, arrange and organise; judge and reason; raise questions and critically discuss answers; and much more besides. All these activities we must be ready to meet half-way with understanding and help, so that they can freely grow further. And it may well be that if we aid them effectively where they first flourish, this will also assist most towards advancing children's formal logical powers.

(V) In commenting on the main misunderstandings to which Piaget's work is liable, I have already indicated, in a piecemeal way, how we can best avoid them. I need therefore only sum up now:

(1) The study of Piaget should start from his account of the basic principles and dynamics of intellectual growth, as set out above all in the two volumes about the first 18-21 months.

(2) We should then view children's further growth as steadily going on in the same way, but on an ever-widening front, and with all the further help of language and language-borne thought (in so far as it is closely harnessed to living learning).

(3) We should realise that the researches on the growth of children's "operational" thinking (as seen in relation to number, space and allied fields of applied logic) cover only one sector, however important, of intellectual development; and even so, we should take great care not to interpret their results too maturationally.

(4) Thus the ages reported for the successive stages must first of all be viewed as only rough general indications, and secondly as in any case not fixed and unchangeable. We may be merely failing to provide the right conditions for readier and more fruitful growth. But of course we may get no response to superficial improvements—only to sufficiently radical ones; in other words, such as are based on the main stream, and the full dynamics, of children's living learning.

(5) Furthermore we should not in any event treat the Piagetian findings as the whole story of children's logical development. On the contrary, every attention must also be given to the concrete working logic which gets so clearly expressed, in real learning situations, from about 4 years onward, but which Piaget's researches, for the reasons I have set out, fail to cover.

SECTION 4 [IMPLICATIONS FOR PRIMARY MATHEMATICS]

General

VI: Turning now to Piaget's work in number: what are the specific implications of his discoveries for the approach to mathematics at primary level?

The answer here is now mainly a matter of applying the above principles to the specific "number" situation.

(1) As already stressed, it does not follow from Piaget's findings that a majority of children are inherently incapable of understanding what number means till some time between 6½ and 8—and therefore cannot do significant number work till after that age. But it does follow that they cannot do such work *until* they have grasped the number idea, whenever that may happen. Even without this grasp they can of course be "taught" numbers, that is, trained (with greatly varying success) to behave in certain prescribed ways in certain kinds of situation. Too often, however, this will mean nothing to them, will lead only to quite poor performance, and may well put children off arithmetic and number for good.

Therefore the first practical implication of Piaget's work would seem to be that each child needs to be *individually tested* (in the ways he has so illuminatingly devised) to make sure that the basic idea is there before we try to build anything on it. Sometimes, as his own findings show, the idea will be there at 6 or 5½, but in most cases under current conditions not till around 7—by which time the practical experiences of life at home will usually have built it up. Once it does get established, progress with most kinds of simple arithmetical operations should become much easier and faster, as well as more interesting and meaningful for the children themselves.

(2) If the notion is found to be completely lacking, as in most 5 year olds, or barely beginning, as is commonly the case between 5½ and 6½, an enterprising teacher might be tempted not to take "inherent unreadiness" too much for granted and to try the effect of some first lessons directly focused on the idea itself. However, if he relied mainly on words, he would probably not get very far with most of his pupils, for the reasons already stated. Verbal explanations mean little to children unless they already inwardly possess (through true living learning) something very close to the notion they are to grasp. With the help of much concrete demonstration, some sort of replica of

the intended idea might get set up in their minds, but only as one more thing "learnt"—in the scholastic, not the living sense.

A genuine element of growth from within must in fact enter in. But this does not signify that everything must wait till the idea somehow comes into being "of its own accord". That would almost certainly mean no more than that it was left to grow out of the child's active experiences *outside school.* There is, however, nothing to prevent it from thus growing within the school itself, and here indeed far more easily, quickly and effectively. And that precisely—in the light of Piaget's work both on number and on basic mental growth—should be the first target in the arithmetical field.[4]

In other words, prior to all "arithmetic teaching", the school must give children their chance to build up the number idea for themselves. If that aim is once accepted, its achievement does not seem too difficult. Many Infant schools already do a great deal towards it, though Piaget's work might well lead to a more fully organised notion both of what to aim at and how it can best be achieved.

Children are in fact interested in a great variety of pursuits which may bring them up against arithmetical relations at any moment. Indeed some of these, like shopping or shopkeeping, turn on just such relations all the time. Others, like building or furnishing or going on journeys or collecting things or sharing them out or arranging them in this or that order, or almost any kind of exploring or finding-out activity, may either lead spontaneously to arithmetical questions or can be very easily steered that way. The important thing is merely that the children should come up against these relations or these questions for themselves, and should *need* the answers before they can get on with whatever they are trying to do. They can then be encouraged to look for the right answers—by discussion and thought, trial and error, or experiment—and if necessary judiciously helped to succeed. The direct value to them of these successes is that each time they will have found the way to surmount an obstacle, and can now go further with what they are actually doing. But each such case will link up with any others of a similar kind that may follow. Children are thus continually gathering further experience of how to make effective use of number relationships; how to link them up into helpful connected patterns; and how to move freely within these patterns, forward and backward and any way round. They are in fact building up a more and more fully structured notion, not merely of number, but of the number-world. And of that world as the one key to a whole host of different problems.

This of course is no more than a series of arrows, to indicate the suggested main movement of advance; but more than that is hardly needed, since the broad ideas involved are familiar enough. I wish merely to make plain here

---

[4] See [chapter] Bibliography – E. Churchill (1961).

how directly they flow out of the psychology of living learning and mental growth which I have outlined. This naturally excludes also any sort of pressure aimed at securing some set standard of arithmetical proficiency at the earliest moment. There is no question of *imposing* the above arithmogenic activities on children and thus turning them back into just a new form of "lessons". If that began to happen, spontaneous interest and living learning would vanish again very quickly. For both depend on children feeling all the time that what they are trying to find the answers to are *their* questions and *their* problems—that the progress they make (with whatever judicious help) is *their* progress—that the discoveries they are led to or the solutions they achieve are *their* discoveries and *their* solutions—and what they are actually doing all along is to make their way forward in grasp and understanding of the real world which *they* live in. And this exactly is what should be happening.

In spite of the lack of pressure we could, I believe, fairly expect that the foregoing way would not only lead to a structured idea of number, but also to quite a wide capacity for successful arithmetical performance. Progress, above all in basic grasp, could be readily checked by means of the Piagetian types of test situations, which are themselves usually of interest to children. Some indeed (or the many changes that can so readily be rung on them) could also be used—if children take them up eagerly enough—to start off further problem-solving pursuits in their own right.

At what point arithmetic should become something to work at for its own sake would not be a very important issue. Most of its main forms would anyhow emerge automatically from the hosts of different situations which call for its help. And since it all *is* a single system based on relatively simple foundations, it can hardly help developing more and more cohesion as it goes along. What would *not* emerge in the above ways would be mainly those laborious exercises which most of us now see anyhow as just a waste of educational time and effort.

But no doubt quite a number of children would find, here as elsewhere, that something that had begun as only a means to other ends presently grew into an object of great interest in itself. This might well be strongly stimulated by the way in which arithmetical questions always keep turning up, in every sort of context, as well as by the endless variety of their forms. A good many children would thus be led to "discover" arithmetic as such; that is, as a large field of its own, to be explored and mapped, studied and learnt about. And for some it would become an exciting game, full of challenges and puzzles, ever-new possibilities and surprising powers and achievements. They would then themselves want to find out more and more about it; and they would therefore welcome the right help in covering the whole ground—and probably in penetrating beyond this into all the further worlds of mathematics.

On the other hand, where children wholly fail to develop such an interest, nothing is really gained by pressing them beyond their elementary needs. Whatever more we manage somehow to drill into them will anyhow be shed again at the earliest moment. Here again we can salvage time and energy from sheer fruitless waste and find some way of turning it to constructive educational use.

(3) The above discussion has dealt only with number, viewed as a field apart, because that is how our school tradition has tended to treat it (at least at the Primary level). But a further important implication of Piaget's work is that this is a mistake, both psychologically and logically. The idea of number has a host of cross-connections with other concepts: with measurement and other spatial ideas; with order, seriation and classification; with speeds and rates, etc. It should therefore from an early stage be linked up with all these other notions, and children should be encouraged to move from one to another, to explore their diverse relationships and to get some sense of what binds them together. This applies of course most of all to the relation between the worlds of number and of space. The concreteness of spatial problems, together with the child's natural keen interest in such activities as measuring, comparing and ordering, can greatly aid him in developing and organising his numerical ideas. These will then in turn help him with many spatial problems; and there is in fact much to be said for treating these two fields from the outset as virtually one.

The foregoing brings together some of the main headings of what Piaget's work on number, and its related themes, implies for our schools. Other implications may, however, well occur to the experienced teacher who makes a close study of this work.

Structural Apparatus

VII: Do you see any contradiction between the use of structural apparatus in mathematics and Piaget's principles?

No contradiction, but not any close relation either. Structural material has the advantage of offering a certain amount of active experience that carries direct arithmetical learning with it. But this is mostly a very limited sort of experience, which need not involve more than just a superior form of *training*. The child may advance further and faster this way than through ordinary verbal teaching—but only within the range of arithmetical performances which the material is designed to foster. No understanding of what these performances mean in the wider world need ensue.

In effect, play with structural material is something segregated and self-contained, without any relation to the main course of the child's interactions with the world around him, or any share in the latter's meaningfulness. Living learning starts from real encounters in that world which arouse the child's direct interest or concern, start up questions or problems for him, offer obstacles to his purposes, etc. He therefore *wants* to find the right answer—that is, one which really satisfies him and about which he can see just why it fits. He wants to be able to feel that he now understands—and has a key which will give him the same insight and power in all similar real situations. But structural material does not belong within this real world, it just moves round and round in its own limited circle, in which the child has anyway only an artificial school-induced interest.

The foregoing, however, only deals with structural material as a supposed main avenue to mathematical learning. What part it might play in a purely supplementary capacity may be left an open question. If the chief stress falls on real activity and experience in the real world and if good progress in essentials has already been made there, it is quite possible that play with structural material could be so introduced as to fit in and render auxiliary service. That would be something to consider as one went along. What needs guarding against is any tendency to set up structural material as an educational medium in its own right—that is, as yet another false *substitute* for living learning.

The Man-Made Structure of Arithmetic

VIII: Our system of decimal numeration, place-value, etc., which forms the structure of arithmetic, is obviously man-made. How could the child at any given age-level gain the concepts of this artificial structure without the use of special apparatus?

As already said, I can see nothing in principle against using special apparatus where it can be clearly seen to give useful *auxiliary* service. But does the fact that the scaffolding of arithmetic is man-made really call for that sort of artificial help? I should say on the contrary that this fact should emerge directly from the man-made problems in the everyday real world through which I should expect number relations to be brought home to children. They would always be re-discovering in how many different ways any one kind of number problem can be handled and resolved—though always in the end through the *same types of answer,* turning on the same few simple and constant principles. The point which we want to see children reach is surely just that of seeing at one and the same time *both* these few fixed principles *and* our freedom to choose through what scaffolding we are going to apply them.

Decimal numeration, place values, etc., should thus come to be viewed as simply a particular scaffolding on which everybody has agreed; though by no means the only possible one and perhaps not even in all respects the best. It has already been shown in recent years how children can learn to appreciate quite early that one could work on bases other than 10, and that this is merely the one nearest to hand which we now all commonly use. It is through concrete daily-life situations that children can best learn both how real are the problems for which we need arithmetic and how *man-made* the different forms of arithmetical apparatus which we use to solve them.

The Right Age-Level for 'Chalk and Talk'?

IX: Finally, in the light of Piaget's work, at what level would you expect a pupil to benefit from the kind of teaching—or instruction if you prefer—in which the conventional "Chalk and Talk" method is used rather than the discovery of knowledge by the pupil?

I should not care to offer any very hard-and-fast answer; I think we still have much to learn about this. If I had to put forward a working guess or hypothesis, on the basis of the general educational approach I have set out, I should be disposed to think in terms of the earlier teens. But at the same time I should emphasise that there should be no sudden break; and that even our strictly "chalk and talk" methods need bringing much closer than in the past to the conditions in which real learning can best flourish.

It would all be a matter of gradual yet flexible development. In the earlier years children would mainly learn through their own discoveries, but even then there would be room at times for informal teacher talks, summings up, historical notes, etc. And as time went on, the teacher's part would tend to increase. When children moved on to more difficult and searching enquiries, they would need more and more background information, guidance about instruments and techniques, and so on. This should also lead to looking up books, reading them, and in general reaching the point previously referred to where the child is really ready and anxious to be *taught all about* some chosen field.

Yet in most fields of knowledge it would still be very important that the verbal teaching stage should preserve continuity with all the vital elements in direct living learning. The main starting-points should still be the arousal of a strong personal sense of real and so far unsolved problems—only then followed by an account of their progressive solutions. There should still be constant emphasis on the ways these came to be found, as well as on the evidence and tests used to establish their correctness. A steady accompaniment both of actual direct experience and of free discussion should be maintained throughout. And what is now known should thus always be seen as something won through acting and experiencing, questioning and exploring, turn by turn with imagining and reasoning, experimenting and testing. The pupil must in effect be so helped to share in the original living learning that it comes to be as if lived and learnt by himself.

Thus for most subjects the "chalk and talk" stage would have to go well beyond the more conventional ways of systematic exposition current in the past. But it should perhaps be added here that although in broad principle much of the foregoing applies even to the mathematical field, this remains in many ways a special case. Here the traditional methods of presentation can—at least beyond a certain point—still claim to be justified. For here we are in effect concerned only with the human mind's own operations, and the structures of concepts thus inwardly built up. Accordingly, after the right foundations have once been laid, most of the forward and backward movement between human minds and the real world which plays so great a part in all other living learning just drops out. What in fact the teacher must finally get across is the idea of a logically self-contained coherent conceptual system. Thus it is logical order, not historical, that is here most vital.

Even if this unique status of mathematics is acknowledged, however, it remains true that the actual history of mathematical knowledge has a great deal in common with that of our progressive new discoveries in the world of fact. Therefore there is still a case, even in the teaching of mathematics, for enabling the learner to re-live this history, as well as to master the resulting self-contained system (or systems). How far a historical approach might continue to be helpful even in the later stages of mathematics can only be thrashed out between a mathematical-minded psychologist like Piaget and philosophic-minded mathematicians.[5] But anyway for the earlier levels, the reasons for a continued "living learning" approach during at least the first years of the "chalk and talk" phase seem clear.

BIBLIOGRAPHY

I. Piaget's books [first English translation]

(1926) *The Language and Thought of the Child.*
(1928) *Judgment and Reasoning in the Child.*
(1929) *The Child's Conception of the World.*
(1930) *The Child's Conception of Causality.*
(1951) *Play, Dreams and Imitation in Childhood.*
(1952) *The Child's Conception of Number* (with A. Szeminska).
(1953) *The Origin of Intelligence in the Child.*
(1954) *The Child's Construction of Reality.*
(1956) *The Child's Conception of Space* (with B. Inhelder).
(1958) *The Growth of Logical Thinking from Childhood to Adolescence* (Inhelder & Piaget).
(1960) *The Child's Conception of Geometry* (with B. Inhelder & A. Szeminska).
(1964) *The Early Growth of Logic in the Child: Classification and Seriation* (Inhelder & Piaget).

[5]E.g. by Z. P. Dienes. See his book *Building up Mathematics* (Hutchinson Educational, 1960) [New York: Humanities Press, 1960].

(Note: The foregoing [list of four early and eight later works, all published by Routledge and Kegan Paul] does not include some translated lesser books by Piaget and a number of untranslated ones. Important among the latter are works on Physical Quantities: Mass, Weight and Volume; on Classes, Relations and Numbers; on Movement and Speed; on Time; on Chance and Probability.)

II. Books and pamphlets about Piaget
    or dealing at length with his work

Churchill, Eileen. *Counting and Measuring: An Approach to Number Education in the Infant School.* Routledge and Kegan Paul, 213 pp., 1961.
Hunt, J. McV. *Intelligence and Experience.* Ronald Press, New York, 363 pp., 1961.
Isaacs, Nathan. *New Light on Children's Ideas of Number: The Work of Professor Piaget* (1960). *The Growth of Understanding in the Young Child: A Brief Introduction to Piaget's Work* (1961). Ward Lock Educational Co., London.
Lawrence, Evelyn; Theakston, T. R.; Isaacs, Nathan. *Some Aspects of Piaget's Work.* National Froebel Foundation, London, 1955.
Lovell, K. *The Growth of Basic Mathematical and Scientific Concepts in Children.* University of London Press, 151 pp., 1962.
Peel, E. A. *The Pupil's Thinking.* Oldbourne, London, 1960.

III. Books dealing more generally
     with children's thinking

Isaacs, Susan. *Intellectual Growth in Young Children.* Routledge and Kegan Paul, 370 pp., 1930.
Wann, K. D.; Dorn, M. S.; Liddle, E. A. *Fostering Intellectual Development in Young Children.* Teachers College Press, New York, 140 pp., 1962.

Memorandum for the Plowden Committee*

In 1963 a committee was formed by the Central Advisory Council for Education in England to "consider primary education in all its aspects." The committee, under the chairmanship of Lady Bridget Plowden, became known as the Plowden Committee, and its final report as the "Plowden Report." This was published in 1967 under the title *Children and Their Primary Schools* (Vol. 1, *Report*; Vol. 2, *Research and Surveys*). It is widely regarded as the official voice of the radical "activity" approach to early education in England.

Isaacs' memorandum to the committee was submitted on behalf of the Froebel Foundation. In it he refers more than once to the Central Council's earlier "Newsom Report" (1963) which, as he put it, had "impressively recorded" that, for approximately half the nation's youth, most of their schooling "has just been wasted." Contending that the limiting factor is not in the minds of poor achievers but in a flawed educational system, he recommends a twenty-year pilot test of a five-stage program that would neither "throw away our greatest asset" ("children's own learning drives") nor neglect the central role of "teaching" (the "planned passing on of our social heritage").

CONTENT OUTLINE

*First published in the *Froebel Journal*, no. 2 (June 1965): 12-33. Reprinted with the permission of Mrs. Evelyn Isaacs and the National Froebel Foundation.

I: A RADICAL THESIS FOR THE LONG TERM

As a member of the Governing Body of the National Froebel Foundation I should first like to associate myself with the detailed evidence already submitted by the Foundation. In addition, however, I wish to raise a very far-reaching issue, which would in any event need to be considered separately just because it is so fundamental.

I believe there is now a new and very strong psychological case for the root-and-branch re-thinking—and eventual reconstruction—of our whole scheme of primary education. But obviously such a case, even if it were to carry reasonable conviction, could not become practical politics unless it were first tried out experimentally, and decisively confirmed. Therefore the present submission can have no more ambitious aim than to show sufficient reasons for a first searching pilot test. This would of itself need much time, since it would involve carrying a number of children right through from infancy to adolescence according to the same consistent educational principles. If, however, the argument has any real merits, there would be urgency about at least getting a test scheme launched.

The principles in question are in substance simply those of the great educational reformers from Rousseau to John Dewey, viz. the education of children through their own live interests, activities and first-hand experiences. The fresh argument, however, is that through Professor Piaget's penetrating work on the basic nature of human learning, these principles are now placed on a massive new foundation of psychological support. By the same token we also gain revealing new insight into the *avoidable* shortcomings of most of our existing educational efforts, and thus perhaps a freshly hopeful explanation of the reasons why so much of our current 'education' fails to educate. (*Vide* the Newsom Report[1].)

II: IS THERE SOMETHING WRONG WITH CURRENT EDUCATION?
THE FRESH PSYCHOLOGICAL EVIDENCE

I cannot in the present memorandum argue my thesis very fully, but hope it will seem significant enough to merit fairly detailed setting out. Its gist is not of course new, but the suggestion is that the case for it has now become both clearer and stronger than at any time before.

(1) Although the above principles have made fair headway at the Infant level and begun to spread also into the earlier Junior years, they are still widely viewed as simply a transitional stage towards education, not education itself. The latter comes when we begin to *teach:* in effect school education is substantially equated with teaching. For what it sets out to do, first of all, is

[1] [Central Advisory Council for Education (England), *Half our Future: A Report* (London: Her Majesty's Stationery Office, 1963).]

to give every child possession of certain skills, and a view over some broad areas of knowledge, which we regard as key elements of our common social heritage. Even in these modest aims, however, we are seeking to pass over to children within a few years a heritage collectively built up over many millennia. And that, as seems self-evident, can only be done through teaching. What we mean by teaching is in fact precisely our best efforts (constantly restudied and where possible improved) to get the selected elements of our heritage 'across' to our children.

This then appears to be simply a matter of who wills the end having to will the means. But the difficulty is that, despite the immense resources we put into the means, in the case of much of our school population the end is just not achieved. Something of the 'basic skills' is picked up, but these are themselves only further means. And the picking up is too often at the expense of any wish ever to use those means where it can be avoided. Even reading is only learnt at the cost of a lasting distaste for it, which nullifies almost all its intended value. As for the elemental knowledge taught, say of geography, history or general science, this frequently leaves not a rack behind. Thus at the end of our ten years' main national teaching effort, there is a large body of school-leavers for whom most of it has just been wasted. This element of waste becomes most evident, of course, during the later school years, because that should be the time of harvesting of what the primary phase of preparation and equipment has made possible. How little in fact those later years mean to many Secondary Modern School pupils is all too impressively recorded in the Newsom report.

Our trouble, however, is that, having become much too accustomed to this state of affairs, we have long tended to treat it as in the nature of things. We put it down, in effect, to the inherent limitations of our average human material; and the harder we have tried to improve our teaching methods, the clearer this conclusion has appeared. Moreover the work of psychologists earlier in the century had seemed to put a final scientific seal on it. Every individual appeared to have his own inborn level of intellectual capacity, which outside influences had little power of altering or improving. And it seemed that in the case of ordinary average children, this level put a severe limit precisely to their educability ('or capacity to profit by education'). Thus the poor results of all our educational strivings for them appeared both inevitable and fully explained.

(2) However, this sort of view has lost much of its former hold. Many psychologists now consider that even if there is such a thing as inborn intelligence, our tests are no direct measure of it. The level of apparent *capacity* which they establish could already have been influenced by a child's early environment. There is indeed positive evidence for this; in particular that the stimulatingness or otherwise of his previous home setting can effect

the 'intelligence' he displays at school. We might well suspect uneasily at this stage that perhaps schools may not be *bringing into action* the intelligence of a good many children—especially among those who have not had the advantages of stimulating home environments. Their own interest may not be sufficiently gripped. That could be the case even if up to a point they were 'responding', that is, faithfully trying to remember or perform as is asked of them, even though the whole business meant nothing to them. So that even 'doing their best' in this way might be no genuine measure of what, in some more spontaneously active state of mind, they could do.

Thus the whole fundamental question ought to haunt us again; *must* almost everything we are aiming at fail for the great numbers of children for whom in fact it does? Is their capacity for sharing in our common heritage really so inherently limited (if not from birth, then anyway by the time they come to school)? Or could it after all be that the limiting factor is not in their minds, but in some entrenched psychological flaw in our school education?

Now on the basis of Piaget's fundamental work we can, I believe, say very confidently that there is such a flaw, and point to its actual mode of operation. How much difference its elimination would make to how many children could only be finally tested by fully eliminating it. But there are weighty grounds for expecting that the difference would be substantial. To see why, we need merely consider, first, the basic dynamics of human intellectual growth as Piaget's work exhibits it, and then the impact on this of our current scheme of school education. In provisional summary terms we shall then note how school *teaching* in the ordinary school setting systematically shuts out all the main means through which the child has previously achieved mental growth and puts in their place something alien and unmeaning to him. Thus we actually throw away our greatest educational asset and instead thrust on children what many at that stage can only feel as a tedious form of bondage.

This in no way conflicts with the fact that eventually teaching, as the planned passing on of our social heritage, must take its place at the very centre of education. But prematurely forced on children, it can itself prevent them from ever getting to the point of *educationally* benefiting by it. What is needed is that it should evolve at its own right time out of a child's intrinsic ways of mental growth, instead of being forcibly imposed much sooner and then just suppressing and supplanting those ways. It should in fact come as an exciting fresh stage of accelerated and more powerful growth, able to take children much further in the very directions they themselves want to go.

For this to happen, however, school education must first of all *take over* children's own learning drives and the activities that both express these and then re-stimulate and strengthen them. The school must work with those processes, encourage them and help them forward, and seek to carry them on to the point where their own demands for something more—something which only planned teaching can supply—becomes plain and even pressing. All this, however, when its implications are fully worked out, is emphatically not just a matter of another transitional year or two. Even the full existing primary period would probably not allow long enough. For a majority of children primary education might well need not only to dedicate its whole present time to their living learning processes, but also to provide for a further 1-2 years of progressive transition to a mainly teaching approach.

III: THE SUBSTANCE OF THE ARGUMENT

The foregoing may serve to indicate the broad nature of the argument but its psychological substance has yet to be filled in:

The Child's Own Learning Growth

What Piaget's fully documented work,[2] particularly on the crucial first 18/21 months, brings out in the most striking way is this. The child learns above all through his own *actions*—begins to do this soon after birth—and does so in ways which continually lead to further learning and build up ever growing knowledge and powers. And he is constantly impelled from within towards action, and then carried on by the interest and satisfactions which his actions bring to him. He is thus led both to pursue fresh experiences and to achieve fresh powers in every direction he can open up for himself.

This is not the place for reproducing the Piagetian picture in any detail. But its main point, from the present angle, is that all the essential motive forces and processes which it describes operate in the same way during subsequent years—and to the same cumulative effect. The first key factors of the continuous dynamics of mental growth, as exhibited by Piaget, can perhaps be briefly set out as follows:

(i) The child's learning is generated by the constant shuttle movement between himself and his surrounding world.

(ii) This learning takes two chief forms:

(a) Self-expanding cycles are formed through the attraction of novel experiences as such. As the infant encounters these, he is stimulated into following them up. This leads to further experiences; which again stimulate further pursuing activities, and so right on. That happens first in separate fields (visual, tactile, etc.), and then in more and more varied and complex combinations of them. And of course it leads also to the active seeking out of new experiences.

(b) Random movements or actions produce effects which excite the child and lead him to repeat them—first just to reproduce the effects, but later in order to master them and be able to produce them at will.

[2] [Piaget, *The Origins of Intelligence in Children,* trans. Margaret Cook (New York: International Universities Press, 1952); Piaget, *The Construction of Reality in the Child,* trans. Margaret Cook (New York: Basic Books, 1954).]

(iii) [Form] (a) develops into a sustained interest in every kind of *exploratory and experimental activity*, usually with keen pleasure in the discoveries to which this leads.

(iv) [Form] (b) develops into a lively and continuing interest in every kind of *'achieving' power and skill*: from the simplest mechanical effects to every sort of making, building, planning and executing enterprise.

(v) These interests and drives become linked by various cross-connections and once more turn readily into further self-expanding cycles. New knowledge and understanding provides the bases for fresh skills and powers, which often lead to new experiences and fresh extensions of knowledge. And so right on again.

It should be added that Piaget follows through, stage by stage, what these various learning processes, in their growing combination and co-ordination with one another, achieve over the first 18/21 months. Thus on the one hand the child builds up a varied range of abilities, not merely to use known means for known ends, but also (i) to exploit known means for attaining new ends, and (ii) to find new means for securing known ends. On the other hand, he is shown gradually constructing working notions of (a) separate persisting objects (b) spatial relations (c) events and their rudimentary time relations (d) cause-and-effect linkages between actions and their results, or happenings and what starts them off. By the age of 18/21 months he has pieced these together into a connected psychic working scheme: that is, of a surrounding world of objects and events joined together in a common order of space and time, and also particularly linked in specific sequences of causes and effects. Children's active command of such a scheme is clearly demonstrated by all the connected courses of movements and actions which at the above age they can already *initiate for themselves* and *successfully carry through*.

Thereafter this basic scheme is always taken for granted as the framework for everything else, and the child's further exploratory and experimental activities are mainly concerned with (i) continually extending its range (ii) constantly doing further filling in (iii) elaborating its multiple relations and connections and more and more fully organising these. In all this it is clear that the same main drives and interests continue at work as before. But they are of course immensely aided by one essentially new factor which now enters the child's intellectual life, viz. the mastery of speech. This needs some brief reference here, not only because of its vital positive role in all the child's later intellectual development, but equally because of some widespread *negative* aspects of that role. These latter in fact play their part also in processes of learning through being taught.

It is obvious that only language can make possible most of the vast later expansion, and all the explicit conceptual structuring, of the child's mental world. But it is important to note likewise

(i) that a tremendous amount had already been psychically achieved prior to it

(ii) that this was basically the work of the child's exploratory, experimental and effect-producing activities, which go on generating further growth and achievement in just the same way

(iii) that since language operates through mainly arbitrary sound-patterns, its first meanings for the child can only stem from his own real doings, experiencings and learnings

(iv) that all fresh communications too must draw their meanings either from the same sources or from some combination of these with fresh real doing, experiencing and learning

(v) and, finally that when we disregard this and try to instruct children through unsupported, or insufficiently supported, verbal 'information' or 'explanations', we constantly find—as indeed we ought to expect—that all we have produced is either complete ununderstanding, or else vague and confused half-understandings which manage to pass muster, but are apt to be even more obstructive to any further intellectual growth.

On the other hand, we see language doing much of its best work where the child himself brings it in, directly in the service of some exploratory drive, that is, as itself a mode of exploration. In other words, where something has stirred up his interest and he tries to get further with it by *asking questions.* Provided he then meets with the right sort of response, he will frequently go to ask further questions, or launch into active discussion in which he is visibly achieving new grasp and understanding. But even so it must be noted that language operates as an essentially secondary and dependent instrument. Poor handling by the person asked can at once defeat it. And where it helps, it does so in the first place by linking on to the child's own past living learning and enabling him to carry this further in imagination; but secondly, it will usually do most for him if it steers him into some fruitful new direction for his own active exploration and forward-moving experience.—Language aids or illuminates only through meanings, and these are not *produced* by it but only by past or present living, doing and experiencing, imagining, thinking and learning. For all these in their more developed forms it is indispensable as a vehicle, support and auxiliary instrument; but it can only *serve* them, not supersede them or take their place.[3]

[3] I am leaving out of consideration here the further vital function of language as a vehicle for "free" phantasying and imagining. This is a world apart, and even quite young children soon have to learn to *keep it substantially apart.* I cannot here try to do justice to the cross-relations between this purely psychic world and children's learning-growth into the real one, which constitutes my main theme. But obviously the fostering of children's imaginative life and growth has its own essential place in education, to which brief reference will be made again later.

The Impact of the School and of Normal School Teaching

(i) The foregoing real learning or growth processes, as they go on up to school age, produce in most children a steady expansion of knowledge, understanding, powers and skills. This is usually reflected in part (but only in part) through the concomitant growth of language from the third year onward. Where all the conditions have been favourable (that is, where a variety of interest-arousing experiences has been combined with every encouragement and help in enquiring and exploring, thinking and discussing, experimenting, trying and achieving, making and constructing, planning and carrying out) we often get an astonishing flowering of children's intellectual powers by around 4-5. In such cases they have in fact already advanced far into their social heritage—the stimulating evidences and expressions of which usually surround them on every side.

Where the conditions have been less favourable, progress will be more limited; but unless they were severely adverse, children will still be habitually interested in the world around them, will still have been stimulated by all the more obvious forms of our social inheritance, and will still enjoy exploring and discovering, making and achieving. Thus most five-year-olds will already have built up much real past learning, but in addition will still possess all the essential drives and potentialities for more.

At this point then comes the intervention, or intrusion, of the school. From now onward a large part of most days will be spent there, under conditions which the school decides and the child just has to accept and comply with, whether it all means anything to him or not. If he is lucky, he may find himself in an Infant School which for some time at least is predominantly a place for playing, and where he may have even better opportunities than at home for carrying out self-chosen learning-and-growing activities. If he is less lucky, teaching, that is class-room teaching, may befall him, in greater or lesser measure, very soon after five. In any case, by seven it will usually be waiting for him, often already armoured cap-a-pie. He will now form part of a class in a classroom, all called upon to attend, listen and watch, that is, to shut out every other thought and give their whole mind to following, careful step by step, wherever the teacher elects to lead. The latter will without doubt be intent on making all this as easy and as interesting as he knows how. But only within the limits of what he is there for, namely to *teach*—and to teach this or that specific subject; that is, to build up in the minds of children a set body of knowledge (or, in some cases, of knowledge plus skills). The whole aim of the teaching situation requires that they shall for the time being abdicate their own lives, drives or self-initiated interests and activities, and place themselves entirely in the teacher's hands.

And furthermore his leadership must be exercised predominantly through language, even though this is of itself enough to put many young children off, or anyway to prevent them from more than half-following. But the teacher himself has no choice. He can bring in specimens, models, pictures, illustrations, actions, or whatever the subject-matter may permit; but all the essential connecting tissue must consist of language. In the last analysis, he must explain, bring together and build up in words. For he is seeking to *transfer* something already existing, and in so far as it is knowledge, existing essentially in the form of words. That applies in large measure even to the verbal information that needs to be mastered in learning the 'basic skills'. Whilst in the case of knowledge proper, the firm installation of this in the minds of the pupils as a connected word-borne whole is the very point of the teaching exercise.

(ii) In these circumstances what ought we to expect the impact of the school teaching situation to be?

(a) First of all, in many children virtually no *educational* response. And that is what we find. It means nothing to them, does not touch them or interest them, and is merely something which grown-ups in their superior wisdom decide to be good for them, and in their position of authority *make* children do. The latter may try, in their varying degrees, to comply with what is expected of them; and they usually do manage some sort of performance, more especially in the lower reaches of the three R's. But fundamentally it is all just school mumbo-jumbo for them.

Meanwhile in some of these children the true living learning processes may of course continue to operate outside the school; and if that happens, they may even at a later stage join up with school education and infuse meaning into some of it, as part of their own larger whole. But more often those processes will just wither away, since 'learning' now *means* for the children school mumbo-jumbo, and anything to do with the world of knowledge is therefore not for them. This will naturally be most marked where, through previous lack of encouragement and help, the living learning processes were anyhow at a low ebb.

(b) The foregoing children make up that part of 'half our future' which represents our great unsolved educational problem and challenge. But what of all those who successfully adapt themselves to the schoolteaching situation and indeed in many cases seem positively to thrive on it? Why are they not affected in the same way? And since to all appearance they are not, can the present argument be valid?—There could be various partial answers to this, which would still leave the main psychological challenge standing. For example, there might exist between children differences in *adaptability* that demanded differences in handling—and some of these could moreover be due merely to unhelpful earlier environments. But the real answer is surely that even among the pupils who seem to respond well to ordinary school-teaching, a large proportion secure little or no *lasting educational gain.* And here again everything works out very much as we should expect.

Of course, for the bare A.B.C. of learning to read and write a ready response to teaching will normally serve the purpose. Thus the mere ability to use these tools will as a rule be lastingly gained, though even here there can be much gratuitous loss and waste. However, mastery of these tools by itself is not education. And once we aim directly at the latter by trying to teach the beginnings of knowledge about the real world (geography, history or science), the limitations of the school-teaching medium even where apparently successful soon show through. In many children interest in some of these subjects *within* the teaching framework can certainly be aroused and can then lead to various degress of authentic school learning. But what is thus learnt tends strongly to stay apart from the pupil's personal life and to build up into carefully pigeon-holed separate bodies of 'school' knowledge, kept in special 'school' compartments in their minds. That then frequently means that when all this world is left behind (even if only at 16 or 18), almost everything that had been identified with it is automatically dropped and forgotten.

Where this is what happens, school education has once more substantially failed to *educate*. For that would only be achieved if the knowledge in question, or anyway a significant core of it, had now become an integral and lasting part of each learner's mind. Of course in a number of cases again true mental growth will continue outside school, strong interests will get formed, and (as already noted) these self-educative processes may eventually pick up, and fuse with the more congenial parts of school education. Moreover, there are always some children in whom the school itself stimulates interests so keen and enduring that these pupils presently turn over to them as their own main channels of growth.

However, these are the more outstanding successes of formal education and against them must be set those other cases where some school interest establishes a real lasting hold, but yet goes typically wrong. It not only stays as segregated as it began, but through its very growth develops into a whole sealed-off world of its own. Here the final result is apt to be some kind of permanent very narrow specialisation, either just unrelated to most of our common world or else virtually displacing this, and in any event again an example of *educational* failure.

And finally there are also all the revealing *half*-successes of taught education. That is, the cases of those of us who are gratefully aware of what we have carried away from it, but know even more certainly how external this has remained by the side of all those transforming learning experiences which we discovered, and lived through, ourselves.

IV: THE MORAL FOR BOTH EDUCATION AND TEACHING

This has already been drawn in principle, and if the underlying psychological case has now been made out, what follows need only be detailed amplification and supplementary comment.

(1) The basic argument so far has been that for young children there is a deep psychological chasm between learning in the sense of their own full-blooded active building up of knowledge, and school-learning as the attempt to take this over from someone else, prepared lesson by lesson, in ready-made verbal form. This chasm can only be bridged if teaching is not brought in until children themselves can actually see it as a more potent continuation of their own direct learning. And that is a very far cry, and needs a long process of psychological building up. Direct learning—always through exploration, experimentation and the striving for fresh achievement—must in fact be steadily re-stimulated and aided to advance further and further, until the help of planned teaching becomes its own next need and active demand.

(2) What the principle of active education implies for the planning and organisation of a school is of course familiar ground. One need merely refer in this connection to such well-known writings as those of Susan Isaacs,[4] Miss Dorothy Gardner[5] and others. But the tendency of educators generally, as already noted, has been to think of the above principle chiefly in the context of Nursery and Infant Schools, whilst the crux of the present psychological argument is that it ought to form the basis for the whole of Primary Education (and indeed right on to around 12-13). This seems to call for at least a brief re-formulation of the kind of school that would be required and above all of the way in which it might be expected to operate over so long a range:

(i) The starting-point would obviously be a carefully planned endeavour to provide optimal conditions for children's living learning—conditions that would be quite beyond the scope of most homes. These would *combine:* (a) ample opportunities for stimulating experiences and challenges (b) plentiful and varied materials and equipment (c) the fullest chances for free discussion, but above all (d) the continual availability of grown-ups able at all times to help, guide, suggest, raise questions, comment and co-operate. And (e) all this sustained day after day and week by week over a steady sequence of years.

---

[4] [Susan Isaacs, *Intellectual Growth in Young Children, with an Appendix on Children's "Why" Questions by Nathan Isaacs* (1930), *The Nursery Years* (1932), *Social Development in Young Children* (1933), *Childhood and After* (1948): Routledge and Kegan Paul, London; *Psychological Aspects of Child Development* (London: Evans Brothers, 1950); *The Children We Teach* (London: University of London Press, 1963); *Children and Their Parents: Their Problems and Difficulties* (London: Routledge and Kegan Paul, 1968).]

[5] [D. E. M. Gardner, *The Children's Play Centre* (1937), *Education Under Eight* (1949), *Education of Young Children* (1956); *Experiment and Tradition in Primary School* (1966): Methuen, London. D. E. M. Gardner and J. E. Cass, *The Role of the Teacher in the Infant and Nursery School* (Oxford: Pergamon Press, 1965).]

(ii) It would be clear that such optimal conditions should be at the service of children as early as they could benefit by them, that is, would be ready for some hours daily of group life. In other words, real equality of educational opportunity for children demands for a start Nursery Schools for all from about three onward. Until these are the general rule we must expect that among the five-year-old entrants into the Infant School a number will already have had their interest and zest depressed by persistent earlier discouragement and disuse. Some will nevertheless rapidly respond to more favourable conditions; others may need special re-encouragement and help for a while. There will no doubt also be some who will require more radical remedial treatment than any straight Infant School can give; and a number may prove permanently incapable of normal mental growth. But these last two groups would usually fare even worse in a conventional school setting.

(iii) The main aim for the years from 3 to 7 or 8 would be the stimulation and expansion of active interest over as wide a field as possible. Beginning from interest-arousing experiences and encounters, children would be encouraged to ask every sort of question, to discuss, explore, experiment and try out. And this would of course apply not only to all the world of knowledge and understanding (about physical happenings, living things, and human affairs—near and far, present and past), but also to that of every kind of productive, constructive or other achievement. And equally to the world of imagination and all its forms of expression.

The help given by the teachers would be primarily guided by the two main principles of mental growth already emphasised. First, children must get actively involved, that is involved through activities of their own which they are eager to pursue. Secondly, these activities must wherever possible be so steered that they bring results which reinforce the initial interest or give rise to some new one—but either way *re*-stimulate children to go on. This aim would obviously not always succeed, and in the earlier years never for long. Interests flag, fizzle out or drop into some repetitive pattern which presently exhausts itself. But the teacher's aid would always be directed to finding the kinds of suggestions, comments or actions that would lead children to real discoveries, or to such other heartening or exciting experiences as would impel them on afresh. For anyone really interested, who identifies with the children and enters into the situation with them, but naturally can always see much further ahead, help on the foregoing lines is not usually very difficult. The possible ways of giving it are indeed well-nigh unlimited. And the feel of such help quickly becomes quite different from that of merely telling, teaching or showing them; or 'helping' them when they do not need or want this; as the children soon demonstrate if there is any relapse into such ways.

(iv) In the years from 7 or 8 to 10 or 11, three things should concurrently happen:

(a) Interests, activities and enterprises should progressively become more sustained and consecutive. This should develop naturally in part because much is already familiar and questions would start from there and press further forward; partly because children's capacity for sustained pursuits grows both with exercise and with overall internal growth; and partly because teachers would all the time be steering children further in this direction (in particular through the second of the above learning principles).

(b) A number of large fields of interests and exploratory activity would begin to take separate shape. And this not through being expressly labelled and set apart, but because of all their *experienced* different characters. Thus in the realm of knowledge living things would come to stand away from physical happenings (though still parts of the same real world): and human beings and their affairs from both, (though still belonging within the domain of living things). The world of action and performance, concerned first with personal skills and powers, and then linking up with the larger powers of machines and instruments, would stand away from that of knowledge, though still linked with it and closely depending on it. And the realm of the imagination and of the expressive and formative activities based on this would appear as an ever-growing world of its own, though once more showing numerous cross-links with the others. Labellings could now increasingly become a helpful ancillary to experiencing, knowing and understanding, instead of a worthless substitute for these.

(c) Individual children would have the opportunity of finding out for themselves what kinds of interests and pursuits meant most to each of them—attracted them most and gave them most satisfaction. This clearly is of vital importance, from both an individual and a social point of view. And the broader their previous range of exploration, the wider and freer would be their choice, and therefore the greater the chance of their discovering their *strongest* interests and bents. One would usually hope that there would in fact be several which they would want to press forward with at the same time. Later on they might have to be content with one or two main choices, or often with a single predominant one. In any case, what might well emerge quite early and very usefully would be the negative counterpart to all this. That is, what meant least to them—what they could not sustain interest in and preferred to put aside, so that they could get on with what they really wanted to know or do.

(v) Thus, with the help of these developments, the stage should be fully set from about 10 or 11 onward for the transition to systematic teaching. There would be (1) a broad basis of active exploratory experience in the most varied directions (2) a considerable amount of sustained and consecutive experience of enquiries followed through and constructive or imaginative enterprises carried out, i.e. experience of methods and ways and means as well as results (3) some developed sense of the general pattern of our world, and its main sub-divisions or distinct domains, and (4) a growing awareness of being strongly drawn in some directions, but not in others.

But with all the foregoing there should also grow up an increasing aliveness to the many points at which checks and defeats had been met. It would become plain in numerous ways how much needed knowledge was missing. Children would discover how many things they just could not understand, even where they most wanted to do so. They would find that they could not get on without being able to *do* various things, or to use a number of unfamiliar tools or instruments. And so on. Yet it would become plain that everything which they lacked, some of the adults round them actually had. They could not possibly find it all out for themselves, but they could take it over, or learn it, from those who already had it.

This, however, would mean quite a different way of behaving from all one's own finding-out—in fact a kind of turning round on oneself. One had to put oneself in the hands of someone who already knew, and listen, watch, note and learn from him. Moreover that could only be done about one field or 'subject' at a time, and had to be gone on with over a long period. On the other hand, if one really wanted to know all about some particular field or subject, here was the surest and quickest way of getting on with this—at any rate up to the point which other people had already reached.

The transition to that stage would not of course happen in this explicit fashion, but would simply be a mounting series of awarenesses, and a growing state of readiness. Teachers could themselves do much, as opportunities arose, to help it forward. As fast as explorations or enterprises became more consecutive, from 7 or 8 onward, the gaps and barriers which could not easily be dealt with would start to show up more clearly. After a while they could begin to be discussed, even though not at all pressed. It would in fact be no help to 'talk' children too soon into being 'properly taught', because at this stage they could probably not *keep up* genuine learning in that form, even if they eagerly launched out on it. But a few more years of building up their own base in breadth and developing it more fully at particular chosen points would make all the difference. Between 10 and 11 the full movement towards teaching could begin.

The natural shape into which this movement would initially fall would simply be that the teacher's share in the child's exploratory and learning activities would constantly grow. Background information of every sort, verbal explanations, demonstrations, reference to suitable books, the help of T.V. and Radio, etc. would all play their part. It would still not be planned lessons or teaching, but an accompaniment to children's own enterprises, aimed at arousing and holding their interest and not pursued beyond this; but more and more of the substance of good teaching would already be present in it.

In most cases by 12 or 13 the time for the final switch should be reached—and would appropriately take the form of the physical move into the Secondary School. But the age for this would not be too closely fixed and would in fact depend partly on teachers' judgments of readiness, and partly on actual free discussions with the children. In some of them real readiness might be attained by 11 or even a little earlier. In such cases there is no reason why a few teaching groups, on a purely voluntary basis, should not be set up within the Primary School. Teachers in regular contact would have little difficulty in judging approximate degrees of readiness, including *probable staying power,* from about 10 onward. But all this could be handled in the most open-minded way, with ample room left for *tentative* tryings-out which could easily be dropped again, or modified, or temporarily adjourned.

(vi) The final proof of readiness can of course only come in the shape of sustained right response to the right teaching. What this means in substance is that the pupil must be able to translate back the verbal presentations and explanations of the teaching into the *living learning*—the actual insight and vision built up—embodied in these verbal forms.

That, however, can be fully expected only where two conditions are fulfilled:

(a) The learner must start from a genuine wish to know *much more* about the particular field in question. In other words, he must already know enough about it to give real meaning and sustained driving power to the wish. Hence the importance of the long prior phase, first of broad all-round exploration and then of the fuller following up of chosen interests. Only a strong drive to know more about something, already well supported by a fair grasp of what the whole business is about, is likely to provide the background needed for the most effective learning from teaching. For this demands first of all the complete self-subjection already referred to—shutting everything else out and placing oneself wholly in the teacher's hands—and then an intent and persisting effort to extract from his words the living meaning that should be behind them.

It follows that extremely little is gained *educationally* by 'making children learn' subjects which they 'ought to know about', but to which they cannot be led to bring any positive drive or interest of their own. This wasted effort might just as well be saved, and the time put to some productive use. In any case, on the basic approach here advocated, the broad foundations built up over the years before the teaching stage should already have ensured, far more educatively, (a) that no main part of our human world has gone entirely by default (b) that the subjects actually chosen for intensive following up retain their connection with the rest of that world, and (c) that there remains a wide groundwork for subsequent revivals of earlier interests, for responses to new stimuli, and for later enlargements of horizons generally.

(b) The second condition, if taught knowledge is to be most fruitfully interpreted in terms of living learning, is almost self-evident. The teaching itself must come as close as possible to these terms. Here the present approach is very much in line with current trends, and seeks only to give these the clearest psychological definition. Learners' minds must from the start be aroused into active participation in their own teaching. A given body of knowledge, or 'subject' must not be presented (in the old time-honoured way) as a closed, static scheme offered in an orderly succession of lessons which will eventually get joined up into an intelligible whole. The learner must on the contrary be enabled, from the beginnning, to see each such body of knowledge as the outcome, so far, of living learning stories which started very much like his own. In other words, from specific live interests, aims and purposes, questions, problems and challenges. Free and full discussion must play a large part throughout. Where formulation in terms of problems is feasible, learners must have every opportunity of taking these over *as problems*–actually experiencing them–thinking about them and debating them–considering possible ways forward–and hearing about actual ways tried which have failed, or only partly succeeded. Only then will come an account, which can now be given its full value, of the best solution so far achieved.–In this exact form such a procedure may not always be suitable or practicable. But it can serve to typify the psychology of the situation; and there are in fact few branches of authentic insight-giving knowledge to which that broad kind of approach could not helpfully be applied.

(vii) This, however, takes the discussion well into the field of Secondary Education. I must not pursue it there beyond recalling that this is where children should be able to harvest everything for which we have been so busily equipping them during the earlier years. That accordingly is the testing period for our basic national scheme of education. The lamentable outcome of the test until now, i.e. the extreme poverty of what a large proportion of school-leavers carry away from school, has already been referred to. But what perhaps merits special stress, as the worst aspect of the indictment, is that from their whole education they have usually not gained a single enduring *interest.* They are thus plunged into the world without anchorage or compass. It could be fairly said, I think, that by far the most important service which our basic education could render would be to leave most of its pupils with some genuine interest, or interests, which they will really want to go on with for themselves. Without this, as we know, they risk becoming the victims of a chronic boredom which makes them a heavy burden to themselves as well as to society.

If anyone is tempted to shrug this off on the old horse-to-the-water grounds, the answer, in the same terms, is surely that we have failed to build up the *thirst* that needs to come first. The argument here has suggested starting from that end and putting into the task not only all our present efforts, but also all the resources of our most searching latter-day psychology of mental nutrition and growth. The crucial question is whether in that way far more children might not end up with a real, meaningful share of their own in our vast and varied contemporary world—some forward-facing interests which they could keep on pursuing with active zest and re-stimulating rewards.

V: SUPPLEMENTARY COMMENTS

The foregoing concludes the main argument, but there are loose ends to gather up and points that call for brief comment.

(1) It may appear that in this discussion there has been one conspicuous omission which largely clips the argument's wings. For most people the first task of Primary Education is to teach children the three R's, or 'basic skills'. And these, they would say, clearly contain much that must just be *learnt*—in the ordinary school sense of this term. Since moreover they are the indispensable bases for the whole rest of education, they should be learnt as early as possible, and in the swiftest and most effective way. In other words, these subjects at any rate must, as soon as practicable, be efficiently *taught*.

But even if such a view could not be gainsaid, it would not need to mean more than that, as a necessary but limited evil, these three bands of conventional teaching must run through part of the earlier Primary years. All the remainder of the large time-span between 5 and 11 (or rather, as suggested here, between 3 and 12-13) would still be available for the kind of active, living learning here described. In fact, however, the above view does not have to be accepted, and is no more than a specially plausible hangover from the very assumptions about education which are here under challenge. But for that very reason, it does need to be further discussed.

The first step, as I see it, is to split off one of the three R's, to which the argument is anyway almost completely inapplicable. Arithmetic includes some elements that need to be 'learnt', in the sense of being practised and memorised; but they are its least significant parts. As far as they matter, they can be easily and quickly taken care of when the *important* learning has been done. And this latter must certainly come under the heading of living learning, through genuine interest, active exploration and experimentation, free discussion and discovery. For arithmetic, educationally, is *not* a skill; it is a branch of insightful logical knowledge (even if of a rather special kind) and must be treated like every other such field.

On the other hand, the two remaining R's, reading and writing, do begin life as artificial social tools, the make-up and use of which *seems* to call mainly for conventional 'learning'. However, when this is assumed to imply conventional class-room teaching, by regularly recurring lessons, we are again back in the kind of situation already dealt with, which just means nothing to many children except an enforced tedious grind. Even if it were true that reading and writing could be learnt in no other way, there would be a strong case for deferring rather than hastening the burdensome task. However, once we get rid of our current misconceived hurry, there is no reason why the mastery of reading and writing should need to be that kind of task. Or why, as already noted, many children should only 'master' these tools to dislike them and to minimise their use for ever after.

Here, as everywhere else, meaningfulness should in fact come first. These two skills can easily be brought before young children in a host of challenging forms, as keys constantly called for by all their other active interests and enterprises. In effect, this should be an outstanding case of their coming themselves to feel in a more and more pressing fashion that here is a gap or lack which badly gets in their way, and which they must do something about. In practice they would actually be asking for help, especially with reading, as they went along. They would thus be picking up bits and pieces in the stride of their other activities—and thereby make further advance progressively easier. Presently most of them would want to get hold of this mystery once and for all and would positively appeal for proper help. They would then be ready to do any necessary memorising and practising with a will—just as children settle down to learning to manage other tools which they want to be able to use, or how to play a game in which they want to take part.

This might perhaps not happen in some cases till 7 or 8, but even that would not really matter. If they were too busy exploring, experimenting, constructing, etc. to want to bother with reading for the first year or two in school, their really important education through living learning would in fact be going on apace. Nothing of importance would be lost through their delay over this particular tool, and eventually they would certainly want to pick it up, since their handicaps through lacking it would constantly get more irksome. But it seems improbable, for just those reasons, that under free learning conditions, many children would in fact want to wait very long.—Writing might follow somewhat later than reading, but the same factors would be at work and should presently lead to the same results. Thus the special case of reading and writing, even if in some degrees different from the world of children's direct exploratory or constructive interests, fits quite readily into the present educational approach, seen as a whole.

(2) This approach has been mainly focused on the field of knowledge—construed in the widest sense to cover every kind of connected understanding of the world around us, physical, living and human, present and past. Knowledge has moreover been considered not only for its own value, but also as a basis for all our powers of foresight and successful action. In this comprehensive sense it does usually rank as the dominant target of education; but the latter would remain radically incomplete if it did not also include the

constant active fostering of children's imaginative life and its chief forms of expression. In effect, though it has not been possible to go into this in detail, the present conception of living learning is just as applicable here as to the worlds of knowledge and of action. That has of course been duly acknowledged in principle, but detailed discussion has not seemed so essential, since this is the one realm where set, formal teaching—anyway during earlier childhood has already lost most of its credit. Here in fact the foregoing principles are already to a large extent accepted. It can, I think, thus be fairly said that they cover the whole educational ground. In the last analysis, indeed, the conception of learning here put forward embraces all mental growth that can be won through the combined operations of human doing, experiencing and thinking. This does not seem to leave anything essential out.

(3) This last point suggests another which we do not normally bring under the head of school education (or at any rate the school education that has hitherto ended at 15), but which has its own closely related importance and even urgency. In so far as school means chiefly class-room teaching of set subjects, it has no direct mandate bearing on the social growth of its children. This may come in more or less incidentally, but only in a limited way. But the kind of Primary school here envisaged might well have a strong influence on that growth, and of a very positive and helpful kind. It would be very much more of a living community, in which children would be doing their learning and mental growing in continual co-operation with one another, in larger or smaller groups. There would be constant give and take, with a need for reciprocal consideration and exchanges of help which in the ordinary way would be virtually taken for granted. Social ways of thinking and feeling would be promoted all the time, and, as in all common enterprises, success would demand that the rules of mutual fairness and co-operation should normally be honoured.

But at the same time the free-ranging interests and activities of the school should in any case throw up questions connected with every sort of human and social relation, which would thereupon get discussed, explored and followed up. Such enquiries would then frequently find relevent material in the way of life of the school itself, so that theory and practice could directly illuminate each other. Thus the children's habitual compliance with the daily demands of their communal life could increasingly join up with reflective understanding of these demands, and the right kind of foundation would be taking shape for the larger social life to follow.

It would of course be essential that the secondary school in its turn should carry further what was thus begun. It is true that, just on the present view, children would now be moving into a world in which the teaching situation proper, and therefore the kind of organisation and relationships demanded by it, would play the central part. But, in the first place, this situation itself would, as already indicated, take a much more participative form than is common at present. Secondly, it could reasonably be expected that children coming from the above kind of Primary School would be far more interested than hitherto in now 'learning properly' about the various chief *human and social* fields of knowledge. This, based in turn on active participation and ample free discussion, would directly link up with all the groundwork done before and should lead straight on to the enlarged reflective grasp now most needed.—Thirdly, as need hardly be said, a considerable part would in any case need to be left for group or collective enterprises of various kinds (some linked with the teaching work, some independent), and there would generally be very much closer links between the work of the school and the personal and social life of its members. Here the recommendations of the Newsom report⁶ would obviously fall into place.

Thus, all in all, the teaching functions of the Secondary School as here conceived would not only fit in well with its important socialising role, but may also be expected to make their own substantial contributions to this.

(4) A final point, but one of key importance. What would follow from the present general educational approach as regards the training—or education—of teachers?

Some colleges already accept this approach, and model their training on it. But those for which education has in the past been mainly planned classroom teaching would no doubt need to do much reconsidering of their curriculum. In particular, the current distinction between the 'professional training' of teachers and their 'further education' would seem to call for a somewhat searching review. What is aimed at under the first heading is of course essentially the preparation and equipment of students for their future role as classroom teachers. This obviously includes the theory of education as well as, in many colleges, a good deal of educational psychology; but, in accordance with current basic assumptions, it is all pivoted on teaching. And indeed the very distinction made between 'professional training' and the student's 'further education' seems still to reflect the narrow conception of the work of the teacher which has remained at the back of almost everyone's mind.

But the present approach would mean that future teachers' 'professional training' would itself have to turn into one of the most liberal of educations. Its two chief poles would continue to be the theory of education on the one hand and psychology on the other. But the latter would first of all signify understanding of that whole story of inward building up, or fundamental learning, which in fact first turns each of us into a potential civilised human. Whilst the theory of education would primarily be the theory of the goals which we most want to help those processes of building up and living growth

⁶[Central Advisory Council for Education (England), *Half Our Future: A Report* (London: Her Majesty's Stationery Office, 1963).]

to reach; in other words, a round survey of our civilised heritage for those values which we should most wish *'all* our future' to have some chance of sharing.

This then signifies that as regards psychology, the student must be enabled to penetrate to some depth, whilst for the goals of education his first need is large horizons and vision in breadth. But what is just as important—above all for the primary, pre-teaching 'teacher'—is a representative grasp of the kinds of roads and bridges, or ways and means, by which children can best make their way forward towards an ever-broadening picture of our common world. Here psychology and the theory of education must meet and interpenetrate, but must join up also with a wide knowledge of the first stages of exploration of many things; plants and animals, physical happenings, engines, human affairs, painting and modelling, etc. etc. In fact anything which can arouse children's interest or questions or wish to find out more.

This very wide informedness can obviously not extend to any distance in more than a few directions. Even so, the demands made both on students and on those who direct their studies are clearly considerable. But they are moderated by the fact that when students begin their 'teacher's' work, they will not be setting out to 'teach' any of the foregoing 'subjects', but merely to join with children in exploring them, and to help with fruitful leads. They will in effect be entering into a give-and-take relation, in which they in turn will be continually re-stimulated, led to see new possibilities, and, where necessary, incited to move further ahead themselves.

Meanwhile in their own education as future teachers they will build up the wide informedness which they need partly through studies of children's exploratory activities both in the literature which is already available (and steadily growing), partly in real life through actual work in Nursery and Infant Schools and some Junior ones, and partly by participative learning through suitable wide-ranging teaching.

'Professional training' and 'further education' will thus become fused into a single comprehensive whole. This whole, however, would not be complete if it did not also include at least one subject (such as is now brought in under the heading of 'further education'), for real intensive study. There needs to be some specific civilised field in which the future teacher is fully at home (as regards knowledge, methods and instruments), to provide another dimension of depth in his overall equipment. For those whose wish is to deal with older children, at the stage of readiness for systematic teaching, the 'special' subject of their choice will naturally become their main teaching one. But even though, in their actual teaching, they might thus become subject specialists, they would still need both the wide civilised framework within which their subject would have to be placed, and also that psychological understanding of real living learning, through which their planned teaching could itself be brought close to this.

On the other side it will be clear that for those students who are attracted to the earlier years (when all our human world is still children's learning field) their 'further education' will even after qualification only be at its threshold. They will constantly be impelled to go on growing with their children, whose own active reachings-out in ever new directions will serve as an incessant challenge. Once the 'teaching' of children from 3 to 13 is seen as essentially the process of helping them to grow into their civilised birthright and to find out what within this most interests and satisfies them individually: once this is seen such 'teaching' should surely stand out as one of the most liberal, exciting and rewarding of professions.

VI: PRACTICAL CONCLUSION

As was emphasised at the beginning of this memorandum, all that it seeks to do at the present stage is to establish a sufficient case for the setting up of a searching pilot test scheme. If this proved decisively successful, great educational changes would have to be initiated, but with the prospect of immensely much being gained. And even if the scheme were only partly successful, a great deal might be learnt from it—or for that matter also from virtual failure. However, quite apart from the theoretical case, there is already a good deal of practical evidence to suggest a high probability of at least some measure of success.

On the other hand something much more comprehensive than has hitherto been attempted would clearly be necessary. A considerable number of children, spread over a number of schools in different areas, would have to be carried right through according to the principles sketched out, in some cases from five, in others from three, right up to the future earliest leaving age of 16. This would have to be done under adequate central guidance and observation, and then followed up for at least some years, so that there would be reasonable evidence as to the kind of adult who would eventually emerge. Furthermore the scheme itself would need a period of preliminary study of all the information already available about the outcomes of the active learning approach, both in this country and in the United States (where the greatest amount of enquiry and comparative testing has already been done). It seems certain, however, that none of this information can compare for conclusiveness with the picture which a fully planned longitudinal scheme of the kind here suggested is likely to yield. But for such conclusive results it might well be necessary to allow something like 20 years (even though interim findings on which partial action could be taken might well begin to emerge much sooner).

In these circumstances all that can be said is that since any major practical consummation must lie so far ahead, we should, if the suggested test commends itself, at least start *planning* it as soon as possible. Whether this can be recommended is now submitted for your Committee's consideration.

Bibliography of Nathan Isaacs' Works

I: WORKS BY ISAACS ALONE, LISTED CHRONOLOGICALLY

"Education and Science." Appendix to *Intellectual Growth in Young Children* by Susan Isaacs. London: Routledge and Kegan Paul, 1930. Reprinted from *Nature*, July 23, 1927.

"Children's 'Why' Questions." Appendix to *Intellectual Growth in Young Children* by Susan Isaacs. London: Routledge and Kegan Paul, 1930.

"Psycho-Logic." *Proceedings of the Aristotelian Society.* 31 (1930-1931): 225-262.

"The Logic of Language." *Proceedings of the Aristotelian Society.* 33 (1932-1933): 259-294.

The Foundations of Common Sense: A Psychological Preface to the Problems of Knowledge. London: Routledge and Kegan Paul, 1949.

"The 'Temporal Correspondence' Approach to Truth." *Proceedings of the Aristotelian Society.* 51 (1950-1951): 47-82.

"Methodology and Research in Psycho-Pathology." *The British Journal of Medical Psychology.* 24 (1951): 13-25.

"Froebel's Educational Philosophy in 1952." In *Froebel and English Education: Perspectives on the Founder of the Kindergarten,* edited by Evelyn Lawrence. London: National Froebel Foundation, 1952. Reprint. New York: Schocken Books, 1969.

"About 'The Child's Conception of Number' by Jean Piaget." *National Froebel Foundation Bulletin,* no. 91 (December 1954): 1-11.

"Piaget's Work and Progressive Education." In *Some Aspects of Piaget's Work,* National Froebel Foundation. London: National Froebel Foundation, 1955.

"What is Required of the Nursery-Infant Teacher in This Country Today?" *National Froebel Foundation Bulletin,* no. 109 (December, 1957): 2-16.

Early Scientific Trends in Children. London: National Froebel Foundation, 1958.

"Some Basic Reflections about Language (Part I)." *National Froebel Foundation Bulletin,* no. 115 (December 1958): 2-10.

"Some Basic Reflections about Language (Part II)." *National Froebel Foundation Bulletin,* no. 116 (February 1959): 18-27.

"What do Linguistic Philosophers Assume?" *Proceedings of the Aristotelian Society.* 60 (1959-1960): 211-230.

"On a Gap in the Structure of our General Psychology." *Journal of Child Psychology and Psychiatry and Allied Disciplines.* 1 (1960-1961): 73-86.

The Growth of Understanding in the Young Child: A Brief Introduction to Piaget's Work. London: Ward Lock Educational Company, 1961. Reprinted, New York: Agathon Press, 1972, in Nathan Isaacs, *A Brief Introduction to Piaget.*

New Light on Children's Ideas of Number: The Work of Professor Piaget. London: Ward Lock Educational Company, 1961. Reprinted, New York: Agathon Press, 1972, in Nathan Isaacs, *A Brief Introduction to Piaget.*

"Some Thoughts about Language and Thought." *National Froebel Foundation Bulletin,* no. 128 (February 1961): 1-16.

"The Case for Bringing Science into the Primary School." In *The Place of Science in Primary Education,* edited by W. H. Perkins. London: The British Association for the Advancement of Science, 1962.

"Children's 'Scientific' Interests." In *Studies in Education: First Years in School.* University of London Institute of Education. London: Evans Brothers, 1963.

"Critical Notice: 'Intelligence and Experience' by J. McV. Hunt." *National Froebel Foundation Bulletin,* no. 141 (April 1963): 1-13.

"Critical Notice: 'Fostering Intellectual Development in Young Children' by K. D. Wann, M. S. Dorn and E. A. Liddle." *National Froebel Foundation Bulletin,* no. 149 (April 1963): 12-20.

"Psychology, Piaget and Practice." Published in three parts in *Teaching Arithmetic* 2 (Summer 1964): 3-10; 2 (Autumn 1964): 2-9; 3 (Spring 1965): 11-16. Reprinted, with minor alterations, London: National Froebel Foundation, 1965, as *Piaget: Some Answers to Teachers' Questions.*

"Memorandum for the Plowden Committee." *Froebel Journal,* no. 2 (June 1965): 12-33.

Piaget: Some Answers to Teachers' Questions. London: National Froebel Foundation, 1965.

II: WORKS WITH CO-AUTHORS

Jebb, Eglantyne; Lawrence, Evelyn; Brearley, Molly; and Isaacs, Nathan. "Future Education and the Training of Teachers: Memorandum Submitted by the Foundation to the Robbins Committee on Higher Education, September 27th, 1961." *National Froebel Foundation Bulletin,* no. 133 (December 1961): 1-15.

Lawrence, Evelyn; Isaacs, Nathan; and Rawson, Wyatt. *Approaches to Science in the Primary School.* London: The Educational Supply Association, 1960.

Index

Active education ("activity" methods, "open" classroom), 1, 132, 134-145, 159, 169-180
Anthropomorphism, 16, 41-43
Arithmetic, 149, 151-155, 175
  Man-made structure of, 155-156
  See also Mathematics, teaching of; Number, Piaget's views on

Belief-testing, 8, 10, 88, 95, 102-103, 118

Causal inquiries:
  See "Why" questions
Central Advisory Council for Education (England):
  Children and Their Primary Schools ("Plowden Report"), 159
  Half Our Future ("Newsom Report"), 159, 160, 161, 178
Child's Conception of Causality, The (Piaget), 157
Child's Conception of Geometry, The (Piaget), 157
Child's Conception of Number, The (Piaget), 113, 133, 157
Child's Conception of Space, The (Piaget), 113, 157
Child's Conception of the World, The (Piaget), 157
Child's Construction of Reality, The (Piaget; U.S. title: *The Construction of Reality in the Child)*, 2, 113, 135, 157
Churchill, Eileen, 158
Cognition, psychology of, reconstructing, 2, 8-10, 98-113
Cognitive history of individual, 9-10, 98, 101-113
  Behavioral study of, 100, 113
  Belief-testing in, 102-103
  Dramatic quality of, 109
  Role of anticipation in, 105-107, 108-110
  Truth-falsity distinction in, 101-107
  See also Infant learning
Cognitive organization (cognitive map, world model, world picture), 3-5, 9-10, 93, 98, 105-106, 109-110, 119
Cognitive "unconscious," 9, 106
Construction of Reality in the Child, The (Piaget; Brit. title: *The Child's Construction of Reality)*, 2, 113, 135, 157
Counting and Measuring (Churchill), 158
Curiosity:
  See "Why" interest; "Why" questions

Développement de la Notion de Temps chez l'Enfant (Piaget), 158
Dorn, M. S., 158

Early Growth of Logic in the Child, The (Piaget), 157
Education, summary of Isaacs' recommendations for, 168-180
Egocentrism, 13, 17, 56-57
Epistemic interest(s), 26, 29-30, 38-40, 49, 53, 62-64
  See also "Why" questions, epistemic
Explanation(s), 16-18, 22-24, 37, 92-97, 126-127
  And education, 14, 51-53
  And language, 139, 165
  By adults, 28-33, 43, 94
  Main functional modes of, 25, 54-55
  Standards of, 8, 29, 52-53, 95
  Types of, 16